DEAN CAHILL, ACCA

Exotic Markets

Investing & trading with foreign stocks

Pervasives

Copyright © 2021 by Dean Cahill, ACCA

All rights reserved. No part of this publication may be reproduced, stored or transmitted in any form or by any means, electronic, mechanical, photocopying, recording, scanning, or otherwise without written permission from the publisher. It is illegal to copy this book, post it to a website, or distribute it by any other means without permission.

Dean Cahill, ACCA has no responsibility for the persistence or accuracy of URLs for external or third-party Internet Websites referred to in this publication and does not guarantee that any content on such Websites is, or will remain, accurate or appropriate.

Disclaimer: The information in this book should not be considered tax, financial, investment, or any kind of professional advice. Only a professional diagnosis of your specific situation can determine which strategies are appropriate for your needs. Pervasives can and do not provide advice unless/until engaged by you.

First edition

ISBN: 979-8-53-655241-4

This book was professionally typeset on Reedsy. Find out more at reedsy.com

Contents

Bookmark cutout v

I Part One

1 Think Relative 3

II Part Two

2 Western Europe 15
3 Nordics 47
4 Balkans 66
5 Eastern Europe 92
6 Central & East Asia 103
7 South-East Asia 149
8 South America 183
9 Central America 206
10 Middle East 220
11 Africa 248

III Part Three

12 Timeframe and broker 291
13 Macro selection 299
14 Industry selection 325
15 Micro selection 345
16 The Tide 358

17 The buffet	369
18 Protection	374

IV Part Four

19 Think Global	383

How can I help you?	387
How can you help us?	388
Recommended tools	389
Recommended books	395
Financial advice disclaimer	396
Image credits	397
Notes	411

Bookmark cutout

This is a $10 Namibian dollar note, which is worth about $0.67 USD.
It can be cut out and used as a bookmark while reading this book.

I

Part One

It's a big world out there, but it's smaller than you think

Join me on this journey through the silk roads. Get onto your magic carpet, envisage the smell of spices, listen to a distant Oud playing the Phrygian dominant scale of Arabic sounds.

1

Think Relative

Investing overseas is way too risky, and the US market is the best market in the world, why would you trust your capital with a bunch of "insert racist word here"?

2019	in USD billions	%
World GDP	87,345	100%
United States	21,433	25%
European Union	15,593	18%
China	14,343	16%
Japan	5,082	6%
India	2,869	3%
Brazil	1,840	2%
Total 6 regions	61,160	70%

There are 7.9 billion people in the world as of 2021. The globe is predicted to grow by 3 billion people by 2050, bringing the total population to 11 billion. Africa, Asia, and Latin America are currently home to 80 percent of the world's population, yet they account for 99 percent of global growth. In today's world, women have an average of 2.9 children over their lives.

This number varies greatly, ranging from 1.2 in Eastern Europe to 5.8 in Sub-Saharan Africa. With a population of 657 million people and a total fertility rate of 5.8 children per woman, Sub-Saharan Africa is by far the world's fastest expanding area. the region is projected to have 1.5 billion inhabitants by 2050. In stark contrast to the developing world, Europe's population continues to drop. As developing-country populations grow and Europe's population declines, Europe will account for only 7% of the world's population in 2050, down from 12% now.

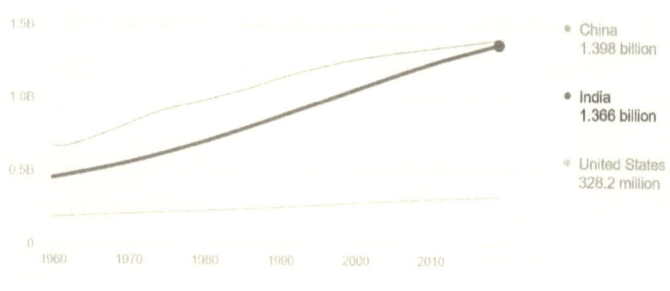

World population data as of 2019

Western media will tell you that all these people are unhappy in their home country and that they will emigrate to developed regions to look for a better life. This is true in part, some will emigrate to Europe or North America in the hope to improve their lives.

But Emigrants are only a tiny percentage of the population of these less developed regions, the vast majority of the population will stay and develop their own country. Western media will also argue that the reasons those regions are not as developed are because of local governments being the direct obstacle to trade and economic growth.

This is also true. But one thing to understand is that local governments can do all they can in their power to prevent a western-style society, but there is only so much they can do in their power, and one should not underestimate the power of private enterprise and free will. Even when the business conditions are at their worst state, enterprising people find a way to improve their lives and trade occurs against all odds.

If we use the COVID 19 pandemic as an example, you will remember the worldwide effort by all governments around the globe to shut down trade for almost 2 years. In reality, companies and individuals adapted and found ways to survive and thrive, whatever the conditions and the governments of the world can do little about it after all.

So why is 70% of GDP mostly in developed regions and not in emerging regions? Will the weighing of GDP include emerging markets more heavily in the coming decades?

Catch 22

- How to buy stocks abroad?
- How to trade stocks in "country name"?
- Are foreigners allowed to trade in this region's market?

- Diversification?
- Political risk?
- Currency risk?
- Wide broker spreads?
- Huge broker commissions?
- Corruption in third-world countries?
- Over-the-Counter?
- Tax?

The increased transaction cost is the most significant impediment to participating in overseas markets. Even though we live in a somewhat globalized and linked world, transaction costs vary significantly depending on which foreign market you invest in. International brokerage commissions are nearly usually greater than those in the United States.

There may be extra costs unique to the local market in addition to the increased brokerage commissions. Stamp duties, levies, taxes, clearing fees, and exchange costs are examples of these.

You must first exchange your US dollars into a foreign currency at the current exchange rate before investing directly in a foreign market (rather than through ADRs).

Let's say you buy a foreign stock and keep it for a year before selling it. That implies you'll have to exchange the foreign money for US dollars. Depending on which way the currency is heading, this might assist or hinder your return.

Liquidity risk is another risk that exists in international markets, particularly in emerging economies. This is the danger of being unable to sell an investment swiftly and profitably at any moment owing to a political or economic catastrophe.

There is no simple solution for the typical investor to protect themselves from foreign market liquidity risk. Foreign assets that are or may become illiquid by the time investors wish to sell should be avoided at all costs.

Many emerging nations, as well as certain developed markets, do not have the same reporting criteria as the US. The Securities and Market Act of 1934, for example, mandates that all businesses listed on a U.S. stock exchange disclose their earnings quarterly and file the necessary paperwork with the Securities and Exchange Commission on a regular basis.

10Ks, 10Qs, and other papers may fall under this category. These rules may not apply in other countries, making it impossible to discover reliable information about the company—to say nothing of the fact that accessing the information may be difficult due to a language barrier.

Purchasing shares in these many marketplaces can be difficult to say the least. Brokers may not always have access to certain markets or be able to execute specific deals. When brokers are able to complete the transaction, reporting and clearing periods may be lengthier than in US markets, resulting in longer settlement delays. Also, if the bank or brokerage firm goes out of business, the shares may not be safe from fraud or theft.

Finally, with foreign taxation, your local CPA accountant may call you and ask, "what's this?", to which you will candidly reply:

You: "oh, this is a new investment I did after I read this shady book, these are Polish stocks with exposure to the local IT sector, I bought them with Polish Zloty."

Accountant: "Ah Ok..., well..., for the next tax year..., don't do that. It's just not worth it. Just buy US stocks."

After this interaction, you will probably follow the advice of your CPA and not do that anymore because it is not worth it. The accountant is partially true in his statement. He says it's not worth it, but his sentence is incomplete. It's not worth it for *him*. Because he has no clue about Polish taxes.

You see, he only charges you a couple of hundred dollars to compute your income tax every year. This takes him roughly an hour or two to do on complete auto-pilot.

Now that you bought a few thousand dollars worth of Polish stocks, he has to go out and figure out the exhaustive tax code in Poland, all within a Friday night, which was supposed to be Oktoberfest Friday!

Paradigm shift

So why would you invest in overseas markets when your home market is perfectly fine and easier to trade?

The answer is dead simple: opportunities. Opportunities is the single reason and it outweighs the disadvantages by a mile. You think it's too risky because generally you only arrive to that conclusion when you don't know much about it. Problems with accessing overseas stocks? You can buy ADRs, GDRs, ETFs, and even go the foreign market directly. Next, currency risk? Currency risk may be mitigated by simply hedging your currency exposure. Currency futures, options, and forwards are among the tools available. Liquidity risk? Lack of liquidity is an opportunity (when you are on the right side), because it moves markets aggressively and is an enabler of volatility.

Major opportunities lies in Emerging and frontier markets,

not so much in developed markets. Emerging market economies have reached a basic degree of development, whereas frontier markets are the least economically developed countries in the global marketplace. This lack of development gives an investing diversity that can't be found in more developed economies. Market, political, and currency risk, as well as the danger of nationalization, are all present in both types of markets.

What's confusing is that the stock exchanges mentioned in Part Two does not exclusively offer stocks from its home country exclusively. They can sometimes offer stocks in different countries, the same way the NYSE offers foreign stocks directly on their exchange, denominated in US dollars (ADRs), or even include stocks from overseas companies on their exchange. Exotic Market is therefore not a collection of stock exchanges by countries, but an intricate interweaving web of financial markets.

You see, the whole point of this is the ease of access. They try to accommodate the investors in that country, by offering them foreign options with no currency risk (denominated in the exchange country's currency) and limited taxation involvement.

You can buy german stocks on the NYSE denominated in US dollars, as much as you can buy US stocks on the Frankfurt stock exchange, denominated in euros.

The only issue with this is that it does not cover everything. You will have limited options in terms of choice, it will only cover the big names with big market caps. Basically, the company's with the least region-specific exposure, and the most global coverage exposure (being multinationals with operations in a lot of countries).

To find the gems that nobody talks about, you will probably have to put in the leg work and go to the desired country's exchange, trade the stock outright (lack of available derivative instruments) in the currency of that country.

This book is not about banning stocks from the US or Europe, and go full-on frontier market with extremely volatile currencies and political conflicts, far from it. This book is simply an invitation to geographically diversify.

People think in absolute terms, you should think in relative terms. Other people: the best deal out there is the one I know of within the limited scope I have and never challenge.

You: what's the best deal out there? what's the best option for me?

This is simply an invitation to widen your scope, remove the preconceived notions given to you from cradle to grave, think relative, and start to dip your toes into new territories.

THINK RELATIVE

	Beginner	**Experienced**	**Advanced**
Capital	$0-$250k	$250k-$1M	$1M+
Brokerage accounts	1 main US account, 1 secondary account for other region	1 main US account, 2-3 secondary accounts for other regions	Multiple main accounts, 1 account for each sub regions (emerging and frontier)
Regions	Developed Emerging developed	Developed Emerging developed Emerging	Developed Emerging developed Emerging Frontier emerging Frontier
Instruments	Stocks ETFs CFDs Options	Stocks ETFs CFDs Options Warrants Certificates	Stocks ETFs CFDs Options Warrants Certificates
Currency risk	ADRs & GDRs Currency ETFs	ADRs & GDRs Currency ETFs Currency Swaps	ADRs & GDRs Currency ETFs Currency Swaps Foreign Exchange
Taxation & accountancy work	As low as possible	Limited and reasonable	1 main holistic accountant + multiple locals outsourced in each region

Table representing beginner to advance levels, the capital range is only a guideline

II

Part Two

The playground
This Section is a near-comprehensive list of markets that are available for you to trade and explore. This is the part where Alice follows the white rabbit and falls into the hole, where an endless list of opportunities and avenues unfold under your scope and present their perks and quirks. Come back to this section whenever you start to arouse your curiosity and unveil the many possibilities at your disposal.

This Part is repetitive, skipping frowned upon, but allowed.

2

Western Europe

The first group of countries are allowing foreigners to buy stocks, have wide access from international brokers, and are business-friendly. The information available pertaining to the stocks listed on these exchanges is accessible and wide.

* * *

Germany

There are 8 stock exchanges in Germany: the Frankfurt Stock Exchange (XFRA), the Xetra Stock Exchange (XETR), the Stuttgart Stock Exchange (XSTU), the Munich Stock Exchange (XMUN), the Berlin Stock Exchange (XBER), the Dusseldorf Stock Exchange(XDUS), the Hamburg Stock Exchange (XHAM), and the Hannover Stock Exchange (XHAN). The Frankfurt Stock exchange is by far the biggest and the one you should look at to get exposure to German equities in the easiest way.

Most German equities are listed on the Frankfurt stock exchange as their primary listing. The different exchanges can offer slightly different capacities and methods of trading. There are also foreign companies that are listed on the Frankfurt exchange.

More than 80 countries list on the Frankfurt Stock Exchange with about 50% from North and South America, 30% from Europe, 14% from Asia, and 6% from Australia and Africa. When filtering for German stocks only, there are 364 stocks available. As Germany is a western European developed economy, you will have plenty of access to its listed equities with any major standard brokers. Stocks are denominated in Euros.

Germany's economy is a well-developed social market economy. It possesses Europe's largest economy, as well as the world's fourth-biggest nominal GDP and fifth-biggest GDP. According to the International Monetary Fund, the country accounted for 28% of the euro area GDP in 2017. Germany had the greatest trade surplus in the world in 2016, at $310 billion, making it the world's largest capital exporter. Germany is one of the world's major exporters, with products and services valued at $1810.93 billion in 2019.

The service sector accounts for over 70% of overall GDP, industry for 29.1%, and agriculture for 0.9 percent. Exports accounted for 41% of total production. Vehicles, machinery, chemical goods, electronic items, electrical equipment, medicines, transport equipment, basic metals, food items, and rubber and plastics are among Germany's top ten exports. Germany's economy is Europe's largest manufacturing economy, and it is less likely to be damaged by a financial crisis. The German "Mittelstand," or small and medium-sized businesses, account for 99 percent of all businesses in the country, with the majority of them being family-owned. In the Fortune Global 2000, 53 of the world's 2000 largest publicly traded firms by revenue are located in Germany, with Allianz, Daimler, Volkswagen, Siemens, BMW, Deutsche Telekom, Bayer, BASF, Munich Re, and SAP in the top ten.

The DAX, or the German stock market index, includes 30 businesses located in Germany. Mercedes-Benz, BMW, SAP, Siemens, Volkswagen, Adidas, Audi, Allianz, Porsche, Bayer, BASF, Bosch, and Nivea are all well-known worldwide brands.

Double taxation treaties are available with most countries therefore you are only liable to pay capital gains tax in your home country in most cases. The most useful information pertaining to that exchange will be the Economic Sentiment Indicators published by the European Union, and the Short term indicators of the Statistisches Bundesamt.

Frankfurt stock exchange, 2015

United Kingdom

The London Stock Exchange (LSE) started in 1698 when John Castaing started keeping tabs on stock prices on a board hanging inside Jonathan's coffee house, which was the place to encounter businessmen with monocles. This exchange/region is by far the least exotic of all as you could argue that the US stock exchange was simply an extension of the London stock exchange at first and that its model was copied from it. Today, the LSE is operated under the London Stock Exchange Group, which used to also own the Borsa Italiana, more on that later.

Good or bad, the recent Brexit gives the opportunity to the UK to take a new direction with its financial market, without having to abide by the EU's way of doing things, all things stock related of course. There are 2483 listed companies on the London Stock exchange, and they are denominated in British Pound Sterlings. The exchange allows foreigners to trade on it with no restrictions. The UK is a developed economy therefore the exchange contains a wide variety of listing both in manufacturing as well as services in all major industry groups. You will have no issues accessing UK listings from abroad as access is very broad, most standard brokers will offer listings on the LSE by default.

The United Kingdom's economy is a well-developed social market and market-oriented economy. It has the world's fifth-largest nominal gross domestic product (GDP), ninth-largest purchasing power parity (PPP), and twenty-first-largest GDP per capita economies, accounting for 3.3 percent of global GDP. The United Kingdom was the world's fifth-largest exporter and importer in 2019. It also has the third-largest inbound and outbound foreign direct investment.

In 2020, commerce with the European Union's 27 member states accounted for 49 percent of exports and 52 percent of imports in the United Kingdom. The service sector dominates, accounting for over 80% of GDP; the financial services industry is especially significant, with London ranking as the world's second-largest financial center. Despite a loss in global supremacy, the United Kingdom has the potential to project enormous power and influence throughout the world in the twenty-first century.

There are no complicated tax burdens on UK stocks for foreigners, and the UK holds a double taxation treaty with most countries in the world, therefore there is little chance of having difficulties on that front. The main hiccup you will come across is when the company of the shares you own is UK property heavy, then there will be taxes to be paid to the UK authorities. Information is widely available for companies listed on the LSE. The best resources for research on UK listings can be found under the Business, industry, and trade section of the Office for National Statistics (UK) website.

The present stock exchange, volume 1 of Old and New London

France

The main exchange in France is Euronext Paris, which was known as the Bourse de Paris prior to its consolidation with Amsterdam, Lisbon, and Brussels exchanges under the Euronext umbrella (second-largest exchange in Europe behind the UK's London stock exchange group). There are 898 companies listed on the exchange and there are no restrictions for foreigners.

Access is also wide, and the top percentile in terms of the market capitalization of stocks is available to trade on any major broker by default. The exchange listings are denominated in Euros. There are listings in both the manufacturing sector and the services sector, with all major industry groups covered.

France's economy is highly developed and based on free markets. It is the world's seventh-largest economy in nominal terms and the tenth-largest economy in terms of purchasing power parity. After Germany and the United Kingdom, it is the third-largest economy in Europe as of September 30, 2020. Paris, a leading global metropolis, has one of the world's greatest city GDPs and is the first city in Europe (and third worldwide) for the number of Fortune Global 500 firms.

In 2017, Ernst & Young named La Défense, Paris' Central Commercial District, as the premier business district in continental Europe and fourth in the world. France was the most-represented European country in the Fortune Global 500 in 2020, with 31 firms, ahead of Germany (27 companies) and the United Kingdom (22 companies). France was also the country with the largest weight on the Eurozone's EURO

STOXX 50 index (representing 36.4 percent of all total assets) as of August 2020, ahead of Germany (35.2 percent). Several French firms, such as AXA in insurance and Air France in air transportation, are among the largest in their respective fields. With L'Oreal as the world's largest cosmetics firm and LVMH and Kering as the world's two largest luxury product firms, luxury and consumer goods are particularly relevant. GDF-Suez and EDF are two of the world's largest energy businesses, while Areva is a big nuclear-energy firm.

Veolia Environnement is the largest provider of environmental services and water management in the world. Large construction companies include Vinci SA, Bouygues, and Eiffage. Michelin is one of the top three tire producers in the world. Capgemini and Atos are two of the most well-known technology consulting firms. In terms of revenue, Carrefour is the world's second-largest retailer. Total is the fourth-largest private oil business in the world. Danone is the world's fifth-biggest food corporation and the largest mineral water supplier. Sanofi is the fifth-largest pharmaceutical firm in the world. Publicis is the world's third-largest advertising firm; Groupe PSA is the world's sixth-largest automobile and Europe's second-largest automaker; Accor is Europe's leading hotel group, and Alstom is one of the world's major rail transportation conglomerates.

Double taxation treaties are plenty with other countries, therefore tax implications are low for the most part, but similar to their European counterparts, property companies will be liable to capital gains to the french authorities regardless of the double taxation treaty. Access to information on French public companies is widely available. In order to explore the french equity market, I recommend the economic outlook/business indicator section of the English version of the INSEE website (Institut National de la Statistique et des Études Économiques), as well as the European Economic Sentiment indicators published by the European Union.

Painting of Louis and Eugène Roland-Gosselin, Parisian stockbrokers, Bourse de Paris, 19th century

La Défense, Paris, home of French listed companies

Italy

The Italian Bourse (Borsa Italiana S.p.A.) is the country's stock market, situated in Milan. The Italian Bourse was a London Stock Exchange Group subsidiary. This changed on October 9, 2020, when the London Stock Exchange Group and Euronext, the pan-European stock exchange group, agreed to a €4.3 billion merger.

The purchase of the Italian Bourse by Euronext was finalized on April 29, 2021. The Commissione Nazionale per le Società e la Borsa regulates the Borsa Italiana (CONSOB). There are roughly 110 Italian companies listed on the Borsa Italiana. One benefit of the Euronext group is that they offer a wide variety of financial instruments such as options and warrants. Individual brokers will also be favorable to allow CFD trading or margin trading. There are no restrictions for foreigners on the exchange, and access is wide therefore standard brokers will give you access by default.

The exchange listings are denominated in Euros. There are listings in both the manufacturing sector and the services sector, with all major industry groups covered.

Italy's economy is the third-largest in the European Union, the eighth-largest in terms of nominal GDP, and the 13th-largest in terms of GDP (PPP). It is the world's tenth-largest exporter, with $632 billion exported in 2019. Its closest trading partners are the other European Union nations, with whom it conducts around 59 percent of its overall commerce.

In terms of market share in exports, Germany (12.5 percent), France (10.3 percent), the United States (9 percent), Spain (5.2 percent), the United Kingdom (5.2 percent), and Switzerland (4.6 percent) are the top trade partners. Italy is a prominent player in manufacturing (the second largest in the EU after Germany) and exporter of a wide range of items, including equipment, automobiles, medicines, furniture, food, apparel, and robotics. Nine of the world's 500 largest stock-market-listed corporations by revenue in 2016, according to the Fortune Global 500, are located in Italy.

Due to the abundance of double taxation treaties with other countries, tax effects are often modest; nevertheless, property firms, like their European counterparts, will be subject to capital gains taxes by the Italian government regardless of the double taxation treaty. There is a lot of information accessible on Italian public corporations.

I recommend reading the "Business Outlook Survey of Industrial and Service Firms" section of the Banca D'Italia website, as well as the European Economic Sentiment indicators published by the European Union if you want to learn more about the Italian equity market.

EXOTIC MARKETS

Borsa di Milano, Paolo Monti, 1968

Netherlands

The Amsterdam Stock Exchange (Dutch: Amsterdamse effectenbeurs) was regarded as the world's earliest "modern" securities exchange. Shortly after the formation of the Dutch East India Company (VOC) in 1602 as a secondary market to trade its shares, stocks began trading on a regular basis.

The Amsterdam Stock Exchange is now part of the Euronext group, which is a European stock exchange with marketplaces in Amsterdam, Brussels, Dublin, Lisbon, London, Milan, Oslo, and Paris. It has over 1,900 listed issuers representing €5.6 trillion in market capitalization in May 2021. The AEX, which originated in 1983 and is comprised of more than 20 of the most frequently traded Dutch firms that trade on Euronext Amsterdam, is by far the most traded and significant index. International corporations such as Unilever, ING Group, Philips, and Royal Dutch Shell are among those represented.

It is one of the primary national indexes of the Euronext stock market group, alongside the BEL 20 in Brussels, the CAC 40 in Paris, and the DAX in Germany. Access will be easy with any standard broker. In terms of financial instruments, Euronext includes equities, exchange-traded funds, warrants and certificates, bonds, derivatives, commodities, and indices. The exchange is denominated in Euros. There are listings in both the manufacturing sector and the services sector, with all major industry groups covered.

According to the World Bank and International Monetary Fund, the Netherlands' economy is the 17th largest in the world in 2019 (in terms of GDP). Its GDP per capita is predicted to be at $57,101 in the fiscal year 2019/20, making it one of the world's highest-earning countries. Today, the Netherlands has more than a quarter of the European Union's total natural gas reserves. The Netherlands has a robust and open economy that is highly reliant on international commerce. The economy is known for its stable labor relations, as well as its relatively low unemployment and inflation.

Industrial activity is predominantly in food processing, chemicals, petroleum refining, high-tech, financial services, creative sector, and electrical machinery. Several big global corporations have their headquarters in the Netherlands. Until 2009, Royal Dutch Shell was the largest firm in the Netherlands by revenue and the largest in the world, but it has since dropped to the seventh position. Other well-known companies include Heineken, Ahold, Philips, TomTom, Unilever, Randstad, and ING. Because of the favorable corporate tax levels, thousands of firms of non-Dutch origin, such as EADS, LyondellBasell, and IKEA, have their headquarters in the Netherlands.

Tax impacts are frequently minor because of the availability of double taxation treaties with other countries; nevertheless, property businesses, like their European counterparts, will be subject to capital gains taxes by the Dutch government regardless of the double taxation treaty.

There is a wealth of data available about Dutch public enterprises. A good place to start researching Dutch stocks would be the business outlook section of the CBS statistics website, and the European Sentiment Indicators published by the European Union.

The Old Stock Exchange in Amsterdam, circa 1680, Painting by Job Berckheyde

Belgium

The Brussels Stock Exchange (French: Bourse de Bruxelles, Dutch: Beurs van Brussel), shortened to BSE, was established in 1801 by Napoleon's edict in Brussels, Belgium. In 2002, the BSE amalgamated with the stock exchanges of Amsterdam, Lisbon, and Paris to form Euronext N.V., renaming the BSE Euronext Brussels and is part of the Euronext group, the leading pan-European exchange. The BEL20 is the most well-known stock market index on the BSE.

There are 181 listed companies on the Brussels Stock Exchange, and they are denominated in Euros. Financial instruments include equities, exchange-traded funds, warrants and certificates, bonds, derivatives, commodities, and indices. The Belgian stock exchange is regulated by the National Bank of Belgium and the Financial Services and Markets Authority.

Belgium's economy is a modern, capitalist economy that has benefited from the country's central geographic location, well-developed transportation network, and diverse industrial and commercial base. Belgium imports raw materials and semi-finished items before processing and re-exporting them. Belgium has few natural resources other than rich soils, with the exception of coal, which is no longer economically viable to mine. Nonetheless, most conventional industrial sectors, such as steel, textiles, refining, chemicals, food processing, pharmaceuticals, autos, electronics, and machinery fabrication, are represented in the economy. Despite the importance of heavy industry, services account for 74.9 percent of GDP.

Like other European countries, double taxation treaties

are in place, and you will have to consult the bilateral agreement between Belgium and the non-resident person's home country. You can find out which of the two nations has the authority to tax capital gains. The most typical regulation is that the beneficiary's nation of residency has the authority to tax them, but there are exceptions, so check the agreement. There is also a tax on stock exchange transactions, that ranges between 0.12% to 1.32% per transaction.

Information about Belgian stocks is widely available. Stock research data can be found in the Enterprise section of the Statistical office website Statbel, as well as the Economic Sentiment indicators published by the European Union.

Brussels stock exchange in the 1920s, postcard

Austria

The Wiener Börse is a stock market located in Vienna, Austria (sometimes called the Vienna Stock Exchange). The Vienna Stock Exchange also owns the Prague Stock Exchange. Wiener Börse was created in 1771 and is one of the oldest exchanges in the world. A total of 264 companies are listed on the exchange. The listed stocks are denominated in Euros. Financial instruments include stocks, certificates and warrants. The exchange is regulated by the Stock Exchange Act.

Austria's economy is a well-developed social market economy, with the country ranking fourteenth in the world in terms of GDP (gross domestic product) per capita. Until the 1980s, many of Austria's major industrial enterprises were nationalized; however, privatization has decreased state ownership to levels comparable to other European countries in recent years.

Although certain sectors, such as various iron and steel works, chemical plants, and oil firms that employ thousands of people, are worldwide rivals, the majority of industrial and commercial firms in Austria are rather tiny on a worldwide scale. The service industry, which accounts for the great bulk of Austria's GDP, is particularly significant. Over the previous few decades, Vienna has evolved into a financial and consultancy powerhouse, establishing itself as the gateway to the East. Vienna's legal firms and banks are among the most prominent organizations doing business with the new EU member nations. Tourism is particularly important to the Austrian economy, contributing for around 10% of Austria's GDP.

Gains on the sale of shares for non-residents are excluded if the individual holds 10% for at least a year. Subject to specific criteria, tax on gains from the sale of movable or immovable property may be deferred.

Information about Austrian stocks is easily available. Stock research data can be found in the Economy section of the Statistics Austria website, as well as the Economic Sentiment indicators published by the European Union.

Wiener Börse in 1914

Spain

The Madrid Stock Exchange (Bolsa de Madrid) is the largest and most international of Spain's four regional stock exchanges (the others being in Barcelona, Valencia, and Bilbao), and was founded in 1831. It trades shares, convertible bonds, fixed income instruments, as well as government and private-sector debt.

Bolsas y Mercados Espanoles owns Bolsa de Madrid. The Madrid Stock Exchange General Index (IGBM) is the main index of the exchange, representing the sectors of construction, financial services, communications, consumer, capital/intermediate goods, energy, and market services. The Bolsa de Madrid's benchmark is the IBEX 35 Index, which is a capitalization-weighted index that includes the 35 most liquid Spanish equities traded in the continuous market.

The Spanish Stock Exchange had at the end of the month of November 2020 a total of 2,750 listed companies. The listed companies are denominated in Euros. Financial instruments available are stocks and warrants, and options are available through The Meff Sociedad Holding de Productos Derivados.

Spain's economy is the fourteenth biggest in the world by nominal GDP and one of the greatest by purchasing power parity. Spain has a mixed capitalist economy. Based on nominal GDP numbers, the Spanish economy is the fifth-largest in Europe, behind Germany, the United Kingdom, France, and Italy, and the fourth-largest in the eurozone. Spain was the world's fifteenth largest exporter and fourteenth largest importer in 2019.

Some Spanish corporations have attained international status during the 1990s, extending their operations in culturally similar Latin America, Eastern Europe, and Asia. After the United States, Spain is Latin America's second-largest foreign investor. Spanish firms have also increased their operations in Asia, particularly in China and India. Spanish enterprises gained a competitive edge over some of their competitors and European neighbors as a result of their early worldwide growth. Another factor contributing to Spanish business' success may be the growing interest in the Spanish language and culture across Asia and Africa, as well as a corporate culture that has learned to take risks in volatile markets.

Spanish companies have invested in fields such as biotechnology and pharmaceuticals, renewable energy (Iberdrola is the world's largest renewable energy operator), technology companies such as Telefónica, Abengoa, Mondragon Corporation, Movistar, Gamesa, Hisdesat, Indra, train manufacturers such as CAF and Talgo, global corporations such as textile company Inditex, petroleum companies such as Repsol, and infrastructural companies such as Ferrovial, Acciona, ACS, OHL, and FCC are six of the ten largest worldwide construction businesses specializing in transportation. Spain also has a strong financial system, with Banco Santander and BBVA being two worldwide systemically significant institutions.

For Non-Residents, any capital gain from the sale or transfer of assets situated in Spain is subject to a fixed tax of 24 percent, with a lower rate of 19 percent if the non-resident is a resident of another European Union nation, Iceland, or Norway. Furthermore, anybody staying in a nation of the European Union or the European Economic Area with whom Spain has an agreement for the exchange of tax information has been eligible for the reinvestment of a habitual residence exemption since 2015. It is not necessary for this new habitual home to be in Spain.

The European Union's Economic Sentiment Indicators and the Spanish Statistical Office Short-Term Indicators will be the most valuable sources of information for research on Spanish stocks.

Bolsa de Madrid, 2011

Ireland

Since 1793, Euronext Dublin (previously The Irish Stock Market, ISE) has served as Ireland's major stock exchange. The Irish Stock Exchange has four markets: the Main Securities Market, which is the main market for Irish and international companies; the Enterprise Securities Market (ESM), which is an equity market designed for growth companies; the Global Exchange Market (GEM), which is a specialist debt market for professional investors; and the Atlantic Securities Market (ASM), which is a market dedicated to companies that want to dual list on both the Irish and international stock exchanges.

There are currently 50 companies with shares listed on the Irish Stock Exchange. The listings are denominated in Euros.

The Republic of Ireland's economy has a highly developed knowledge economy, with high-tech, life sciences, financial services, and agriculture, particularly agrifood, as its main sectors. Ireland is an open economy that ranks first in high-value foreign direct investment (FDI) flows (5th on the Index of Economic Freedom). Ireland is ranked 4th out of 186 countries in the IMF table and 4th out of 187 countries in the World Bank table in terms of GDP per capita.

Chargeable profits resulting from the sale of shares are subject to Irish CGT at a rate of 33% for non-Irish residents only when the corporation derives the majority of their capital assets for the purposes of commerce carried on in Ireland through a permanent establishment.

As a result, if the value of the shares in the Irish business is not derived from Irish land, buildings, mineral, or exploration rights, no Irish CGT will be imposed on the individual's disposal of the shares in the Irish business. Information about Irish stocks is easily available. Stock research data can be found in the Economy section of the Central Statistical Office website, as well as the Economic Sentiment indicators published by the European Union.

The Dublin Stock Exchange, 1924, Lafayette photography agency

Switzerland

Switzerland is not only banks, high-end timepieces, and chocolate. Switzerland's main stock exchange, SIX Swiss Exchange (formerly SWX Swiss Exchange), is headquartered in Zurich (the other being Berne eXchange). Other securities traded on SIX Swiss Exchange include Swiss government bonds and derivatives such as stock options.

The securities are denominated in Swiss Francs. SIX Swiss Exchange manages a number of important indices. The SMI, or Swiss Market Index, is the most well-known index, consisting of the SPI's 20 biggest and most liquid firms. The SPI, or Swiss Performance Index, includes over 200 companies that are listed on the exchange and meet certain criteria. The SLI, or Swiss Leader Index, is a capped index that includes the top 30 companies in Switzerland. The exchange contains over 40,000 products in the form of Shares, Bonds, ETFs, ETPs, Sponsored Funds and Structured Products.

Switzerland's economy is one of the most advanced free-market economies in the world. The service sector, especially the Swiss banking industry and tourism, has come to play a significant economic role. The city of Zurich, is the most important economic center of the country and one of the world's major financial centers.

In terms of economic sectors, the Swiss economy follows the traditional developed world model. The primary or agricultural sector employs only a small percentage of the workforce, while the secondary or industrial sector employs a greater proportion (27.7 percent in 2012). The tertiary or service sector of the economy employs the vast majority of the working population (71.0 percent in 2012). Switzerland is a major exporter of high-end timepieces and watches. The majority of the world's high-end watches are made in Switzerland. Switzerland's manufacturing sector is diverse, with internationally competitive companies in a variety of industries.

Most notably, food processing companies like Nestlé, computer and robot manufacturers like ABB, Bobst SA, and Stadler Rail, automotive and construction chemicals companies like Sika AG, and military equipment companies like Ruag. In addition, Switzerland has one of the most competitive pharmaceutical industries in the world. The majority of Swiss exports are precision or 'high tech' finished goods, since it is a developed country with a trained labor force. Medication (13 percent), heterocyclic compounds (2.2

percent), watches (6.4 percent), orthopaedic equipment (2.1 percent), and precious jewelry (2.1 percent) are the top export categories in Switzerland.

In early 2000s, the financial sector employed approximately 196,000 workers (136,000 of whom work in the banking sector), accounting for about 5.6 percent of the total Swiss workforce. Zurich is known for banking (UBS, Credit Suisse, Julius Baer) and insurance (Swiss Re, Zurich insurance), while Geneva is known for wealth management (Pictet Group, Lombard Odier, Union Bancaire Privée) as well as commodity trading, trade finance, and shipping (Cargill, Mediterranean Shipping Company, Louis Dreyfus Company, Mercuria Energy Group, Trafigura, Banque de Commerce et de Placements).

If you are a non-resident, it is most likely that you will not pay tax on your gains. For Swiss residents, whether or not you pay capital gains tax on trading profits depends on whether the tax office categorizes you as a private investor or as a professional investor. Private investors do not pay tax on capital gains achieved through investing their assets. Professional investors, on the other hand, must account for capital gains in their taxable income.

Information about Swiss stock is widely available. A good place to start would be the Swiss Federal Statistics Office website.

Zurich, Switzerland

Luxembourg

The Luxembourg Stock Exchange, LuxSE (French: Bourse de Luxembourg) is based in Luxembourg City. The Luxembourg Stock Exchange specializes in the listing of foreign bonds, and as of August 2016, it was the first in Europe with 25,831 debt securities listed. It was the first exchange in the world to list a Eurobond, a foreign bond denominated in a currency other than the country where it was issued, when it issued Italian Autostrade bonds in 1963.

Luxembourg has held a leading position in European bond issues to this day, accounting for about 40% of all cross-border securities traded in Europe. The LuxX Index, a weighted index of the nine most valuable stocks by free-float market capitalization, is the primary share index of the Luxembourg Stock Exchange. The stocks are denominated in Euros. Today, the Luxembourg Stock exchange has more than 37 000 listings, in the form of bonds, warrants, shares, and funds.

Luxembourg's economy is heavily reliant on the banking, steel, and manufacturing sectors. Luxembourgers have the world's largest per capita gross domestic product. The main industries are banking and financial services, construction, real estate services, iron, metals, and steel, information technology, telecommunications, cargo transportation and logistics, chemicals, engineering, tires, glass, aluminum, tourism, and biotechnology.

Despite being dubbed the "Green Heart of Europe" in tourist literature, Luxembourg's pastoral land coexists with a highly industrialized and export-intensive region. Luxembourg's economy resembles Germany's in several ways. Luxembourg enjoys a degree of economic stability that is uncommon among developed democracies. Luxembourg's banking industry is the largest in the country. Luxembourg was ranked the 25th most competitive financial center in the world in the 2019 Global Financial Centres Index, and the third most competitive in Europe after London and Zürich. The country has made a name for itself in the field of cross-border fund administration.

Luxembourg's financial center is mostly foreign due to the country's limited domestic market. Political stability, good communications, easy access to other European centers, professional multilingual workers, a banking secrecy tradition, and cross-border financial expertise have all aided the financial sector's development.

If the holding period is less than six months and the gross capital gains exceed EUR 500, capital gains resulting from the sale of movable assets are subject to Luxembourg progressive income tax rates (0 percent to 45.78 percent). If movable assets are sold more than six months after purchase, capital gains are not taxable unless the owner has a significant stake in the company (material interest). After the six-month cycle, capital gains from the sale of material interest are charged as exceptional profits at half the overall combined tax rate (maximum 22.89 percent).

The information available on Lux stocks is easily accessible. The Luxembourg Statistical Office (STATEC) is a great resource as well as the European Sentiment Indicators published by the European Union.

Luxembourg city

Portugal

The Euronext Lisbon stock exchange is located in Lisbon, Portugal. It is a member of Euronext, a pan-European stock exchange. It was founded in 1769. There are 56 listings on the exchange, and they are denominated in Euros. Equities, public and private shares, participation bonds, warrants, corporate warrants, investment trust units, and exchange-traded funds are all traded on Euronext Lisbon.

Listed shares on the official market are included in the BVL General index, which is the exchange's official index. Long-term interest rate futures, three-month Lisbor futures, stock index futures and options on the PSI-20 Stock index, and Portuguese stock futures are among the derivatives available.

The economy of Portugal is ranked 34th in the World Economic Forum's Global Competitiveness Report for 2019. The European Union (EU), whose countries earned 72.8 percent of Portuguese exports and were the source of 76.5 percent of Portuguese imports in 2015, accounts for the vast majority of foreign trade. Since the third quarter of 2014, the Portuguese economy has been steadily growing.

The economy's expansion has been followed by a steady decline in unemployment (6.3 percent in the first quarter of 2019, compared with 13.9 percent registered at the end of 2014). In addition, the government's budget deficit has decreased from 11.2 percent of GDP in 2010 to 0.5 percent in 2018. Portugal is home to a number of notable leading companies with worldwide reputations, such as The Navigator Company, a major world player in the international paper market; Sonae Indústria, the largest producer of wood-based panels in the world; Amorim, the world leader in cork production; Conservas Ramirez, the oldest canned food producer; Cimpor, one of the world's 10th largest producers of cement; EDP Renováveis, the 3rd largest producer of wind energy in the world; Jerónimo Martins, consumer products manufacturer and retail market leader in Portugal, Poland, and Colombia; TAP Air Portugal, highly regarded for its safety record, and one of the leading airlines linking Europe with Africa and Latin America (namely Brazil).

The tertiary sector is currently the most important component of the Portuguese economy, accounting for 75.8 percent of the gross value added and employing 68.1 percent of the labor force. It is followed by the industry sector, which accounts for 21.9 percent of gross value added and provides 24.5 percent of jobs. Machinery, electrical and electronics industries, automotive and shipbuilding industries, injection moulding, plastics and ceramics industries, textile, footwear and leather industries, oil refinery, petrochemistry and cement industries, beverages and food industries, and furniture, pulp and paper, wood and cork industries are currently the major industries in Portugal.

Some large Portuguese service companies, such as retailer Jerónimo Martins, which owns Poland's largest supermarket chain and is also investing in Colombia, have committed to internationalizing their services. The largest Portuguese banks are Banco Comercial Português and the state-owned Caixa Geral de Depósitos. Portuguese banks have strategic stakes in other sectors of the economy, such as insurance. Foreign bank participation is moderate, as is state ownership via the Caixa Geral de Depósitos (CGD). Overall, Portugal's financial system is sound, well-managed, and competitive, with short-term risks and vulnerabilities well contained and a strong financial policy framework supporting the system. Despite its small size and concentration, Portugal's banking system compares favorably to that of other European Union countries in terms of efficiency, profitability, and asset quality, with solvency close to European levels.

The entire gain from the sale of a property, shares, securities, or bonds in Portugal is taxable at a flat 28 percent rate for non-Portuguese residents. If you are an EU resident, you can elect to be taxed as a Portuguese resident at the scale income tax rates instead. However, you would need to declare your worldwide income in order to calculate the applicable tax rate on the gain, so this may not be the most tax-efficient approach. Information about Portuguese equities is widely available.

To research Portuguese stocks, start by looking at the business section of the Statistic Portugal Office web portal as well as the European Economic Sentiment Indicators published by the European Union.

Lisbon, Portugal

3

Nordics

Denmark

The Nasdaq Copenhagen, originally known as the Copenhagen Stock Exchange (Danish: Københavns Fondsbørs), is a global exchange for Danish assets such as stocks, bonds, treasury bills, and notes, as well as financial futures and options. One of the Nasdaq Nordic Exchanges is Nasdaq Copenhagen.

Nasdaq Nordic dates back to the 2003 merger of OM AB and HEX plc to establish OMX and has been a part of Nasdaq, Inc. since February 2008. (formerly known as NASDAQ OMX Group). For futures and options trading, the C25 Index, a weighted market value index comprised of 20 Danish blue chips, was created (members include the A.P. Moller-Maersk Group).

On the KVX Growth Market, the KFX Index includes growth businesses in the medical, telecommunications, biotechnology, and information technology sectors. The

KAX Index is the exchange's all-share index. The listed companies are denominated in Danish Krones.

Denmark's economy is a contemporary mixed economy with high living standards, extensive government services and transfers, and a strong reliance on international commerce.

The service industry employs 80 percent of the workforce, while manufacturing employs 11 percent and agriculture employs 2 percent. In 2020, the nominal gross national income per capita was $58,439, the fifth-highest in the world.

Denmark, being a small open economy, favors a free trade policy, with exports and imports accounting for around half of GDP. Denmark adheres to a fixed exchange rate system by maintaining an independent currency: The Danish krone, which is pegged to the euro.

Capital gains on publicly traded Danish shares are taxed at a rate of 22%. On the sale of shares in Danish enterprises, foreign shareholders are normally exempt from Danish capital gains tax but exceptions may apply.

The European Union's Economic Sentiment Indicators and the Denmark Statistics website Short-Term Indicators will be the most valuable sources of information for research on Danish stocks.

Københavns Fondsbørs, 1895, Peder Severin Krøyer painting

Sweden

The Nasdaq Stockholm AB, previously the Stockholm Stock Exchange (Swedish: Stockholmsbörsen), is a Swedish stock exchange located in Frihamnen, Stockholm. It was founded in 1863 and has since grown to become the principal securities exchange for the Nordic nations.

As of March 2021, there are a total of 832 firms listed on Nasdaq Stockholm - 385 on the main market and 447 on secondary marketplaces (Nasdaq First North and Nasdaq First North Premier). The exchange is part of the Nasdaq group which operates the Nasdaq exchanges in the US (New York, Boston, Philadelphia) but also all exchanges in the Nordic countries of Europe. In terms of financial instruments, Nasdaq offers trading and clearing in Swedish options and futures. Stocks on the Stockholm exchange are denominated in Swedish Kronas.

Sweden's economy is a developed export-oriented economy supported by wood, hydropower, and iron ore. These are the foundational resources of a trade-oriented economy. Motor cars, telecommunications, pharmaceuticals, industrial machinery, precision equipment, chemical products, household goods and appliances, forestry, iron, and steel are among the major industries.

Today, Sweden is developing internationally competitive engineering, mining, steel, and pulp sectors, as indicated by businesses such as Ericsson, ASEA/ABB, SKF, Alfa Laval, AGA, and Dyno Nobel.

Sweden's economy is competitive and highly liberalized, with an open market economy. The great majority of Swedish businesses are privately held and market-oriented, with a large welfare state that includes transfer payments amounting to up to three-fifths of GDP. Volvo, Ericsson, Vattenfall, Skanska, Hennes & Mauritz, Electrolux, Volvo Personvagnar, Preem, TeliaSonera, Sandvik, ICA, Atlas Copco, Nordea, Svenska Cellulosa Aktiebolaget, Scania, Securitas, Nordstjernan, SKF, ABB Norden Holding, and Sony Mobile Communications AB were the 20 largest Sweden-registered companies.

Sweden's industry is predominantly under public and governmental control; the most visible example is LKAB, a state-owned mining firm mostly engaged in the country's north, with the highest recognized market share of all domestic rivals.

If you have never been a resident of Sweden and have capital gains from the sale of Swedish listed shares or units in Swedish trusts, you will not be taxed in Sweden. Capital gains are taxed in your country of residence in line with that nation's own legislation. Information pertaining to Swedish stocks is widely available.

A great place to find such information is the business activity section of the statistical database SCB website, as well as the Economic Sentiment indicators published by the European Union.

Offices in Kista, Stockholm, 2011

Norway

The Oslo Stock Exchange (OSE: OSLO) is a stock exchange in the Nordic nations that now provides Norway's sole regulated marketplaces for securities trading. Equities, derivatives, and fixed income products are all available on the stock exchange.

The Euronext consortium of European stock exchanges operates the Oslo Stock Exchange. *OBX* – The index comprises the 25 most traded shares listed on Oslo Børs. There are 220 listed companies on the Norwegian exchange.

They are denominated in Norwegian Krones. The Oslo Stock Exchange contains equity certificates issued by Norwegian savings banks in addition to Norwegian and international corporations having shares listed. The distinction between shares and equity certificates has to do with who owns the company's assets and how much power banks have in their administrative bodies.

Norway's economy is a well-developed mixed economy with governmental ownership in key industries. Despite being susceptible to global business cycles, Norway's economy has grown steadily since the industrial revolution began. In comparison to other European nations, the country boasts a very high quality of life and a well-integrated social system.

Norway's sophisticated industrial and welfare systems rely on a financial reserve generated by natural resource extraction, primarily North Sea oil. Presently, The North Sea's oil output has reached its peak. In the broad Norwegian sections of the Norwegian Sea, new oil and gas resources have been discovered and exploited.

In contrast to other Nordic nations like Sweden and notably Finland, there has been minimal government motivation to assist in the creation and foster new sectors in the private sector since the 1970s because of the oil boom. However, in recent decades, national and municipal governments have begun to provide incentives to foster the establishment of new "mainland" businesses that are internationally competitive. Aside from expectations for a high-tech economy, there is significant interest in fostering small company growth as a potential source of employment.

Most nations have double taxation treaties with Norway, therefore in most circumstances, you will only have to pay capital gains tax on the sale of Norwegian shares in your own country.

The European Union's Economic Sentiment Indicators and the Norwegian Statistics SSB Short-Term Indicators will be the most valuable sources of information for research on Norwegian stocks.

Oslo at night, 2014

Finland

The Nasdaq Helsinki was originally known as the Helsinki Stock Exchange (Finnish: Helsingin Pörssi, Swedish: Helsingforsbörsen). It has been a part of Nasdaq Nordic since September 3, 2003. (previously called OMX).

OMX Helsinki 25 (OMXH25) is a stock market index for the Helsinki Stock Exchange. There are 141 listed Finnish companies on the exchange, and they are denominated in Euros. Stocks, bonds, futures, and options are available to trade.

Finland's economy is highly industrialized and mixed, with per capita production comparable to that of major western European economies such as France, Germany, and the United Kingdom. Services account for 72.7 percent of Finland's GDP, followed by manufacturing and refining (31.4 percent). Manufacturing is the most important economic sector in terms of international commerce.

Electronics (21.6%), equipment, cars, and other engineered metal goods (21.1%), the forest sector (13.1%), and chemicals (13.1%) are the most important industries. Finland boasts a diverse range of natural resources, including timber, minerals, and freshwater. Finland ranks second behind Ireland in high-technology manufacturing in an OECD study.

Knowledge-intensive services are also the smallest and slowest-growing industry, coming in second only to Ireland. The investment was lower than projected. The short-term prognosis was positive, and GDP growth was higher than many EU counterparts. Behind Sweden, Denmark, and the United Kingdom, Finland has Europe's fourth-biggest knowledge economy.

Finland's economy is ranked first in the World Economic Forum's Global Information Technology 2014 report for coordinated output between the corporate sector, scholarly production, and government aid in information and communications technology.

Finland's economy is highly connected, with foreign commerce accounting for a third of GDP. The European Union accounts for 60% of all commerce. Germany, Russia, Sweden, the United Kingdom, the United States, the Netherlands, and China have the highest trade flows. Since the 1990s, as more traditional sectors have declined due to globalization, Finland's industry, which had relied on the country's enormous woods for centuries, has become more dominated by electronics and services. More production was outsourced abroad as a result of outsourcing, with the Finnish industry focusing more on R&D and high-tech devices.

Instru, Vaisala, and Neles (now part of Metso) are examples of Finnish enterprises that have thrived in fields like industrial automation, medical technology, and meteorological technology. Notable companies in Finland include Nokia, the former market leader in mobile telephony; Stora Enso, the world's largest paper manufacturer; Neste Oil, an oil refining and marketing company; UPM-Kymmene, the world's third-largest paper manufacturer; Aker Finnyards, the world's largest cruise ship manufacturer (such as Royal Caribbean's Freedom of the Seas); Rovio Mobile, the video game developer best known for creating Angry Birds; KONE, an elevator and escalator manufacturer; Wärtsilä, a power plant and ship engine manufacturer; and Finnair, the largest Helsinki-Vantaa airline.

Foreign-registered corporations own around 70-80 percent of the equity listed on the Helsinki Stock Exchange. The majority of the income for the larger corporations comes from outside the nation, and the bulk of its workers work elsewhere as well. Cross-shareholding has been outlawed, and an Anglo-Saxon model of corporate governance is becoming more popular. However, just around 15% of inhabitants have invested in the stock market, compared to 20% in France and 50% in the United States.

Finland does not tax gains of non-residents (except on disposals of companies whose main assets are real estate and on certain disposals by non-resident companies with a permanent establishment in Finland).

Information about Finnish stocks is easily available. Stock research data can be found in the Economic Trends section of the Statistics Finland website, as well as the Economic Sentiment indicators published by the European Union.

Helsinki Stock Exchange, 1965

Lithuania

The Nasdaq Vilnius (Vilnius Stock Exchange, VSE) is a stock exchange based in Vilnius, Lithuania, that was founded in 1993. Nasdaq Nordic, which also runs the Helsinki Stock Exchange and the Stockholm Stock Exchange, owns it. VSE, along with Riga Stock Exchange and Tallinn Stock Exchange, is a member of the Baltic Stock Exchange, which was created to reduce investment obstacles between Estonian, Latvian, and Lithuanian markets (OMX Baltic 10).

There are 30 listings available on the exchange, and they are denominated in Euros. Being part of the Nasdaq group, investors can expect a relatively good amount of available financial instruments to trade from.

Lithuania's economy is the most developed of the three

Baltic republics. Lithuania is a member of the European Union, with the second-highest GDP per capita in the Baltic region, trailing only Estonia. Lithuania was the first country to proclaim independence from the Soviet Union in 1990, and it quickly transitioned from a centrally planned to a market economy, enacting a slew of liberal reforms in the process.

It, along with the other Baltic republics, saw rapid development after entering the European Union, giving rise to the concept of a Baltic Tiger. Since regaining independence in 1990, Lithuania's economy (GDP) has grown by more than 500 percent. In the Ease of Doing Business Index, Lithuania is placed 11th in the world. Agricultural, furniture, logistics, textile, biotechnology, and laser industries have long been dominant in Lithuania.

Maxima is a retail chain with locations in Lithuania, Latvia, Estonia, Poland, and Bulgaria. It is the largest Lithuanian capital firm and the Baltic republics' largest employment. Girteka Logistics is the largest transportation firm in Europe. Biotechpharma is a biopharmaceutical research and development business that specializes in the development of recombinant protein technology. The BIOK Laboratory is the largest manufacturer of natural cosmetics in Lithuania, having been developed by biochemistry specialists. UAB SANITEX is Lithuania's and Latvia's largest wholesale, distribution, and logistics firm, with operations in Estonia and Poland as well. UAB SoliTek Cells is a major solar cell manufacturer in Northern Europe. UAB Teltonika is one of Europe's leading manufacturers of cellular IoT gateways. More than half of the firms in Coface's "Baltic Top 50," a ranking of the largest Baltic nations enterprises, are from

Lithuania (29). Information and communication technology are one of the most important sub-sectors (ICT).

9.5 percent of total FDI went to ICT. Lithuania is home to 13 of the Baltic States' top 20 IT businesses. Some of the most promising sectors include the development of shared services and business process outsourcing. The financial sector is mostly concerned with the domestic market. The Bank of Lithuania has issued licenses to nine commercial banks and eight international bank branches. The majority of the banks are owned by multinational firms, mostly from Scandinavia. The country has been attempting to establish itself as the EU's major fintech center, promising to grant European operational licenses within three months, compared to a year in nations like Germany or the United Kingdom.

Only 35 FinTech businesses started in Lithuania in 2017. In comparison to the other Baltic countries, Lithuania's industrial sector accounts for a substantially higher portion of the economy's structure. Lithuania is closer to certain Central European nations in this way, such as the Czech Republic and Germany. Manufacturing accounts for the majority of Lithuania's gross value added.

The sale of shares by a non-resident is not taxed in Lithuania.

Market information is pretty accessible. The Lithuanian Department of Statistics and the European Economic Sentiment Indicators (published by the European Union) are great places to research the Lithuanian market.

Downtown Vilnius, 2019, Lithuania

Latvia

The Nasdaq Riga, formerly known as the Riga Stock Exchange, is Latvia's only stock exchange. Nasdaq, which also owns exchanges in Denmark, Sweden, Finland, Iceland, Lithuania, and Estonia, owns it. The Riga Stock Exchange, along with the Vilnius Stock Exchange and the Tallinn Stock Exchange, form the joint Baltic market, which was formed to reduce investment barriers between the Latvian, Lithuanian, and Estonian stock exchanges. OMX Riga (OMXRGI) is an all-share index that includes all of the Riga Stock Exchange's listed securities. The listings in the exchange are denominated in Euros.

Latvia's economy is a decentralized economy in Northern Europe that is a member of the European Union's (EU) single market. Main industries are processed foods, processed wood products, textiles, processed metals, pharmaceuticals, railroad cars, synthetic fibers, and electronics. During 2006–07, Latvia's economy grew at a rate of more than

10% per year, but the country fell into a deep recession in 2009. The European Union, the International Monetary Fund, and other international donors offered considerable financial assistance to Latvia as part of an agreement to protect the currency's peg to the euro in return for the government's adherence to strict austerity measures, which was triggered by the failure of Parex Bank, the country's second largest bank. Latvia's GDP increased by 5.5 percent in 2011, putting it back among the European Union's fastest-growing economies.

If a non-resident sells shares in a real estate company in Latvia, the gross proceeds will be subject to a 3% tax. For regular shares, double taxation treaties apply.

The Riga Stock Exchange, circa 1900-1918

Estonia

The Nasdaq Tallinn AS, originally the Tallinn Stock Exchange, is an Estonian stock exchange based in Tallinn. The only regulated secondary securities market in Estonia is Nasdaq Tallinn. Nasdaq Tallinn, formerly known as TALSE, is the main stock market index. There are 15 listings on the exchange, and they are denominated in Euros. Because it is part of the Nasdaq group, a good selection of financial instruments is available to trade.

Estonia's economy is sophisticated, and the nation is a member of both the European Union and the eurozone. The economy of Estonia is highly impacted by the economies of Finland and Sweden. Estonia was ranked 21st on the World Bank Group's Ease of Doing Business Index in 2013. The economy's core industries are oil shale energy, telecommunications, textiles, chemical goods, banking, services, food and fishing, lumber, shipbuilding, electronics, and transportation. The Estonian economy's long-term prospects remain among the most promising in Europe.

Estonia's real GDP growth was 8.0 percent in 2011, and according to CEPII predictions, GDP per capita might reach the levels of the Nordic nations of Sweden, Finland, Denmark, and Norway by 2025. According to the same forecasts, Estonia might overtake Luxembourg as the most productive country in the EU by 2050, and therefore join the world's top five most productive nations. Tallinn has established itself as the country's financial hub. The benefits of the Estonian financial industry, according to Invest in Estonia, include unbureaucratic collaboration between enterprises and government, as well as a relative quantity of educated individuals. Swedbank, SEB Pank, and Nordea are the three largest banks. Over 60% of Estonia's workforce is employed in the service industry. Estonia's information technology sector is robust.

Non-residents' capital gains from the sale of Estonian firm shares are generally exempt from taxation in Estonia. The selling of shares in a real estate corporation by non-residents is subject to a 20% income tax. Information on Estonian stocks is available, the first stop for researching Estonian stocks will be the Statistics Estonia website, as well as the European Economic Sentiment Indicators published by the European Union.

Downtown Tallinn during sunset, Estonia

Iceland

The Nasdaq Iceland, formerly known as the Iceland Stock Exchange (XICE), is an Icelandic stock exchange. It was founded in 1985. Many of the companies traded on the XICE are small and illiquid due to the small size of the Icelandic economy and the low cost of going public. There are 18 listings on the exchange and they are denominated in Icelandic Kronas. Because of the market's limited size and illiquidity, no international corporation has ever listed directly on the XICE. In contrast, few Icelandic companies have gone public in other countries.

Iceland's economy is small and prone to high uncertainty. The main industries of Iceland are tourism, fish processing; aluminum smelting; geothermal power, hydropower; and medical/pharmaceutical products. Iceland's economy is a combination of free trade and government interference, with a high degree of free trade.

Gains from the sale of shares of Icelandic companies are subject to WHT at a rate of 22% for individuals and 20% for anyone else. These rates refer to transactions involving two non-residents as well.

Reykjavik, capital of Iceland

4

Balkans

Turkey

The Borsa Istanbul (abbreviated as BIST) is Turkey's sole exchange entity, bringing together the former Istanbul Stock Exchange (ISE) (Turkish: Istanbul Menkul Kymetler Borsas, IMKB), the Istanbul Gold Exchange (Turkish: Istanbul Altn Borsas, AB), and the Derivatives Exchange of Turkey (Turkish: Vadeli şlem Opsiyon Borsas, VOB) under one roof.

Its slogan is *worth investing*. Borsa Istanbul was founded in 1866 as the Dersaadet Securities Exchange. Borsa Istanbul's shareholders include the Turkish government with 49 percent, 41 percent IMKB, 5 percent VOB, 4 percent IMKB members, 1 percent IMKB brokers, and 0.3 percent IAB members. All of the government's shares are expected to be put up for sale.

ISE is home to 320 national companies and 411 total listings. The indices are ISE National-All Shares Index, ISE National-30, ISE National-50, ISE National-100, and Sector and sub-sector indices. The stocks are denominated in the Turkish Lira.

Short selling is not banned when it comes to the BIST-30 index components—the top 30 most traded stocks on the Istanbul exchange—but the uptick rule is in place, meaning you can only send a short-sell order at one level above the last effective price on the trading board. Short sellers are generally disliked by the Turkish government, which is the de facto dominant participant in all of Turkey's asset markets. It penalized several brokerage firms that were exempt from the uptick regulation in July 2020. They were permitted to short shares on the Borsa Istanbul thanks to the exemptions, and they did so with zeal. Providing such exemptions to a few participants on a regulated market, on the other hand, looks odd.

According to the International Monetary Fund, Turkey's economy is classified as an emerging market economy. According to the CIA World Factbook, Turkey is one of the world's developed countries. Economists and political scientists classify Turkey as one of the world's newly industrialized countries.

Turkey has the world's 20th highest nominal GDP and 11th biggest PPP GDP, with a population of 83.4 million as of 2021. Agriculture, textiles, motor cars, transportation equipment, building materials, consumer electronics, and home appliances are among the country's top exports. The economic and social components of Turkey's economy have seen significant changes during the last 20 years.

Since 2000, there has been a rise in employment and income. Among the country's major industrial conglomerates are Koç Holding, Sabanc Holding, Anadolu Group, Eczacbaş

Holding, and Zorlu Holding, which operate in a variety of industries. In 2014, the Forbes Global 2000 list included 12 Turkish firms. The banking business has the most firms on the list, with five, followed by the telecommunications business, which has two. There are also two conglomerates, having one company each in the transportation and beverage industries.

As of 2016, Turkey's largest trading partners include Germany, Russia, and the United Kingdom, as well as the UAE, Iraq, Italy, and China, with several of them ranking first in both export and import. The automobile industry accounts for a substantial portion of Turkey's commerce, with autos accounting for $13.2 billion in exports. Gold, delivery trucks, auto components, and jewelry are the country's other top exports, at $6.96 billion, $5.04 billion, $4.64 billion, and $3.39 billion, respectively.

Turkey is also a source of FDI in Central and Eastern Europe and the Commonwealth of Independent States, with more than $1.5 billion invested. Turkey's Black Sea neighbors, Bulgaria and Romania, have received 32 percent of the investment, mostly in the natural resources and construction sectors. Turkish corporations also have significant FDI holdings in Poland, estimated to be worth over $100 million. Construction and contracting firms such as Enka and Tekfen have played a key role in the economy of the country.

Non-residents' gains are usually not taxed in Turkey unless the non-resident has a permanent establishment or a permanent representation in Turkey and the income can be traced back to them. Capital gains generated from the sale of shares by a non-resident are subject to a special tax regime.

Information on Turkish markets is wide and available. The European Union's Economic Sentiment Indicators and the Turkish Statistical Institute website Short-Term Indicators will be a great resource for research on Turkish stocks.

Founded in 1866, Dersaadet Securities Exchange, the predecessor of the Borsa Istanbul

Levent financial district in Istanbul, 2013

Greece

The Athens Stock Exchange (ASE or ATHEX) is Greece's stock exchange, located in Athens, the country's capital. It was established in 1876. ATHEX currently operates five markets: regulated securities, regulated derivatives, alternative market, carbon market (for EUAs), and OTC market. Investors can trade stocks, bonds, ETFs, and other related securities in the regulated securities market.

Currently, 172 stocks representing 166 companies are traded on the stock exchange. The listings are denominated in Euros. ATHEX has more than 30 indices. The six major indices are the Composite Index (GD), the FTSE/Athex Large

Cap (FTSE, also known as the FTSE 25), the FTSE/Athex Mid Cap Index (FTSEM), the FTSE/Athex Market Index (FTSEA), the FTSE/ATHEX Global Traders Index Plus (FTSEGTI), and the FTSE/ATHEX Factor-Weighted Index (FTSEMSFW).

At the height of the Greek debt crisis, After being closed since June 27, 2015, due to the ongoing debt crisis, the stock market crashed when it reopened on August 3, 2015. The overall index lost more than 16 percent of its value on the day, with bank stocks losing the maximum allowed 30 percent.

Greece has the fourteenth largest economy in the 27-member European Union as of 2021. Greece's GDP per capita in 2021, according to IMF figures, is $19,673 in nominal terms and $30,495 in purchasing power parity terms. Greece is a developed country with an economy based on the service (80%) and industrial sectors (16%), with agriculture accounting for an estimated 4% of national economic output in 2017. Tourism and shipping are important Greek industries. The Greek Merchant Navy is the world's largest, with Greek-owned vessels accounting for 15% of the global deadweight tonnage in 2013. Because of the increased demand for international maritime transportation between Greece and Asia, the shipping industry has seen unprecedented investment.

Non-resident individuals who do not have permanent residency in Greece should not be taxed on capital gains from the sale of shares. The sale of shares listed on the Athens Stock Exchange, on the other hand, is subject to a 0.2 percent transfer duty borne by the seller.

Information on greek stocks is widely available. Research on greek stocks can be done through the Hellenic Statistical authority, and the European Economic Sentiment Indicators published by the European Union.

Stock exchange of Athens

Hungary

By market size and liquidity, the Budapest Stock Exchange (BSE) is the second biggest stock exchange in Central and Eastern Europe. It is located at 7 Liberty Square in Budapest, Hungary, in Center V, the city's major business district. Previously, it was housed in the Budapest Stock Exchange Palace building from 1864 until a larger trading floor was required under the Austro-Hungarian Empire. Listed issuers,

Hungarian private investors, and the central bank all have a say on the exchange. The BSE is a member of the Federation of European Securities Exchanges and the World Federation of Exchanges.

There are 98 listings on the Budapest Stock Exchange, and they are denominated in Hungarian Forints. The exchange is regulated by the Hungarian National Bank (Securities and exchange surveillance). BUX is a blue-chip stock market index that includes up to 25 important Hungarian firms that trade on the Budapest Stock Exchange.

Hungary's economy is a high-income mixed economy, with the Economic Complexity Index ranking it as the 9th most complicated economy in the world. With $265.037 billion in yearly production, the Hungarian economy ranks 57th in the world (out of 188 nations surveyed by the IMF), and 40th in terms of GDP per capita calculated by purchasing power parity.

Hungary has an export-oriented market economy with a strong focus on international commerce; as a result, it is the world's 35th biggest export economy. Hungary is one of the most attractive countries in Central and Eastern Europe for foreign direct investment. Germany, Austria, Romania, Slovakia, France, Italy, Poland, and the Czech Republic were Hungary's main commercial partners in 2015.

Food processing, pharmaceuticals, automobiles, information technology, chemicals, metallurgy, manufacturing, electrical products, and tourism are all major businesses. Hungary is Central and Eastern Europe's largest electronics manufacturer. Electronics manufacturing and research are two of the country's most important sources of innovation and economic growth. MOL Group, OTP Bank, Gedeon

Richter Plc., Magyar Telekom, CIG Pannonia, FHB Bank, Zwack Unicum are examples of well-known corporations; Hungary also has a huge number of specialized small and medium firms, such as numerous automotive sector suppliers and technological start-ups.

Budapest is Hungary's financial and business capital. The capital is an important economic center, having been categorized as an Alpha-world city in research by the Globalization and World Cities Research Network, and being Europe's second-fastest-growing metropolitan economy. Heavy industry (mining, metallurgy, machine and steel manufacture), energy production, mechanical engineering, chemicals, food industry, and car manufacture are the key areas of the Hungarian industry.

In 2007, the tertiary sector accounted for 64 percent of GDP, and its importance in the Hungarian economy has gradually increased over the previous 15 years as a result of consistent expenditures in transportation and other services. Hungary's geostrategic location, in the center of Central Europe, plays a vital role in the expansion of the service industry, since the country's central location makes it ideal and profitable to invest in.

Capital gains, in general, are taxed at the regular rate of 9 percent and are included in the income tax base. With the exception of Hungarian property firms, capital gains deriving from the sale of shares in Hungarian corporations by non-resident individuals are tax-free.

Information on Hungarian stocks is somewhat accessible. The first stop for researching Hungarian stocks would be the Hungarian Central Statistics Office and the European Economic Sentiment Indicators published by the European

Union.

Building in Budapest Financial district (district V)

Romania

The Bucharest Stock Exchange (BVB) is Romania's stock exchange, based in Bucharest. BVB's market capitalization climbed 23.4 percent to EUR 37.8 billion in 2019, compared to the previous year.

There were 83 firms listed on the BVB at the end of 2019. Banca Transilvania (TLV) is the most liquid business on the BVB's main market, with around 30% of the total traded value. The FTSE Russell rating agency advanced the

Bucharest Stock Exchange from the Frontier Market to the Secondary Emerging Market category in September 2020.

The Bucharest Stock Exchange's history may be traced back to 1839, when the commodities-trade exchanges in Bucharest were created. Shares, rights, bonds, fund units, structured products, and futures contracts are among the financial instruments traded on BVB. The listings on the exchange are denominated in Romanian Leus.

BVB's initial index is known as BET. BET tracks the performance of the top 15 most liquid businesses on the BVB regulated market, excluding financial investment firms. BVB is home to some of Romania's most well-known enterprises. OMV Petrom S.A., S.N.G.N. Romgaz S.A., Banca Transilvania, BRD – Groupe Societe Generale S.A, Fondul Proprietatea, S.N.T.G.N. Transgaz S.A., and Societatea Energetica Electrica S.A. are the top corporations by market capitalization.

Romania's economy is a fast-growing, high-income mixed economy with a high Human Development Index and a skilled labor force, ranking 12th in total nominal GDP and 7th when adjusted for purchasing power parity in the European Union. Romania's economy is ranked 35th in the world, with an annual production of $585 billion dollars (PPP).

Romania has seen some of the strongest growth rates in the EU in recent years, with rates of 4.8 percent in 2016, 7.1 percent in 2017, 4.4 percent in 2018, and 4.1 percent in 2019. In purchasing power parity terms, its GDP per capita reached 69 percent of the European Union average in 2019, up from 44 percent in 2007, the EU27's greatest growth rate.

Vehicles, machinery, chemical goods, electronic items,

electrical equipment, medicines, transport equipment, basic metals, food items, and rubber and plastics are among Romania's top ten exports.

Romania required cash injection, entrepreneurial and management skills after communism, and the quickest way to get these was through foreign direct investment. Romania received 81 billion EUR in foreign direct investment in 2018.

Romania has growing middle and upper classes with relatively high per-capita income. In recent years, Romania has made significant progress in expanding its industrial sector. Industry and construction contributed 32 percent of the gross domestic product, a sizable contribution even when associated services are excluded. Romania is a world-class manufacturer of autos, machine tools, and chemicals.

Romania's car industry had a revenue of 28 billion Euros in 2018. Romania has one of the greatest machine tool market shares in the world in 2004. (5.3 percent). Dacia, Petrom, Rompetrol, Bitdefender, Romstal, and Mobexpert, all established in Romania, have expanded their businesses throughout the area. Small and medium-sized manufacturing businesses, on the other hand, make up the majority of Romania's industrial sector.

The service sector accounts for 55 percent of GDP and employs 51.3 percent of the workforce. Financial, rental, and commercial operations account for 20.5 percent of services; commerce, hotels and restaurants, and transportation account for 18 percent; and other service activities account for the remaining 18 percent (21.7 percent). Romania's service industry has grown in recent years, now employing almost half of Romanians and contributing to slightly more than half of GDP.

The retail industry, which employs about 12% of Romanians, is the largest employer. The retail business is dominated by a limited number of chain businesses that are grouped together in shopping malls.

Romania is pushing and expanding its biotechnology industry vigorously. Hundreds of millions of euros have been invested in the sector to improve infrastructure, support R&D, and attract top foreign experts to Romania. In crucial fields such as pharmacogenomics, protein engineering, glycoengineering, tissue engineering, bioinformatics, genome medicine, and preventive medicine, Romania has one of the world's newest competitive bio-industries.

Non-residents' capital gains from the sale of shares in Romanian enterprises are taxed at the corporate income tax rate of 16 percent in Romania. Treaty-country sellers are excluded from corporate income tax if the holding requirement of 10% for one year is satisfied at the time of sale.

Information on Romanian stocks is relatively accessible. The best resource to research Romanian stocks are the Romanian National Statistics Institute, and the European Economic Sentiment Indicators published by the European Union.

Almaty Financial District buildings, Bucharest

Slovakia

The Bratislava Stock Exchange is a stock exchange in Bratislava that commenced operations on March 15, 1991, after a decision by Slovakia's Ministry of Finance in 1990. The official stock index for the Bratislava Stock Exchange is SAX. The listings are denominated in Euros.

Slovakia's economy is dependent on the country joining the EU in 2004 and adopting the euro at the beginning of 2009. Bratislava, Slovakia's capital, is the country's major financial center. The unemployment rate was 5.72 percent in the first quarter of 2018.

The Slovak economy was dubbed the Tatra Tiger because its GDP grew at a rapid pace from 2000 to 2008, with an annual growth rate of 10.4% in 2007. Slovakia has seen significant growth in foreign direct investment. Slovakia's key benefits for foreign investors include cheap and skilled labor, a 19 percent flat tax rate for both enterprises and people, no dividend taxes, weak labor laws, and a desirable geographical position.

During the previous ten years, the Slovak service industry has expanded quickly, presently employing over 69 percent of the population and contributing over 61 percent of GDP. Slovakia was mostly industrialized in the second part of the twentieth century. Industry (which includes construction) accounted for 35.6 percent of GDP in 2010, compared to 49 percent in 1990.

Automotive, electronics, mechanical engineering, chemical engineering, and information technology are the primary industries with promise for growth today, based on a longstanding history and a highly trained labor force. Due to recent substantial investments by Volkswagen (Bratislava), Peugeot (Trnava), Kia Motors (ilina), and, from 2018, Jaguar Land Rover in Nitra, the automotive sector in Slovakia is one of the fastest expanding.

In the Slovak Republic, there is no separate capital gains tax. Gain on the sale of non-business property is tax-free if the individual has held the property for at least five years or has used it for non-business activities for at least five years. Capital gains are included in a person's taxable income and are subject to income tax. If held for more than one year, capital gains from the sale of shares listed on a recognized stock exchange are tax-free. The Statistical Office of the Slovak Republic is a great resource to research Slovakian equities.

Bulgaria

The Bulgarian Stock Exchange (abbreviated BSE) is a stock exchange in Sofia, Bulgaria's capital. It was established as a joint-stock corporation on October 10, 1991, as the First Bulgarian Stock Exchange. The Bulgarian Stock Exchange is 44 percent controlled by the Bulgarian government, and it is seeking possible international investors, including the Frankfurt Stock Exchange, Athens Stock Exchange, OMX, and Prague Stock Exchange.

There are four indices listed on the exchange, SOFIX, BG40, BGTR30, and BGREIT. The listings are denominated in Bulgarian Leva and Euros.

Bulgaria's economy is based on free-market principles, with a large private sector and a smaller public sector. According to the World Bank, Bulgaria is an industrialized upper-middle-income country that is a member of the European Union. The lev is the strongest and most stable currency in Eastern Europe.

The Main industries are electricity, gas, water; food, beverages, tobacco; machinery and equipment, automotive parts, base metals, chemical products, coke, refined petroleum, nuclear fuel; and outsourcing centers.

Energy, mining, metallurgy, machine building, agriculture, and tourism are the strongest sectors of the economy. Clothing, iron and steel, machinery, and refined fuels are the primary industrial exports.

Sofia is Bulgaria's capital and economic heart, and it is home to the majority of the country's major Bulgarian and international corporations, as well as the Bulgarian National Bank and the Bulgarian Stock Exchange of course. Bulgaria also has the lowest rates of personal and corporate income tax in the European Union.

Capital gains are taxed on an annual basis with a 10% flat tax rate for residents, but double taxation treaties are in place, therefore making it unlikely to be liable to tax as a foreigner.

Croatia

The Zagreb Stock Exchange (ZSE) is a Croatian stock exchange based in Zagreb. It is the only stock exchange in Croatia. Shares of Croatian firms, as well as bonds and commercial bills, are traded on the exchange. There are 150 listings on the exchange and they are denominated in Croatian Kunas. The Zagreb Stock Exchange is housed in the Eurotower skyscraper. There are two main indices, the CROBEX for stocks, and the CROBIS for bonds.

Croatia's economy is a high-income service-based economy in the early stages of growth, with the tertiary sector accounting for 60% of total GDP. Croatia has one of the most strong economies in Southeast Europe.

The main industries are chemicals and plastics, machine tools, fabricated metal, electronics, pig iron, and rolled steel products, aluminum, paper, wood products, construction materials, textiles, shipbuilding, petroleum and petroleum refining, food and beverages, and tourism. The industrial sector is dominated by shipbuilding which accounts for over 10% of exported goods. Food processing and chemical industries also account for significant portions of industrial output and exports.

The industrial sector represents 27% of Croatia's total economic output while agriculture represents 6%. The industrial sector is responsible for 25% of Croatia's GDP, with agriculture, forestry, and fishing accounting for the remaining 5% of Croatian GDP.

Double taxation treaties are in place making it unlikely to be liable for capital gains tax in Croatia on top of your country of residence.

Panorama of Zagreb, Croatia

Serbia

The Belgrade Stock Exchange (abbreviated as BELEX and romanized as Beogradska berza) is a stock exchange in Belgrade, Serbia. Following the King's proclamation of the Stock Exchange Law of 1886, the Stock Exchange was established in the Kingdom of Serbia in 1894.

There are 436 listings available on the exchange, and they are denominated in Serbian Dinars. The Belgrade Stock Exchange currently has two indices: BELEXline, the general benchmark index of the Belgrade Stock Exchange, and BELEX15, representing the 15 most liquid stocks.

Serbia's economy is a service-oriented upper-middle-income economy, with the tertiary sector accounting for two-thirds of total GDP, and it is based on free-market principles. In 2021, nominal GDP is expected to hit $61.244 billion, or $8,842 per capita.

Energy, automotive industry, machinery, mining, and agriculture are the strongest sectors of Serbia's economy. Automobiles, base metals, furniture, food processing, machinery, chemicals, sugar, tires, clothing, and pharmaceuticals are the most common industrial exports.

Serbian economic production is heavily reliant on trade. Germany, Italy, Russia, China, and neighboring Balkan countries are the major trading partners.

Belgrade is Serbia's capital and economic hub, and it is home to most of the country's major Serbian and foreign corporations, as well as the National Bank of Serbia and the Belgrade Stock Exchange. After Belgrade, Novi Sad is the second-largest city and the most significant economic center. The Serbian dinar is the country's official currency. It went through a spell of hyperinflation in 1992 and 1993. The inflation rate has been stable since the early 2000s, and in recent years, a relatively low level of inflation has been reported.

Night view of Belgrade, capital of Serbia

Cyprus

The Cyprus Stock Exchange (CSE) is a European stock exchange based on the island of Cyprus. There are 60 equity listings available on the exchange at the time of writing, and they are denominated in Euros.

The Emerging Companies Market (ECM) allows private

and public companies to list their bonds, while the ECM allows public companies to list their securities.

The World Bank classifies Cyprus' economy as a high-income economy, and the International Monetary Fund added it to its list of advanced economies in 2001. The main industries in Cyprus are tourism, food and beverage processing, cement and gypsum, ship repair and refurbishment, textiles, light chemicals, metal products, wood, paper, and stone and clay products.

Cyprus has a service-based economy with some light manufacturing that is open, free, and competitive. Cyprus promotes its geographic position as a "bridge" between East and West, as well as its skilled English-speaking population, low local prices, strong airline connections, and telecommunications, on an international level.

Cyprus has had a stable economic record since gaining independence from the United Kingdom in 1960, as evidenced by strong growth, full employment, and relative stability. The colonial underdeveloped agrarian economy has been converted into a modern economy with thriving services, industrial, and agricultural sectors.

For non-resident persons, the selling of shares in a corporation that owns real estate is subject to capital gains tax at a rate of 20%. For non-residents, the sale of ordinary shares is not subject to capital gains tax in Cyprus, although it may be in their home country.

Nicosia, capital of Cyprus

Malta

The Malta Stock Market (Maltese: Bora ta' Malta), formerly the Casino della Borsa, is the island nation of Malta's stock exchange. Since its inception in 1992, the Exchange has played an important role in the private sector's capital raising through the issuance of corporate bonds and equity, while the Government of Malta has issued virtually all of its national debt in the form of Malta Government bonds and treasury bills, which are listed and traded on the secondary market.

Over 75,000 individual investors make up the investor base, which is a large figure given Malta's economic size and population. The Malta Stock Exchange's primary goal is to continue to grow and assist the local market while also inviting multinational firms to list on the Exchange and benefit from the passportability that this provides inside the EU.

There are 27 listed equities on the exchange at the time of writing this book. You can also access 73 different types of Corporate bonds, 50 government bonds and 45 treasury bills.

Malta's economy is heavily industrialized and service-oriented. The International Monetary Fund classifies it as an advanced economy. Malta's economic strengths include its strategic location in the Mediterranean Sea, at a crossroads between Europe, North Africa, and the Middle East, as well as its fully developed open market economy, multilingual population (88 percent of Maltese speak English), productive labor force, low corporate tax, and well-developed finance and ICT clusters.

Foreign commerce, industry (particularly electronics), tourism, and financial services are all important to the economy. The main industries of Malta are tourism, electronics, shipbuilding and repair, construction, food and beverages, pharmaceuticals, footwear, clothing, tobacco, aviation services, financial services, and information technology services. There are more than 250 foreign-owned, export-oriented businesses in the industrial sector.

The selling of shares in the future may be subject to capital gains tax at a rate of 35%, but there is an exemption if the transfer is undertaken by a non-resident person and the Maltese business (in which the share transfer is effected) has no immovable property in Malta.

The Malta stock exchange, located in a historical church building

Montenegro

The Montenegro Stock Exchange (MNSE) is a stock exchange in Podgorica, Montenegro. It is the only stock exchange in Montenegro.

There are 410 listings on the exchange, and they are denominated in Euros. It completely integrated NEX Stock Exchange, also in Podgorica, on January 10, 2011, resulting in a single Montenegrin capital market. Short and long-term stocks, six mutual funds, bonds, and shares from government fund portfolios are all traded on the MNSE. The MONEX20 and MONEXPIF are the Montenegrin Stock Exchange's main stock indices.

Montenegro's economy is currently in transition, as it deals with the consequences of the Yugoslav Wars, the collapse of manufacturing following the fall of the Socialist Federal Republic of Yugoslavia, and UN economic sanctions. In 2006 and 2007, Montenegro witnessed a real estate boom, with wealthy Russians, Britons, and others purchasing property along the coast.

Montenegro's banking sector is highly concentrated, with a large share of foreign money. Most banks in Montenegro provide non-resident accounts to both natural persons and legal entities, and most offer both retail and corporate banking products under one roof.

Non-residents are subject to a final withholding tax of 9% on capital gains and rental income from movable and immovable property. At the end of the fiscal year, all capital gains will be taxed.

Information on the Montenegro market is somewhat accessible. The Statistical Office of Montenegro is a great place to start for Montenegro stocks.

BALKANS

Podgorica, capital of Montenegro

5

Eastern Europe

Poland

The main stock exchange in Poland is the Warsaw Stock Exchange (WSE), and was founded in 1817. The State Treasury established the WSE as a joint-stock enterprise. The Treasury owns a 35 percent stake in the company. Shares, bonds, subscription rights, allotments, and derivatives such as futures, options, and index participation units are all traded on the WSE.

At the end of June 2017, the capitalization of 432 local businesses listed on the Main Market totaled PLN 645.0 billion (EUR 152.6 billion). There are fifteen indices on the Warsaw Stock Exchange, the WIG, WIG20, WIG30, mWIG40, and sWIG80. The sector indices are WIG-BANKI, WIG-BUDOW, WIG-CHEMIA, WIG-DEWEL, WIG-ENERG, WIG-INFO, WIG-MEDIA, WIG-PALIWA, WIG-PL, WIG-SPOZYW, WIG-SUROWCE, and WIG-TELKOM. the listings on the exchange are denominated in Polish Zlotys.

Poland's economy is an industrialized, mixed economy with a developed market, ranking sixth in the European Union and first among the former Eastern Bloc members of the EU. Since 1988, Poland has pursued an economic liberalization policy, and it now stands as the greatest success story of all the post-communist states of Europe: its economy was the only one in the EU to avoid recession during the 2007–08 economic downturn, and the Polish economy has been growing steadily for the past 28 years, a record high in the EU and only surpassed by Australia in the world.

At purchasing power parity, GDP per capita has increased by 6% each year on average. The service sector accounts for the majority of the country's economy (62.3%), followed by industry (34.2%) and agriculture (3.5 percent). Poland's economic foundation was centered on the coal, textile, chemical, mechanical, iron, and steel sectors prior to World War II.

Fertilizers, petrochemicals, machine tools, electrical machinery, electronics, automobile manufacturing, and shipbuilding are now all part of it. The Polish Financial Supervision Authority oversees the banking industry in Poland (PFSA). During the 1992–97 transition to a market economy, the government privatized some banks, recapitalized the remainder, and implemented legal changes to make the industry more competitive. These changes, as well as the sector's overall health and relative stability, attracted a number of important international investors. Despite the fact that Poland's economy is catching up to that of Western Europe, the pace remains gradual. Poland has managed to pass Portugal in terms of social progress so far. There is a lot of difference between regions.

Unless a so-called "real estate clause" in a relevant tax treaty applies or stocks are listed, non-residents are not liable to tax in Poland on gains on the sale of shares in a Polish firm. Every deal involving a real estate company should be thoroughly scrutinized.

Information on Polish stocks is widely available. The European Economic Sentiment Indicators provides a great deal of information on Polish stocks, as well as the Central Statistics Office of Poland.

Warsaw Stock Exchange, 1877

Russia

The largest stock exchange group in Russia, the Moscow Exchange (Russian: Moskovskaya Birzha, IPA: lit. 'Moscow Bourse'), operates trading markets in equities, bonds, derivatives, the foreign exchange market, money markets, and precious metals.

There are 219 listings on the exchange, and they are denominated in Russian Rubles. The Equity & Bond Market is an important venue for Russian companies to raise capital and for domestic and foreign investors to access equity and debt investment opportunities. The market is where Russian stocks, as well as government, municipal, and corporate bonds, are traded.

Many of Russia's largest firms, including Gazprom, Sberbank, Rosneft, Lukoil, and VTB, are listed on the Moscow Exchange. Moscow Exchange is concentrating on growing its domestic investor base in addition to attracting foreign investors to trade on its platform. Recent reforms to pension fund law, as well as changes to the listing regulations, have made it possible for non-state pension funds to spend more of their assets in the market.

In terms of financial instruments available, The Moscow Exchange is one of the top ten global derivatives exchange sites. The Derivatives Market allows traders to trade options and futures contracts on indices, as well as shares of Russian and foreign firms. In 2013, the majority of global investment banks started offering DMA access to the Russian market to their clients.

The shares of the Moscow Exchange are exchanged on the stock exchange under the symbol MOEX. The MOEX

Russia Index, formerly the MICEX Index, is the Russian stock market's largest ruble-denominated benchmark. The composition of the index is identical to that of the RTS Index in dollars.

Domestic investors prefer the MOEX Russia Index, while international investors prefer the RTS Index. Around 57 percent of shares were in the free float as of April 2016, with the Central Bank of Russia (11.75 percent), Sberbank (9.9 percent), Vnesheconombank (8.4 percent), and European Bank for Reconstruction and Development (EBRD) holding blocks of shares (6.1 percent).

Russia's economy is a mixed and transitional economy of upper-middle-income, with vast natural resources, especially oil and natural gas. It is Europe's fifth-largest economy, the world's eleventh-largest economy by nominal GDP, and the world's sixth-largest economy by purchasing power parity.

Russia's vast geography is a key determinant of its economic activity, with some estimates claiming that the country holds over 30% of the world's natural resources. The estimated amount of Russia's natural capital, according to the World Bank, is $75 trillion dollars. Energy sales account for more than 80% of Russian exports to other countries. Oil and gas revenues accounted for 36% of federal budget revenues in 2016. Russia is regarded as a global energy powerhouse.

Russia is also a major mineral and gold producer and exporter. Russia is the world's largest diamond producer, with over 33 million carats produced in 2013, accounting for 25% of global output valued at over $3.4 billion, and state-owned ALROSA accounting for approximately 95% of all Russian production.

In 2019, the nation was the world's third-largest producer

of gold, second-largest producer of platinum, fourth-largest producer of silver, ninth-largest producer of copper, and third-largest producer of nickel. The Moscow international business center (MIBC) is a major financial hub in Europe, with the continent's largest concentration of skyscrapers.

Capital gains on shares sold by a foreign legal entity or individuals are not taxed in Russia unless the Russian target's assets have more than 50% immovable property in Russia.

The information available on Russian stocks is widely available. The first stop for research on Russian stocks is the Russian Federal State Statistics Service website.

The Moscow international business center, 2018

Czech Republic

The Prague Stock Exchange (PSE) is the Czech Republic's largest and oldest securities market organization. It reopened in 1993 after a 50-year break caused by World War II and the Communist dictatorship.

As a result, the PSE restarted the functions of the Prague Commodities and Stock Exchange, which had been established in 1871. PSE was advised by a group of top Central and Eastern European academics, including Raymond Staples, an American businessman. By legislation, PSE is a joint-stock corporation. Wiener Börse AG, the company's largest stakeholder, owns 99.54 percent of the company. The listings are denominated in Czech Korunas.

The Czech Republic's economy is a well-developed export-oriented social market economy centered on services, industry, and innovation, with a high-income welfare state and a European social model. As a member of the European Union, the Czech Republic participates in the European Single Market and is, therefore, a component of the European Union's economy, although it uses its own currency, the Czech koruna, rather than the euro. Industry contributes for 37.5 percent of the economy, with services accounting for 60% and agriculture accounting for 2.5 percent.

High-tech engineering, electronics, and machine-building, steel manufacturing, transportation equipment (automotive, rail, and aerospace sectors), chemicals, advanced materials, and medicines are the most important businesses.

Research and development, ICT and software development, nanotechnology, and biological sciences are among the primary services. Cereals, vegetable oils, and hops are the principal agricultural products. As of June 2019, the unemployment rate in the Czech Republic was the lowest in the EU at 1.9%.

There is no separate capital gains tax in the Czech Republic. Capital gains constitute part of the aggregate individual income tax base, therefore non-residents will not be liable to Capital Gains Tax in the Czech Republic in most cases, but will be in their home country.

The information available for Czech stocks is widely available. The Czech Statistical Office website is a great resource to research Czech equities, as well as the European Economic Sentiment Indicators published by the European Union.

Prague Business district

Ukraine

The PFTS Stock Exchange is a leading stock exchange in Ukraine that was legally considered a trading system for a long time (until 2006), hence its name, the First Stock Trading System (PFTS).

On the PFTS, approximately 220 companies are listed, with a total market capitalization of around $140 billion. The exchange is denominated in Ukrainian Hryvnias, the local currency. Supposedly, derivatives such as options and futures are offered on the exchange, but most definitely only to institutional investors. Retail investors will find it almost impossible to get their hands on derivatives, and will probably struggle just to buy traditional shares.

Ukraine's economy is a developing free-market economy. It expanded rapidly from 2000 to 2008, when the global Great Recession began and reached Ukraine as the 2008–2009 Ukrainian financial crisis. The economy began to recover in 2010 and continued to improve until 2013. The Ukrainian economy experienced a downturn from 2014 to 2015, with GDP in 2015 being slightly more than half of what it was in 2013.

In 2016, the economy began to recover. By 2018, the Ukrainian economy had grown rapidly, reaching nearly 80% of its 2008 size. The World Bank reported in April 2020 that economic growth in 2019 was solid at 3.2 percent, driven by a good agricultural harvest and sectors reliant on domestic consumption.

Household consumption increased by 11.9 percent in 2019, driven by large remittance inflows and the resumption of consumer lending, while domestic trade and agriculture increased by 3.4 and 1.3 percent, respectively. The country possesses many of the characteristics of a major European economy, including fertile farmlands, a well-developed industrial base, highly skilled labor, and an excellent educational system.

Power generation, fuel, ferrous and non-ferrous metallurgy, chemical and petrochemical and gas, machine-building and metal-working, forest, wood-working and wood pulp and paper, construction materials, light, food, and other industries are all present in Ukraine.

Capital gains realized by non-residents of Ukraine on the sale of Ukrainian shares or equity interests are technically subject to a 15% withholding tax (WHT). Under a tax treaty, this WHT can be completely eliminated or partially mitigated.

Kiev industrial center

Belarus

The Belarusian currency and stock exchange (BCSE) is the main stock exchange based in Belarus. It was founded in 1998 by the National Bank of the Republic of Belarus. The listings are denominated in Belarusian Rubles, as well as US dollars for some securities.

Belarus has the world's 72nd-largest economy by purchasing power parity (PPP), with a GDP of $195 billion dollars ($20,900 per capita) in 2019. The main industries are metal-cutting machine tools, tractors, trucks, earthmovers, motorcycles, synthetic fibers, fertilizer, textiles, refrigerators, washing machines and other household appliances, Agricultural products: grain, potatoes, vegetables, sugar beets, flax; beef, and milk.

Belarus had a relatively well-developed industrial base as part of the former Soviet Union; it maintained this industrial base, as well as a strong agricultural base and a high education level, following the disintegration of the USSR.

It has the most soviet-style economy of the former Soviet republics, with many state-owned companies, utilities, and services, as well as strict restrictions on land ownership and banking.

6

Central & East Asia

China

There are two main stock exchanges in China, the Shanghai Stock Exchange, and the Shenzhen Stock exchange. The Shanghai Stock Exchange (SSE) is a Chinese stock exchange located in Shanghai. The Shanghai Stock Exchange, with a market value of US$4.0 trillion as of November 2018, is the world's fourth biggest stock exchange by market capitalisation. The Shanghai Stock Exchange, unlike the Hong Kong Stock Exchange, is still not completely accessible to international investors and is frequently influenced by central government decisions due to capital account limitations imposed by Chinese mainland authorities.

There are 1,860 listings on the exchange, and they are denominated in Chinese yuans. As a competitor to the NASDAQ, the Shanghai Stock Exchange created the STAR Market in 2019, which features exclusively technology-related firms. On the Shanghai Stock Exchange, there are two categories of stocks: "A" shares and "B" shares. The local renminbi yuan currency is used to price A shares, whereas the US dollar is used to price B shares.

Trading in A-shares was initially confined to local investors exclusively, but trading in B shares was open to both domestic and foreign investors. Foreign investors are now authorized (with restrictions) to trade in A-shares through the Qualified Foreign Institutional Investor (QFII) program, which was officially started in 2003, after changes were completed in December 2002. A total of 98 foreign institutional investors have been granted permission to acquire and sell A-shares at this time.

The most widely utilized indicator to represent SSE's market performance is the SSE Composite (also known as Shanghai Composite) Index. All Shanghai Stock Exchange-listed stocks (A shares and B shares) are included in the SSE Composite Index.

Shenzhen Stock Exchange (SZSE) is a stock exchange located in Shenzhen, China. It is the 9th biggest stock exchange in the world, and the 4th largest in East Asia and Asia, with a market value of about US$2.504 trillion in 2019.

There are 2375 listings on the exchange, and they are also denominated in Chinese yuan. Because of the restrictions on foreigners to buy shares directly on these exchanges, most foreigners will buy American Depository Receipts of Chinese shares listed on US exchanges, instead of buying on the Chinese exchange directly. Also, Chinese companies are listed in other overseas markets such as Hong Kong and Singapore, but the access and choice are then limited.

The People's Republic of China's economy is a growing market-oriented economy with economic planning included through industrial policies and strategic five-year plans. The economy, which is dominated by state-owned companies (SOEs) and mixed-ownership firms, also has a substantial domestic private sector and is open to international corporations, making it a socialist market economy.

State-owned firms accounted for approximately 60% of China's market capitalization in 2019 and would produce 40% of China's GDP of US$15.66 trillion in 2020, with the remaining 60% made up of local and international private businesses and investment. The total assets of all Chinese SOEs, including those in the banking sector, hit US$78.08 trillion by the end of 2019. Ninety-one of these SOEs are Fortune Global 500 businesses in 2020.

China has the world's second-biggest economy by nominal GDP, and the world's largest economy by purchasing power parity (PPP) since 2014, which some believe is a more accurate assessment of an economy's real size. Since 2010, it has been the second biggest by nominal GDP, relying on market exchange rates that fluctuate. According to government projections, China will overtake the United States as the world's largest economy in nominal GDP by 2028. For much of the two millennia from the 1st to the 19th centuries, China was one of the world's most powerful economic powers.

Under Deng Xiaoping's leadership, the government launched economic reforms in 1978. As a result, China has the world's fastest-growing major economy, with average annual growth rates of over 10% during the last 30 years. China boasts four of the top 10 most competitive financial hubs in the world, more than any other country (Shanghai, Hong Kong, Beijing, and Shenzhen). By market capitalization and transaction volume, China boasts three of the top 10 stock exchanges in the world (Shanghai, Hong Kong, and Shenzhen).

Foreign investors had purchased a total of US$440 billion in Chinese equities as of the end of June 2020, accounting for roughly 2.9 percent of the total value and indicating that foreign investors had purchased a total of US$156.6 billion in the stocks alone in the first half of 2020. As of the beginning of September 2020, the entire value of China's bond market has surpassed US$15.4 trillion, placing it ahead of Japan and the United Kingdom, and second only to the US with US$40 trillion.

Despite a 44.66 percent year-on-year growth, foreign ownership of Chinese bonds reached US$388 billion at the end of September 2020, accounting for 2.5 percent of the entire value. China's public sector employed 63 percent of the country's workforce in 2019. According to the IMF, China's GDP (nominal) and GDP (PPP) per capita income ranked 59th and 73rd, respectively, in 2020. In 2020, China's gross domestic product (GDP) was $15.66 trillion (101.6 trillion yuan).

The country's natural resources are valued at $23 trillion, with coal and rare earth metals accounting for 90% of the total. China's overall banking sector assets are about $45.838 trillion (309.41 trillion CNY), with total deposits and other liabilities totaling $42.063 trillion. Direct foreign investment in China, which reached over US$1.6 trillion as of the end of October 2016, provided roughly one-third of China's GDP and a quarter of its jobs directly and indirectly.

China's FDI stock reached US$2.947 trillion at the end of June 2020, while China's departing FDI stock was US$2.128

trillion. China's total foreign financial assets and liabilities totaled US$7.860 trillion and US$5.716 trillion, respectively, making it the world's second-largest creditor nation behind Japan. As of 2020, China is the world's greatest receiver of foreign direct investment, with $163 billion inflows.

It has the second-largest outward foreign direct investment, with US$136.91 billion in 2019, after only Japan with US$226.65 billion. China ranked first in the world in total number of billionaires and second in total number of millionaires in 2018, with 658 billionaires and 3.5 million millionaires. According to Credit Suisse Group's 2019 Global Wealth Report, China has surpassed the United States in terms of wealth among the top ten percent of the world's population. China is home to the Fortune Global 500's top firms, with 129 of them located in the country as of 2020.

China also has the world's greatest number of privately held technology firms (tech unicorns), with each having a valuation of over $1 billion. China boasts the world's highest foreign exchange reserves, valued at $3.1 trillion, but when foreign assets held by China's state-owned commercial banks are included, the reserve value increases to over $4 trillion.

China is the greatest manufacturer and exporter of products in the world. It is also the world's fastest-growing consumer market and the world's second-largest goods importer. In terms of services, China is a net importer. It is the world's largest commercial nation and a major player in international commerce. In 2001, China joined the World Trade Organization (WTO). ASEAN, Australia, New Zealand, Pakistan, South Korea, and Switzerland are among the countries with whom it has free trade agreements. The United States, the European Union, Japan, Hong Kong,

South Korea, India, Taiwan, Australia, Vietnam, Malaysia, and Brazil are China's most important commercial partners.

As of 2020, China's labor force will be the world's biggest, with 778 million workers. On the Ease of Doing Business Index, it is ranked 31st, while on the Global Competitiveness Report, it is ranked 28th. China is the only middle-income economy, the only recently industrialized economy, and the only rising country among the top 30 countries on the Global Innovation Index.

China leads the world in patents, utility models, trademarks, industrial designs, and creative products exports, and it also boasts two of the world's top five science and technology clusters (Shenzhen-Hong Kong-Guangzhou and Beijing, respectively, in second and fourth place). China's 5G subscribers have already reached 300 million by the end of April 2021.

The gains generated by nonresident enterprise owners through the transfer of equity interest in China resident firms are subject to a 10% income tax under Chinese law and regulations.

For equity research on the Chinese market, the National Bureau of Statistics of China is a great resource.

Shanghai, China

Hong Kong

The Stock Exchange of Hong Kong (SEHK, or Hong Kong Stock Exchange) is the main stock exchange in Hong Kong. It has surpassed Chicago-based CME as the world's largest exchange in terms of market value. It has 2,538 listed firms (denominated in Hong Kong dollars) with a total market value of HK$47 trillion by the end of 2020. It is said to be Asia's fastest growing stock market. The Hong Kong stock exchange gives access to Chinese stocks through the Shanghai-Hong Kong Stock Connect platform.

Hong Kong's economy is a well-developed free-market economy with minimal taxes, almost unfettered port commerce, and a well-established international financial sector. The Hong Kong dollar, which is linked to the US dollar, is lawfully issued by three major international commercial banks. Individual banks in Hong Kong set interest rates to guarantee that they are market-driven. Although the Hong Kong Monetary Authority serves as a financial regulatory authority, there is no officially recognized central banking system.

Its economy is regulated by positive non-interventionism and is heavily reliant on global commerce and finance. As a result, it is considered one of the best areas to start a business. Indeed, according to recent research, Hong Kong has grown from 998 registered start-ups in 2014 to over 2800 in 2018, with eCommerce (22%), Fintech (12%), Software (12%), and Advertising (11%) firms accounting for the majority.

In 2015, Hong Kong was ranked first in the Economic Freedom of the World Index, with a score of 8.97. A healthy banking system, almost no public debt, a robust legal system, substantial foreign exchange reserves (approximately US $408 billion as of mid-2017), strict anti-corruption measures, and close links with mainland China are among Hong Kong's economic strengths. Due to Hong Kong's highly internationalized and modernized financial industry, as well as its capital market in Asia, its size, regulations, and available financial tools, which are comparable to London and New York, the Hong Kong Stock Exchange is a favorable destination for international firms and firms from mainland China to be listed.

Between 1961 and 1997, Hong Kong's gross domestic output increased 180-fold. In the same time period, the GDP per capita increased by 87 times. Its economy is somewhat greater than Israel's or Ireland's, and in 2011, its GDP per capita at purchasing power parity was the sixth highest in the world, ahead of the United States and the Netherlands but slightly below Brunei. As a result of the global financial crisis, Hong Kong's real economic growth decreased by 2.8 percent in 2009.

Hong Kong was the world's seventh-largest port by the late twentieth century, second only to New York and Rotterdam in terms of container traffic. The World Trade Organization recognizes Hong Kong as a full member. Hong Kong maritime owners were second only to those of Greece in terms of overall tonnage holdings in the world, with the Kwai Chung container complex being the largest in Asia.

Hong Kong has also had a steady supply of labor from the surrounding regions. Opportunities for external commerce, investment, and recruiting were maximized thanks to a competent labor force and the adoption of contemporary British/Western business practices and technology. Prices and salaries in Hong Kong are very variable, depending on the economy's success and stability. Due to its low tax policy, Hong Kong generates money through the sale and taxation of land, as well as luring foreign enterprises to contribute cash for its public finances.

In terms of attracting foreign direct investment, Hong Kong, according to Healy Consultants, has the most appealing business climate in East Asia. Hong Kong was the world's third-largest receiver of foreign direct investment in 2013. The Tax Justice Network's 2011 Financial Secrecy Index put Hong Kong fourth.

In 2016, the Hong Kong Government was placed 13th globally and fourth in Asia in the World Economic Forum's Network Readiness Index (NRI), a measure of a government's information and communication technology. The Heritage Foundation, on the other hand, has removed Hong Kong from the Index of Economic Freedom, citing evidence that its economic policies are ultimately controlled by Beijing in recent years. Hong Kong will be examined in the context of China, according to the economic freedom index, demonstrating degraded independence and increased governmental control over the city's capitalist system.

The sale of capital assets in Hong Kong is exempt from profits tax. The Census and Statistics Department of Hong Kong is a great resource for equity research in that market.

Hong Kong skyline by night

Taiwan

The Taiwan Stock Exchange Corporation (TWSE) is a financial organization in Taipei, Taiwan, with headquarters in Taipei 101. The TWSE was founded in 1961, and it became a stock exchange on February 9, 1962. The Financial

Supervisory Commission oversees it.

There are 898 firms listed on the Taiwan Stock Exchange (denominated in New Taiwan dollars), with a total market value of NT$ 24,519,622 million. Before opening a trading account with a local securities company in Taiwan, international investors must first register with the TWSE to receive an "Investor ID."

Taiwan's economy is a highly developed capitalist economy, with the majority of government businesses having been privatized. Taiwan is the seventh biggest economy in Asia and the 20th largest in the world by purchasing power parity, allowing the IMF to classify it as an advanced economy and the World Bank to classify it as a high-income economy.

Taiwan is the world's most technologically advanced computer chip manufacturer. Telecommunications, financial services, and utilities are the three highest-paying industries in Taiwan as of 2018. In the 2015 Global Entrepreneurship Index, Taiwan's economy was placed first in Asia (GEI). During the previous three decades, real GDP growth has averaged around 8%, thanks to technocracy-centered economic planning until 1987.

Since World War II, exports have increased, while inflation and unemployment have remained low, and the country's foreign reserves have risen to the fourth biggest in the world. Major economic indicators of Taiwan's economy are released by the Directorate-General of Budget, Accounting, and Statistics and the Ministry of Economic Affairs. Taiwan is currently dealing with many of the same economic problems as other industrialized countries.

With the potential of more labor-intensive sectors being

relocated to nations with lower labor costs, such as mainland China, the Philippines, and Vietnam, Taiwan's future development will have to rely on further transformation to a high-tech, service-oriented economy. Taiwan has effectively diversified its trading markets in recent years, reducing its percentage of exports to the US from 49 percent in 1984 to 20 percent in 2002.

Taiwan's reliance on the US should continue to fall as its exports to Southeast Asia and mainland China increase and its efforts to expand European markets bear fruit. The admission of Taiwan to the World Trade Organization (WTO) and its aim to become an Asia-Pacific "regional operations center" are driving more economic liberalization. Taiwan's economy is experiencing de-internationalization and reduced pay as a result of its economic marginalization in the global economy. As a result, human resource professionals are looking for work elsewhere.

Small and medium-sized businesses in Taiwan suffer the most, which thwarts the Taiwanese government's attempts at economic change. The Gross Business Receipts Tax (GBRT) and Value-added Tax (VAT) make up Taiwan's indirect tax system. Over the last 40 years, Taiwan's fast expansion has been fueled by foreign commerce. Taiwan's economy is export-oriented, making it reliant on an open global trade environment and vulnerable to global economic downturns.

Capital gains tax of 45% will be liable on the sale of Taiwanese stocks. the Department of Statistics of Taiwan can be used to do equity research on Taiwanese stocks.

Skyline of Taipei, Taiwan

Japan

There are two main stock exchanges in Japan, the Tokyo stock exchange, and the Osaka stock exchange. The Tokyo Stock Exchange is a stock exchange in Tokyo, Japan, abbreviated as Tosho or TSE/TYO. It is the world's third-largest stock exchange by total market capitalization of its listed businesses, and Asia's largest. As of February 2019, it has 2,292 listed firms (denominated in Japanese yen) with a total market value of $5.67 trillion.

The Japan Exchange Group (JPX), a holding company that also trades on the stock exchange, owns the exchange. The Osaka Exchange merged with JPX to become JPX. In terms of volume of business, Osaka Exchange, Inc. is Japan's second-biggest securities exchange. The Osaka Securities Exchange had 477 listed firms with a total market value of $212 billion.

The minimum purchase quantity per transaction for each firm's shares is determined by the company that issued the stock. If a firm requires a minimum of 100 shares per transaction, for example, you must have the cash to buy the minimum 100-share lot. The majority of firms listed on the TSO/TYO have a minimum transaction size of 100 shares.

When placing an order on a Japanese online trading platform, you can place a "Sashine" order, which is similar to a limit order in that you set a price and wait for the market to trade at that price, but the order is canceled at the conclusion of the trading session. You can also place a "Nariyuki" order, which is the Japanese counterpart of a market order in which the price of your relatively immediate stock fill is set by the current market price.

When you sell Japanese stock, you must disclose the profit or loss on your Japanese yearly earnings statement. The amount you earned or lost is taken into account by the tax office, which then determines how much tax you must pay. You should not neglect the formal need to record gains or losses on your stock transactions because it is a crucial step in terms of your tax liability.

The majority of the largest and most well-capitalized Japanese equities may be purchased and sold using American Depository Receipts (ADRs). These receipts are either listed on major U.S. exchanges such as the NASDAQ and the New York Stock Exchange (NYSE) or traded over-the-counter (OTC) in the United States.

Japan's economy is a well-developed free-market economy. It is the world's third-largest economy in terms of nominal

GDP and fourth-largest in terms of purchasing power parity (PPP), as well as the world's second-largest developed economy. Japan is a member of both the G7 and the G20 groups. The country's per capita GDP was $41,637, according to the International Monetary Fund for 2020. Japan's GDP, measured in dollars, varies dramatically due to a fluctuating currency exchange rate. Using the Atlas approach to account for these variations, Japan's GDP per capita is projected to be about $39,048.

The Nikkei 225 is the world's third-largest stock exchange by market capitalization, and it publishes a monthly report of top blue-chip shares on Japan Exchange Group. Japan was the fourth-largest importer and fourth-largest exporter in the world in 2018. It has $1.3 trillion in foreign exchange reserves, the world's second-largest. On the Ease of Doing Business Index, it is ranked 29th, whereas, on the Global Competitiveness Report, it is ranked 5th. The Economic Complexity Index ranks it #1 in the world. Japan is also the third-largest consumer market in the world.

Japan is the world's third-biggest automotive manufacturer, has the world's largest electronics products sector, and is frequently recognized as one of the world's most inventive countries, leading numerous worldwide patent filing metrics. Faced with rising competition from China and South Korea, Japanese manufacturing increasingly concentrates on high-tech and precise items including optical equipment, hybrid cars, and robots. Aside from the Kant area, the Kansai region is one of Japan's most important industrial clusters and manufacturing regions.

Japan is the largest creditor country on the planet. Japan maintains a significant net foreign investment surplus and runs an annual trade surplus. Japan had the world's third-biggest assets, at $15.2 trillion, or 9% of the global total as of 2017. Japan is home to 51 Fortune Global 500 businesses. In terms of overall wealth, the country ranks third in the globe. Japan used to have the second-largest assets and wealth, trailing only the United States in both categories, but in 2015, China surpassed Japan in both categories.

Japan was also the world's second-largest economy by nominal GDP behind the United States until 2010, when China overtook Japan. Japan's manufacturing sector used to be second only to that of the United States (and almost surpassed it in 1995), but China's manufacturing sector surpassed Japan's in 2007 and the United States in 2010. As a result, Japan is the world's third-largest manufacturer. The bursting of Japan's asset price bubble in 1991 ushered in a period of economic stagnation known as the "lost decade," also referred to as the "lost 20 years," during which the country's nominal GDP dropped from $5.33 trillion to $4.36 trillion.

The Bank of Japan began a unique strategy of quantitative easing in the early 2000s to stimulate economic development. In the aftermath of the Global Financial Crisis in 2007-08, the Tsunami in 2011, and the COVID-19 epidemic that began in late 2019, debt levels have continued to increase. Japan's national debt, at 257 percent of GDP as of 2021, is substantially larger than that of any other wealthy country. Japanese nationals possess the majority of this debt. An elderly and falling population, which peaked at 128 million in 2010, poses significant difficulties to the Japanese economy. According to projections, the population will continue to decline, possibly falling below 100 million by the end of the twenty-first century.

Capital gains on Japanese shares are subject to national income tax, which is levied at a rate of 15% on individual gains on stock sales.

The Bank of Japan's quarterly Tankan survey of business mood is used to forecast the Japanese economy. Equity research on Japanese stocks can be done with The Statistics Bureau of Japan website.

Tokyo, Japan

India

There are 8 stock exchanges in India. The Bombay Stock Exchange (BSE) and the National Stock Exchange (NSE) are the two stock exchanges in India that handle the majority of the stock market's trade (NSE). The BSE has been around since 1875. The National Stock Exchange, on the other hand, was established in 1992 and began trading in 1994. The BSE had 5,518 listed companies as of February 2020, compared to 1,799 on the competitor NSE as of December 31, 2019.

Only around 500 of the BSE's listed companies account for more than 90% of its market value; the remainder is very illiquid shares. Only in the 1990s did India begin to allow foreign investment. Institutional investors can provide exposure to Indian stocks to foreign companies and individuals.

Retail investors are increasingly interested in India-focused mutual funds. Participatory notes (PNs), depositary receipts (ADRs) and global depositary receipts (GDRs), exchange-traded funds (ETFs), and exchange-traded notes (ETNs) are some of the offshore products that may be used to make investments. Although restricted for retail investors, Indian shares are available through Interactive Brokers as they must have gain access themselves as institutional investors.

India's economy is classified as a middle-income emerging market economy. It has the sixth-largest nominal GDP and the third-largest purchasing power parity economy in the world. According to the International Monetary Fund, India ranks 145th by nominal GDP and 122nd by nominal GDP per capita.

From 1947 until 1991, successive administrations used the License Raj to push protectionist economic policies with considerable state intervention and economic regulation, which is known as dirigism. Following the conclusion of the Cold War and a severe balance-of-payments crisis in 1991, India adopted wide economic liberalization. Annual average GDP growth has been 6% to 7% since the turn of the century, and from 2013 to 2018, India was the world's fastest-growing major economy, overtaking China. From the first through the nineteenth centuries, India had the world's greatest economy for the majority of the two millennia.

The Indian economy's long-term development prospects remain strong, thanks to its young population and low dependence ratio, robust savings and investment rates, and rising globalization and integration into the global economy. Due to the shocks of "demonetization" in 2016 and the implementation of the Goods and Services Tax in 2017, the economy slowed.

Domestic private consumption accounts for almost 60% of India's GDP, and the country remains the world's sixth-largest consumer market. Apart from individual consumption, government expenditure, investment, and exports all contribute to India's GDP. India was the ninth-largest importer and twelfth-largest exporter in the world in 2019. Since January 1, 1995, India has been a member of the World Trade Organization.

On the Ease of Doing Business Index, it is ranked 63rd, while on the Global Competitiveness Report, it is ranked 68th. As of 2019, India's labor force is the world's second-largest, with 500 million employees.

India boasts one of the greatest concentrations of billionaires in the world, as well as significant economic disparity. Because India has such a large informal sector, just around 2% of Indians pay income taxes. During the global financial crisis of 2008, India used stimulus measures (both fiscal and monetary) to promote growth and generate demand; the economy recovered in later years. According to a 2017 research by PricewaterhouseCoopers (PwC), India's GDP at purchasing power parity might surpass that of the US by 2050.

According to the World Bank, India must focus on public sector reform, infrastructure, agricultural and rural development, removal of land and labor regulations, financial inclusion, boosting private investment and exports, education, and public health in order to achieve sustainable economic development. The United States, China, the United Arab Emirates, Saudi Arabia, Switzerland, Germany, Hong Kong, Indonesia, South Korea, and Malaysia were India's top 10 trading partners in 2020.

Foreign direct investment (FDI) inflows into India totaled $74.4 billion in 2019–20, with the service sector, computer, and telecom industries continuing to be the major sectors for FDI inflows. India has free trade agreements in place or in the works with a number of countries, including ASEAN, SAFTA, Mercosur, South Korea, Japan, and a number of others.

The service sector accounts for half of GDP and is still developing at a rapid pace, while the industrial and agricultural sectors employ the bulk of the workforce. India is the world's sixth-largest manufacturer, employing over 57 million people and accounting for 3% of global manufacturing output.

Rural India accounts for over 66 percent of the population and accounts for roughly half of the country's GDP. It has $585 billion in foreign exchange reserves, which places it fourth in the world. India's national debt is enormous, at 89 percent of GDP, and its fiscal deficit is 9.5 percent of GDP. Government-owned banks in India are grappling with rising bad debt, resulting in sluggish lending growth, while the

NBFC sector is mired in a liquidity crisis.

India is dealing with moderate unemployment, growing income disparity, and declining aggregate demand. In FY 2019, India's gross domestic savings rate was 30.1 percent of GDP. Independent experts and financial organizations have accused the government of faking key economic figures, particularly GDP growth, in recent years.

India is the world's largest maker of generic medicines, and its pharmaceutical industry supplies more than half of the world's vaccination need. With $191 billion in sales and over four million employees, India's IT sector is a significant exporter of IT services. The chemical sector in India is very diverse, with a market value of $178 billion. The tourist sector employs about 42 million people and provides around 9.2% of India's GDP. India is the world's second-largest producer of food and agriculture, with $35.09 billion in agricultural exports. In terms of direct, indirect, and induced impacts in all sectors of the economy, the construction and real estate industry ranks third among the 14 key industries.

The Indian textiles sector is worth $100 billion, contributing 13% of industrial output and 2.3 percent of GDP while directly employing nearly 45 million people. By the number of mobile phones, smartphones, and internet users, India's telecommunications industry is the world's second-biggest. It is both the world's 25th and third-largest oil producer and consumer. India has the world's fifth-largest car sector in terms of output. Its retail sector is approximately $1.17 trillion, accounting for nearly 10% of India's GDP, and it boasts one of the world's fastest-growing e-commerce marketplaces.

India possesses the world's fourth-largest natural

resources, with the mining industry accounting for 11% of industrial GDP and 2.5 percent of overall GDP. It's also the second-largest coal producer, second-largest cement producer, second-largest steel producer, and third-largest electricity generator on the planet.

Following indexation, the tax burden on the sale of Indian equity is 20%. The gain is categorized as short-term capital gain if the equity shares and equity-oriented mutual fund units are sold within 12 months after purchase. Such a short-term capital gain will be taxed at a rate of 15%.

Equity research on Indian shares can be done with the Ministry of Statistics and Programme Implementation website.

Mumbai skyline, India

South Korea

The Korea Exchange (KRX) is the country's only securities exchange. Its headquarters are in Busan, with a cash markets and market supervision office in Seoul. Under the Korea Stock & Futures Exchange Act, the Korea Exchange was formed by combining the Korea Stock Exchange (KSE), Korea Futures Exchange, and KOSDAQ Stock Market.

Korea Exchange has 2,409 listed firms as of December 2020, denominated in Korean wons, with a total market capitalization of 2,314 trillion KRW ($2.1 trillion USD). Financial instruments available include Stocks, Bonds, Exchange Traded Funds (ETFs), Exchange-Linked Warrants (ELWs), and Real Estate Investment Trusts (REITs).

In terms of derivatives products, you can find Index instruments like the KOSPI 200 Index Futures, KOSTAR Futures, KOSPI 200 Index Options, Single Stock Futures, Equity Options, Interest Rate Instruments, Foreign Exchange Instruments, USD denominated Options, and Commodity Instruments.

South Korea's economy is a highly developed mixed economy controlled by Chaebols, family-owned corporations. It has Asia's fourth-largest GDP and the world's tenth-largest GDP. It belongs to the OECD and the G-20. It is one of the Next Eleven countries, which have the potential to dominate the world economy by the middle of the twenty-first century.

South Korea's demanding educational system, as well as the creation of a highly motivated and educated population, are primarily responsible for the country's high-tech boom and rapid economic progress. South Korea adopted an export-oriented economic strategy to fuel its economy, despite having almost no natural resources and a high population density in its territory, which prevented continued population growth and the formation of a large internal consumer market.

In 2019, South Korea was the eighth-largest exporter and eighth-largest importer in the world. The International Monetary Fund, for example, has praised South Korea's economic resilience in the face of different economic crises, noting low state debt and substantial fiscal reserves that can be rapidly deployed to handle any foreseeable financial crisis. Korea, along with BRIC and Indonesia, is described by other financial institutions like the World Bank as one of the fastest-growing major economies of the next generation.

South Korea was one of the few industrialized countries to avoid recession during the global financial crisis, with an economic growth rate of 6.2 percent in 2010, a significant increase from 2.3 percent in 2008 and 0.2 percent in 2009 when the global financial crisis struck. Despite the global economic crisis, the South Korean economy recovered with a record current account surplus of US$70.7 billion at the end of 2013, up 47 percent from 2012, with technology products exports being the primary economic output.

Despite its high growth potential and apparent structural stability, the South Korean economy suffers permanent damage to its credit rating in the stock market as a result of North Korea's belligerence in times of deep military crises, which has a negative impact on the South Korean economy's financial markets.

Furthermore, the chaebols' dominance, which many South Koreans regard as very corrupt and influential in the political system, is likely to continue, posing the risk of delaying the transformation of the South Korean economy for future generations. Corruption is still a major issue in South Korea; all four living past presidents have been condemned to jail for offenses ranging from abuse of power to bribery and embezzlement, with two of them still serving their terms.

Many South Koreans of the younger generation believe that they do not profit from economic progress and have condemned the country's increasingly tough socioeconomic position and social stratification, calling it "Hell Joseon." They've also labeled themselves as members of the Sampo generation, who have given up on dating, marriage, and having children as a result of high living costs and unemployment.

In the industrialized world, the country also has the greatest rates of poverty among the elderly. According to a Goldman Sachs estimate from 2009, with a united Korea (North and South), GDP might be greater than Japan's by 2050.

If a domestic tax exemption is not available, a treaty-based tax exemption may be possible. Otherwise, a non-capital resident's gains will be taxed in Korea at the rate of 11 percent of the selling proceeds or 22 percent of the capital gain, whichever is lower.

The Bank of Korea and the Korea Development Institute publish important economic statistics and trends on a regular basis. Equity research on Korean stocks can be done with the Statistics Korea website.

Seoul by night, South Korea

Georgia

The Georgian Stock Exchange is the country's most important stock exchange. The "Joint Stock Company Georgian Stock Exchange Charter," which was registered and approved in 1999, gave birth to it. Its abbreviation in English is GeSE, and it is located in Tbilisi, Georgia's capital city. There are 9 companies listed, and 26 bonds listed on the exchange, they are both denominated in US dollars and Georgian laris.

Georgia's economy is a developing free-market economy. Following the demise of the Soviet Union, its gross domestic output plummeted, but it recovered in the mid-2000s, expanding in double digits thanks to the peaceful Rose Revolution's economic and democratic changes.

Since then, Georgia's economy has continued to improve, "going from a near-failed state in 2003 to a generally well-functioning market economy in 2014." Georgia was dubbed the World Bank's number one economic reformer in 2007 and has continuously ranked at the top of its ease of doing business ranking.

Georgia's economy is bolstered by the country's relatively open and transparent environment. Georgia is the least corrupt country in the Black Sea region, according to Transparency International's 2018 report, beating all of its immediate neighbors as well as surrounding European Union states. Georgia is also the only country in its immediate neighborhood with a mixed news media environment where the press is not considered unfree.

Since 2003, large amounts of foreign direct investment have been a driving force behind Georgia's rapid economic expansion. The country is an appealing location for FDI because of its attractive and liberal business climate, as well as its equal treatment of local and foreign investors. Stable economic growth, liberal and free-market economic policies, just six taxes and lower tax rates, fewer licenses and permissions, dramatically simplified administrative procedures, preferential trade regimes with other countries, favorable geographic location, well-developed, integrated, and multimodal transportation infrastructure, educated, skilled, and competitive workforce are some of the benefits that make Georgia competitive on the global market. Georgia also features Free Industrial Zones, where businesses are exempt from all corporate taxes, among other benefits.

Capital gains for non-residents in Georgia can be either 5% or 20%, depending on certain conditions.

Tbilisi, Georgia

Kazakhstan

In Almaty, Kazakhstan, the Kazakhstan Stock Exchange (KASE) was founded in 1993. the exchange offers financial instruments of over 80 issuers, mainly stocks of local and foreign companies.

The total shares market capitalization makes up more than US$42.5 billion. The main bulk of the market is occupied by companies from mining, energy and financial sectors. There are 127 listings on the exchange and they are denominated in Tenges.

Kazakhstan's economy is the largest in Central Asia in terms of both absolute and per capita GDP, however, the currency suffered a significant decline between 2013 and

2016. It has mineral and metal deposits, as well as oil reserves. It also has a lot of agricultural potential, thanks to its extensive steppe areas, which may be used for both livestock and grain production. Apples and walnuts are major crops in the southern mountains, where both species grow wild. The extraction and utilization of these natural resources are the backbones of Kazakhstan's industrial sector.

Cyril Muller, the World Bank's Vice President for Europe and Central Asia, visited Astana (now known as Nur-Sultan) in January 2017 and applauded the country's development throughout the World Bank's 25-year collaboration. Muller also discussed Kazakhstan's improved ranking in the World Bank's Doing Business Report 2017, in which the country was placed 35th out of 190 countries. Kazakhstan was placed 36th in the Ease of Doing Business report released in 2018. The report's rankings place a premium on the ease with which firms can comply with legislation and the strength of their property rights.Kazakhstan came in third place in the 2018 Global Innovation Index's Central and South Asia regional ranking (GII).

Kazakhstan has made non-oil sectors of the economy a priority, with non-oil sectors accounting for 85 percent of the country's economic growth in 2019. Kazakhstan exported much more items in the first seven months of 2020 than it did the previous year, including a seven-fold rise in automotive exports. The country's GDP fell by 3% as a result of the COVID-19 pandemic's impact on the service sector, but the real sector of the economy rose dramatically.

In the first eight months of the year, production in agriculture, construction, and manufacturing all increased. The automotive industry (+53.6 percent), pharmaceuticals (+39.7%), processed metal products (+19.5 percent), mechanical engineering (+16.5 percent), and light industry (+16.4 percent) all had the most increase in 2020. Construction (+10.7 percent) and information and communications (+8.2 percent) were two of the service sector's fastest-growing industries.

Non-residents will be subject to capital gains on the sale of shares at a rate of 15%.

Research on equities can be done with the website of the Bureau of national statistics of the Agency for strategic planning and reforms of the Republic of Kazakhstan.

Astana, Kazakhstan

Bangladesh

There are two stock exchanges in Bangladesh. The Dhaka Stock Exchange (DSE) and the Chittagong Stock Exchange. There are 750 listings on the Dhaka Stock Exchange, and there are 250 listings on the Chittagong Stock Exchange, both are denominated in Takas.

Bangladesh's economy is classified as a developing market economy. It is the world's 37th largest economy in nominal terms and 31st largest by purchasing power parity; it is a frontier market and one of the Next Eleven emerging market medium-income nations. Bangladesh's economy grew at an annual pace of 8.3 percent in the first quarter of 2019, making it the world's sixth-fastest expanding economy.

The country's main financial hubs are Dhaka and Chittagong. Bangladesh's financial industry is the third-largest on the Indian subcontinent. Bangladesh's GDP has grown at a rate of 4.5 percent per year on average since 2004, thanks primarily to ready-made garment exports, remittances, and the local agriculture sector. Textiles, shipbuilding, fish and shellfish, jute, and leather items are among the country's most important export sectors. Pharmaceuticals, steel, and food processing have all evolved into self-sufficient businesses.

Bangladesh's telecommunications industry has experienced a tremendous expansion in recent years, thanks to significant international investment. Bangladesh has significant natural gas reserves and is Asia's sixth-largest gas producer. Offshore exploration operations in its maritime area in the Bay of Bengal are growing. It also has huge limestone resources.

As part of its attempts to boost the country's burgeoning

information technology industry, the government promotes the Digital Bangladesh initiative. Bangladesh is strategically vital for Nepal's and Bhutan's economy because Bangladeshi seaports give marine access to these landlocked nations. Bangladesh is also seen as a possible entry point for China's landlocked southwest, which includes Tibet, Sichuan, and Yunnan.

Poverty fell by about a third in the previous decade, thanks to considerable improvements in the human development index, literacy, life expectancy, and per capita food consumption. Since 1992, the economy has grown at a rate of about 6% per year, lifting more than 15 million people out of poverty.

Bangladesh imposes a 10% capital gain tax on non-resident shareholders. Research on Bangladesh equities can be through the Bangladesh Bureau of Statistics website.

Dhaka, Bangladesh

Pakistan

The Pakistan Stock Exchange (PSX) is a stock exchange with trading floors in Karachi, Islamabad, and Lahore. In May 2017, PSX was reclassified as an MSCI Emerging Market, although the FTSE categorizes it as a Secondary Emerging Market. There are around 220,000 retail investors on the exchanges, as well as 1,886 international institutional investors and 883 local institutional investors.

The Karachi Stock Exchange, one of the PSX's component stock exchanges, was ranked among the world's top-performing frontier stock markets between 2009 and 2015, with an average annual return of 26%. There are 540 listings on the exchange, and they are denominated in Pakistani Rupees.

Pakistan's economy is ranked 22nd in the world in terms of purchasing power parity and 45th in terms of nominal gross domestic product. Pakistan has a population of more than 220 million people, making it the world's fifth-largest country. However, Pakistan's undocumented economy is believed to account for 36% of the country's total GDP, which is ignored when calculating per capita income.

Pakistan is still a developing nation. The economy is semi-industrial, with the Indus River serving as a development corridor. Textiles, leather products, sports products, chemicals, and carpets/rugs are among the most important export items. Internal political strife, a rapidly rising population, and a mixed amount of foreign investment have all harmed the economy in the past.

Pakistan is pursuing an economic liberalization process that includes the privatization of all government enterprises in order to attract international investment and reduce the country's budget deficit. Pakistan was designated one of the ten rising economies in a 2016 BMI Research report, with an emphasis on its industrial hub.

Pakistan's government has forecast that future growth rates will be 5%, one of the highest in South Asia, as of May 2021. Pakistani poverty dropped from 64.3 percent in 2002 to 2.3 percent in 2018, according to the World Bank. Pakistan's debt outlook has been upgraded to "stable" by Moody's due to the country's improved macroeconomic situation.

Pakistan is concentrating on developing its own EV, biomedical, electromagnetic, smartphone, and semiconductor industries. Samsung and Realme have announced plans to open a manufacturing facility in Pakistan. Many new auto sector giants, such as France's Renault, South Korea's Hyundai and Kia, Chinese JW Forland, and German auto giant Volkswagen, are considering entering the Pakistani auto market through joint ventures with local manufacturers like Dewan Farooque Motors, Khalid Mushtaq Motors, and United Automobile Industries.

Exxon Mobil, the world's largest oil and gas company, has returned to Pakistan after a nearly three-decade absence, acquiring a 25% stake in offshore drilling in May 2018, with preliminary surveys indicating the potential for substantial hydrocarbon reserves to be discovered offshore.

According to the Wall Street Journal, as much as 42 percent of Pakistan's population may now belong to the upper and middle classes, based on income and the purchasing of consumer goods. If these figures are true, or even suggestive in the broadest sense, 87 million Pakistanis belong to the middle and upper classes, a population greater than Germany's. Official statistics also reveal that the percentage of homes with motorcycles and washing machines has increased dramatically in the last 15 years.

Because of the rapid expansion of the population in recent decades, a huge number of young people are now entering the job market. Despite being one of Asia's six most populated countries. Excessive red tape in the past made dismissing employees and, as a result, hiring difficult. Because of significant advances in taxes and business reforms, many businesses are no longer forced to operate in the shadow economy.

In 1947, agriculture contributed to roughly 53% of GDP. While agricultural output per capita has increased since then, it has been surpassed by non-agricultural development, and agriculture now accounts for about one-fifth of Pakistan's GDP. In recent years, the country's industries (such as clothing, textiles, and cement) and services have experienced tremendous expansion (such as telecommunications, transportation, advertising, and finance).

Capital gains on the sale of shares are subject to a rate of 15% even for non-residents unless the shares were held for more than 24 months. The best place to research equities in the Pakistani market is the Pakistan Bureau of Statistics website.

Clifton beach, Karachi, Pakistan

Mongolia

Mongolia's main stock exchange is the Mongolian Stock Exchange (MSE). Its headquarters are in Ulaanbaatar. It was founded in January 1991 by a Mongolian government decision to privatize state-owned assets. Since 2006, the MSE has experienced tremendous development. The MSE was the best-performing stock market in the world in 2010, with a gain of 121 percent.

With a 57.8 percent rise, MSE was the world's second-highest performing stock exchange, trailing only Venezuela's Caracas Stock Exchange, which climbed by 80.8 percent.

There are 218 businesses listed as of February 2019, and they are denominated in Mongolian Tugriks. During the majority of Mongolia's post-socialist period, there were few limitations on foreign investments.

Mongolia's economy has historically relied on agriculture and cattle. Mongolia also has abundant mineral resources, with copper, coal, molybdenum, tin, tungsten, and gold accounting for a significant portion of the country's industrial output. Soviet aid, which accounted for one-third of GDP at its peak, vanished virtually suddenly in 1990–91, when the Soviet Union fell apart.

Mongolia has been thrown into a profound economic slump. After slowing in 1996 owing to a succession of natural calamities and rises in international copper and cashmere prices, economic development resumed in 1997–99. Due to the effects of the Asian financial crisis, government income and exports plummeted in 1998 and 1999.

In 1997, Mongolia became a member of the World Trade Organization (WTO). At the final Consultative Group Meeting in Ulaanbaatar in June 1999, the foreign donor community committed more than $300 million each year. Mongolia's economy has recently developed at a rapid speed as a result of increased mining, with Mongolia's GDP growing at a rate of 11.7 percent in 2013. However, because most of this development is reliant on exports, Mongolia is feeling the effects of the global mining downturn brought on by China's slowing development.

In their study "Mongolia: "Blue-sky potential," Renaissance Capital claims that Mongolia is on its way to becoming the next Asian tiger, or "Mongolian wolf," as they like to call it, with "unstoppable" economic development. The 'Wolf Economy' is said to be poised to pounce, based on recent changes in the mining industry and an increase in foreign interest at an amazing rate. The term's assertive moniker reflects the country's capital market mentality, and newer mineral possibilities give it a chance to keep its status as one of the world's fastest-growing economies.

The banking sector is highly concentrated, with five banks controlling about 80% of financial assets.

Non-residents of Mongolia must pay a 20% withholding tax on income earned in Mongolia. Dividends, interest, royalties, services fees paid overseas, and revenue from items sold on Mongolian soil are all included.

For equity research on the Mongolian market, you can consult the National Statistical Office of Mongolia website.

Inside the Mongolia stock exchange

Nepal

Nepal's only stock exchange is the Nepal Stock Exchange Limited (abbreviated as NEPSE). It's in Kathmandu. The stock market capitalization of the firms listed on NEPSE was roughly US$30 billion as of February 8, 2021.

There are 285 listed firms as of March 16, 2021, including commercial banks, hydropower businesses, insurance businesses, and finance businesses, among others, and they are denominated in Nepalese rupees. The following sector subindexes are available: Banking, Development Bank, Finance, Microfinance, Manufacturing and Processing, Hydropower, Non-Life Insurance, Life Insurance, Hotels, Mutual Fund, Trading, Investment, and Other. Shares, Preferred shares, Mutual funds, government bonds, and debentures are the financial instruments available on the exchange.

Nepal's economy is primarily based on agriculture and remittances. The continual shift in political circumstances, which have ranged from monarchy to being governed by the Nepal Communist Party, has complicated and hampered economic growth. Until the mid-twentieth century, the nation was an isolated, agricultural culture.

Since the 1950s, however, the country has made headway toward sustainable economic growth and has opened up to economic liberalization, resulting in economic development and improved living conditions. The country's main difficulties in attaining greater economic growth are frequent changes in political leadership and corruption.

Agriculture continues to be Nepal's most important economic sector, employing around 65 percent of the population and accounting for 31.7 percent of GDP. Only around 20% of the total land area is cultivable; the other 40.7 percent is wooded (i.e., covered with shrubs, pastureland, and woodland); and the majority of the rest is mountains. Non-Resident Nepalis, who engage in a variety of industries, bring in a large number of small foreign investments to Nepal.

Hydroelectricity has great potential in Nepal. As a result, a huge number of international firms want to invest in Nepal, but the process has been stymied by political unrest. Since 2000, Nepal has signed agreements with ten nations (PSRD) to prevent double taxes (all in credit method). Since 1983, it has had investment protection agreements with five nations. Nepal limited foreign aid in 2014 by imposing a minimum ceiling on foreign grants, soft loans, and commercial loans from development partners.

Capital gains (profits from the sale of shares in a publicly traded firm) are subject to a 10% withholding tax for natural persons and a 15% withholding tax for others.

Kathmandu, Nepal

Uzbekistan

The Tashkent Stock Exchange is Uzbekistan's main securities trading platform and the country's only corporate securities exchange. It was established by the government in 1994 as an open joint-stock corporation in Tashkent, Uzbekistan's capital. Tashkent RSE is slated to become a potential partner of Korea Exchange, with KRX purchasing 25% of the equity capital. Meanwhile, RSE is owned by the country's major commercial banks and the government.

Uzbekistan's securities market arose from the substantial privatization of state-owned companies in the 1990s, following the collapse of the Soviet Union and the country's independence from Moscow. In contrast to the Russian Federation, the Uzbek government progressively privatized SOEs, first reorganizing them as joint-stock companies and then selling just a portion of their equity capital through stock exchanges. There are 104 listings on the exchange and they are denominated in Uzbekistani so'ms.

Uzbekistan's economy has remained a Soviet-style command economy since independence, with a gradual transition to a market economy. Although progress on governmental economic policy reforms has been slow, Uzbekistan has made significant progress overall.

The economy continues to be harmed by its restrictive trade regime and generally interventionist policies. Significant structural change is required, notably in the following areas: enhancing the investment climate for foreign investors, strengthening the banking system, and decentralizing the agriculture sector.

The investment climate in Uzbekistan remains one of the worst in the CIS, with only Belarus and Turkmenistan's rating lower. Foreign investment inflows have dwindled to a trickle due to the poor investment climate. Uzbekistan is thought to have the CIS's lowest level of foreign direct investment per capita.

U.S. companies have invested about $500 million in Uzbekistan since independence, although many overseas investors have left or are contemplating leaving owing to deteriorating investor trust, harassment, and currency convertibility issues.

Skyline of Tashkent, Uzbekistan

Azerbaijan

The Baku Stock Exchange (BSE) is Azerbaijan's primary stock exchange. BSE is structured as a closed joint-stock corporation with 19 stockholders. Short-term treasury bonds, common stocks (mainly from privatized former state-owned firms, including food and beverage, construction, and banking businesses), and foreign currency futures are traded on the Baku Stock Exchange. There are 29 companies listed on the exchange, and they are denominated in Azerbaijani manats.

Azerbaijan's economy has completed its post-Soviet transition from a state-led economy to a largely oil-based economy (with the completion of the Baku-Tbilisi-Ceyhan Pipeline). As projects came online during the shift to oil production, impressive growth numbers emerged, reaching 26.4 percent in 2005.

The real GDP growth rate was projected to be 3.7 percent in 2011, however, it was just 0.1 percent. Azerbaijan's economy relies heavily on its vast oil reserves. The Azerbaijani manat, the country's currency, remained steady in 2000, losing 3.8 percent versus the dollar. In 2000, the budget deficit was 1.3 percent of GDP. Economic reform has lagged behind macroeconomic stability in general.

Although the government has implemented regulatory changes in several sectors, including a significant liberalization of trade policy, the effectiveness of these changes is limited due to inefficient public administration in which commercial and regulatory interests are mixed. Agricultural areas and small and medium-sized businesses have been largely privatized by the government.

The government began a second-stage privatization initiative in August 2000, in which several big state companies were sold. Azerbaijan is the region's biggest agricultural basin. Azerbaijan's agricultural areas account for 54.9 percent of the country's total area. The mining and hydrocarbon sectors accounted for nearly all of Azerbaijan's GDP.

The economy's diversification into manufacturing industries is a long-term challenge. Azerbaijan's military sector has developed into a self-contained entity with rising defense manufacturing capabilities. The ministry collaborates with Ukraine's, Belarus's, and Pakistan's military sectors. Azerbaijan's GDP growth rates during the previous several years have made the country one of the world's fastest-rising economies.

However, Azerbaijan's banking industry has yet to realize the enormous development potential that the country's strong economic development should provide. As a result, the banking industry in Azerbaijan remains tiny in comparison to the size of the economy. Azerbaijan had the greatest foreign investment per capita among Commonwealth of Independent States (CIS) countries in 2014.

Azerbaijan does not have a separate capital gains tax. Ordinary taxable income includes proceeds from the sale of capital assets.

Baku city at night, Azerbaijan

Armenia

The Armenia Securities Exchange, or "AMX," previously NASDAQ OMX Armenia, is the country's only stock exchange. It is situated in Yerevan, Armenia's capital. The Central Bank of Armenia is the official regulator for the stock exchange and the Armenian securities market (CBA). Stocks, corporate bonds, government bonds, currencies, SWAP, and REPO (repurchase agreements) on corporate securities are among the instruments being traded on AMX. There are 10 companies listed on the exchange, and they are denominated in Arminian Drams.

In 2020, the Armenian economy declined by 5.7 percent. In contrast, it expanded by 7.6% in 2019, the highest rate since 2007, while GDP increased by 40.7 percent between 2012 and 2018, and key banking metrics such as assets and credit exposures nearly doubled.

Armenia's economy was mainly focused on the industry—chemicals, electrical products, equipment, processed food, synthetic rubber, and textiles—until independence, and it was heavily reliant on outside resources. Copper, zinc, gold, and lead are all mined in Armenia.

GDP growth is expected to recover halfway in 2021, reaching 3.4 percent, before rising to 4.3 percent in 2022. The recovery will be gradual since the economy will most likely not recover to pre-COVID yield levels until 2023. The services industry, together with the construction industry, has been the driving force behind Armenia's recent strong economic growth rate. Armenia's level of living has increased, as has its income, resulting in an improvement in the retail sector. The retail industry employs the most people.

While the industry is improving, it is still concentrated in Yerevan and not in other Armenian cities.

Capital gains received by non-residents on the sale of securities are taxed at 0%.

Financial district of Yerevan at night, Armenia

7

South-East Asia

Australia

The Australian Securities Exchange is the country's main stock exchange. The exchange is owned and administered by ASX Limited, and it is also known as the ASX. Despite the fact that the exchange and the operational firms are two different entities, they are frequently referred to as one due to their interconnected nature. State-based stock markets were the first security exchanges in Australia in the 1800s. The Australian Stock Exchange was established on April 1, 1987, as a result of legislation passed by the Australian Parliament that merged the six state securities markets.

In 2006, the Australian Securities Exchange amalgamated with the Sydney Futures Exchange to become The Australian Securities Exchange. The exchange sells stocks, bonds, derivatives, and commodities, among other things. According to ASX Limited's 2020 Annual Report to Shareholders, it is a "top 10 global securities exchange by value and Asia's largest interest rate derivatives market".

There are 2258 listings on the exchange, and they are denominated in Australian dollars. Shares, futures, options, warrants, contracts for difference, exchange-traded funds, unlisted managed funds (mFund), real estate investment trusts, listed investment companies, and interest rate securities are among the products available for trading on ASX.

Australia's economy is a well-developed mixed economy. Australia has the 12th-largest nominal GDP, the 18th-largest PPP-adjusted GDP, the 25th-largest goods exporter, and the 20th-largest goods importer as of 2021. With the 103rd financial quarter, Australia set a new record for the longest period of unbroken GDP expansion in the developed world, marking 26 years since the country had a technical recession (two consecutive quarters of negative growth).

As of 2021, its GDP was expected to be A$1.7 trillion. The service sector dominates the Australian economy, accounting for 62.7 percent of GDP and employing 78.8 percent of the workforce. With a total value of US$19.9 trillion in 2019, Australia has the tenth largest total estimated value of natural resources.

In 2009-10, when the mining boom was at its peak, the mining industry's total value-added was 8.4% of GDP. Despite recent declines in the mining industry, Australia's economy has remained resilient and steady, with no recessions from 1991 to 2020. In terms of domestic market capitalization, the Australian Securities Exchange in Sydney is the world's 16th biggest stock exchange, and it contains one of the largest interest rate derivatives markets in the Asia-Pacific area.

Commonwealth Bank, BHP, CSL, Westpac, NAB, ANZ,

Fortescue Metals Group, Wesfarmers, Macquarie Group, Woolworths Group, Rio Tinto, and Telstra are just a few of Australia's major corporations. The Australian dollar is the currency of Australia and its territory, which it shares with many Pacific nation-states. The economies of East and Southeast Asia, often known as ASEAN Plus Three, are deeply linked with Australia's, accounting for around 64 percent of exports in 2016. China, in particular, is by far Australia's most important export and import partner.

Australia is a member of the Asia-Pacific Economic Cooperation, the G20, the OECD, and the World Trade Organization. ASEAN, Canada, Chile, China, South Korea, Malaysia, New Zealand, Peru, Japan, Singapore, Thailand, and the United States have all signed free trade agreements with the country.

The ANZCERTA deal with New Zealand has substantially strengthened economic integration. The main industries are: Financial and insurance services, Construction, Healthcare and social assistance, Mining, Professional services, scientific and technical services, and Manufacturing.

In most cases, a non-resident does not pay capital gains tax on the sale of shares in Australia. Equity research on Aussie stocks can be done with the Australian Bureau of Statistics website.

Melbourne, Australia

New Zealand

The New Zealand Market (the NZX), is the country's national stock exchange and a publicly traded corporation. Smartshares, LifeSaver (a financial service for KiwiSaver), and Wealth Technologies are all owned by NZX. The NZX has 258 listed securities with a combined market value of NZ$184.87 billion, and they are denominated in New Zealand dollars.

New Zealand's economy is a well-developed free-market economy. When measured in nominal gross domestic product, it is the 52nd biggest in the world, and when assessed in purchasing power parity, it is the 63rd largest. New Zealand has a huge GDP for its population of 5 million people, and revenue sources are dispersed around the country. The country's economy is one of the most globalized, relying heavily on foreign commerce, particularly with Australia, Canada, China, the European Union, Japan, Singapore, South Korea, and the United States.

New Zealand's economy is quite similar to Australia's. The service sector accounts for 63 percent of all GDP activity in New Zealand's diversified economy. Aluminum production, food processing, metal fabrication, and wood and paper goods are all large-scale industrial businesses.

16.5 percent of GDP was accounted for by mining, manufacturing, power, gas, water, and waste services. Despite accounting for only 6.5 percent of GDP, the primary sector continues to dominate New Zealand's exports.

The information technology industry is rapidly expanding. The New Zealand Exchange is the country's main stock exchange (NZX). The New Zealand dollar (affectionately known as the "Kiwi dollar") is also accepted in four Pacific Island territories. The New Zealand dollar is the world's tenth most traded currency. The main industries are Food processing, textiles, machinery and transportation equipment, finance, tourism, and mining.

Even if you are not a resident, New Zealand does not have a capital gains tax, therefore you will not be taxed on the selling of your shares in New Zealand. Research on Kiwi stocks can be done with the Statistics New Zealand website.

Auckland, New Zealand

Singapore

Singapore Exchange Limited (SGX: S68) is a Singapore-based investment holding company that offers a variety of services including securities and derivatives trading. The Singapore Exchange is a member of the World Federation of Exchanges and the Federation of Asian and Oceanian Stock Exchanges.

There are 776 listings on the exchange, and they are denominated in both Singapore dollars and US dollars. Out of these listings, 483 are domestic companies, while the rest are foreign companies, with the majority from China. Companies listed on SGX are divided into two categories: those listed on the SGX Mainboard and those listed on the SGX NASDAQ. A firm must meet certain SGX standards in order to be listed on the mainboard, but a listing on NASDAQ is not subject to any additional restrictions.

Singapore's economy is a well-developed free-market economy. The World Economic Forum has classified Singapore's economy as the most open, the third-least corrupt, and the most pro-business in the world. Singapore has low tax rates and the world's second-highest purchasing power parity per capita GDP. Singapore is the headquarters of the Asia-Pacific Economic Cooperation.

State-owned businesses play a significant part in Singapore's economy, in addition to its business-friendly image. Temasek Holdings, Singapore's sovereign wealth fund, owns majority stakes in several of the country's largest companies, including Singapore Airlines, SingTel, ST Engineering, and MediaCorp.

The Singaporean economy is a significant outflow financier of foreign direct investment. Due to its extremely favorable investment climate and stable political environment, Singapore has benefited from an inflow of FDI from global investors and institutions in recent years. Singapore's position as a regional center for wealth management, as well as its exports, notably in electronics, chemicals, and services.

Because water is limited in Singapore, it is considered a valuable resource. Due to the scarcity of fertile land in Singapore, agricultural output is reliant on agrotechnology parks. Another critical problem for the Singaporean economy is human resources. With the inclusion of Biopolis, Singapore's economy was placed second overall in the Scientific American Biotechnology ranking in 2014.

In the wafer fabrication sector and oil refining, Singapore may be considered to rely on an extended idea of intermediate commerce to entrepôt trade, by acquiring raw products and refining them for re-export. Singapore has a key port, making it more competitive than many of its neighbors when it comes to doing business. Singapore has one of the highest trade-to-GDP ratios in the world, averaging about 400 percent.

Singapore's port is the world's second-busiest in terms of cargo tonnage. From the 17th to the 20th of August, Singapore will host the World Economic Forum 2021. Singapore has made steps to foster innovation, stimulate entrepreneurship, and retrain its workforce in order to maintain its worldwide status and economic success in the twenty-first century.

In Singapore, there are around 243,000 foreign domestic workers. The main industries are electronics, chemicals, financial services, oil-drilling equipment, petroleum refining, biomedical products, scientific instruments, telecommunications equipment, rubber, food and beverages, ship repair, offshore construction, life sciences, and re-exportation.

Many major financial experts, economists, and politicians believe Singapore to be a worldwide financial center, with Singapore banks providing world-class corporate bank account services. Singapore was ranked sixth most competitive financial center in the world and fourth most competitive in Asia in the 2020 Global Financial Centers Index.

Multiple currencies, online banking, telephone banking, checking and savings accounts, debit and credit cards, fixed-term deposits, and wealth management services are just a few of the options available. For a variety of reasons, including increased fees placed on Swiss accounts and a weakening of Swiss bank secrecy, Singapore has attracted assets previously held in Swiss institutions. In 2005, Credit Suisse, Switzerland's second-largest bank, relocated its head of worldwide private banking to Singapore. The country has been called the "Switzerland of Asia" as a result of this.

Gains from the sale of a home, shares, or financial instruments are typically not taxed in Singapore. Gains from "dealing in properties" may, nevertheless, be taxed. Equity research on Singapore stocks can be done with the Singapore Department of Statistics website.

Singapore Marina Bay

Thailand

The Stock Exchange of Thailand, often known as the SET, is Thailand's main and only stock exchange. SET is ASEAN's second-largest stock exchange, with a market value of US$473 billion as of June 2020, but it is the region's largest IPO market, with total money raised of USD 17.8 billion from 2015 to 2020. As of June 2020, SET is also ASEAN's most active stock exchange, with an average daily trading transaction of USD 2.16 billion.

There were 556 businesses listed on the SET at the end

of 2019, 169 on the Market for Alternative Investment, and 228 bonds on the Thailand Bond Exchange. SET also lists other forms of securities such as warrants, derivative warrants, depositary receipts, exchange-traded funds, real estate investment trusts, and infrastructure funds. The listings are denominated in Thai bahts.

SET has 8 industry groups and 28 sectors.

Thailand's economy is reliant on exports, which accounted for around 60% of the country's gross domestic product in 2019. Thailand is a recently industrialized country, according to the World Bank, with a GDP of 16.316 trillion baht (US$505 billion) in 2018, making it Asia's eighth biggest economy.

Thailand has an average inflation rate of 1.06 percent and a trade surplus of 7.5 percent of GDP as of 2018. In 2019, the Thai economy is anticipated to increase by 3.8 percent. In 2017, the Thai Baht, the country's currency, was the tenth most widely used payment currency in the world. The industrial and service sectors make for the majority of Thailand's GDP, with the former accounting for 39.2 percent.

The agriculture industry in Thailand accounts for 8.4% of GDP, which is lower than the trade, logistics, and communication sectors, which account for 13.4% and 9.8% of GDP, respectively. The building and mining industries contribute 4.3 percent to the country's GDP. Other service sectors make for 24.9 percent of the country's GDP, including banking, education, and hotel and restaurant industries.

Telecommunications and service trade are becoming hotbeds of industrial growth and economic competitiveness. Thailand is Southeast Asia's second-largest economy, after Indonesia. However, following Singapore, Brunei, and

Malaysia, it ranks fourth in Southeast Asia in terms of per capita GDP (US$7,273.56).

Thailand has US$237.5 billion in overseas reserves, making it the second-largest in Southeast Asia (after Singapore). In 2018, the country's current account surplus ranked ninth in the world, at US$37.898 billion. Thailand is the second-largest exporter in Southeast Asia, after Singapore.

In terms of social and development indices, the World Bank has named the country "one of the great development success stories." According to the Office of the National Economic and Social Development Council's new poverty baseline, despite having a low per capita gross national income of US$6,610 and ranking 83rd in the Human Development Index. The percentage of people living in poverty decreased from 65.26 percent in 1988 to 8.61 percent in 2016.

Thailand has one of the world's lowest unemployment rates, with a rate of one percent. This is owing to the fact that a substantial percentage of the population is employed in subsistence agriculture or other susceptible occupations (own-account work and unpaid family work).

The main industries are automobiles and automotive parts (11%), financial services (9%), electric appliances and components (8%), tourism (6%), cement, auto manufacturing, heavy and light industries, appliances, computers and parts, furniture, plastics, textiles and garments, agricultural processing, beverages, and tobacco.

Capital Gains tax on the sale of Thai shares by a non-resident will be 15% but can be exempted either with a double taxation treaty or other provisions. Equity research on Thai stocks can be done with the National Statistical Office of

Thailand website.

Bangkok by night, Thailand

Malaysia

Malaysia's stock exchange is known as Bursa Malaysia. It is located in Kuala Lumpur and was originally known as the Kuala Lumpur Stock Exchange.

There are 801 listings on the exchange, denominated in Malaysian ringgits. the total market capitalization of the exchange is close to 400 Billion US dollars. Malaysia has a significant Islamic population, therefore is offering a wide range of Shariah-compliant products on the exchange.

According to the International Monetary Fund in 2020, Malaysia's economy is the fourth biggest in Southeast Asia. It is also the world's 36th largest economy. Due to a high density of knowledge-based businesses and the adoption of cutting-edge technologies for manufacturing and the digital economy, labor productivity in Malaysia is substantially greater than in neighboring Thailand, Indonesia, the Philippines, or Vietnam.

Malaysia's economy is ranked 27th most competitive in the world, according to the Global Competitiveness Report of 2019. Malaysians live in relative luxury compared to virtually all other ASEAN countries, only coming close with only Singapore and Brunei. This is due to a rapidly developing export-oriented economy, a low national income tax, extremely inexpensive local food and transportation fuel, and fully subsidized single-payer public healthcare.

Malaysia has a freshly industrialized market economy that is open and state-led. Malaysia's economy is strong and diverse, with high-tech items exporting at the second-highest level in ASEAN, behind Singapore. After Indonesia, Malaysia exports the second-largest volume and value of palm oil products in the world.

Despite government initiatives aimed at increasing per capita income in order to accelerate Malaysia's transition to a high-income nation by 2020, wage growth has been sluggish, trailing behind the OECD average. Cost of Living Assistance, a social welfare benefit with direct cash benefit transfer, has also been in existence since 2011. To cut deficits and satisfy federal debt commitments in 2018, the government ramped up steps to generate income by implementing the Sales and Service Tax at a rate of 6%.

International commerce is highly important to Malaysia's economy since it is one of three nations that govern the Strait of Malacca. It was formerly the world's greatest producer of tin, rubber, and palm oil. Manufacturing has a significant impact on the country's economy, accounting for more than 40% of GDP.

Malaysia also has the largest Islamic banking and financial center in the world. In the 1970s, Malaysia's economy began to shift from a mining and agricultural-based economy to a more multi-sectoral one.

Malaysia will become the world's 21st largest economy by 2050, according to a 2012 HSBC estimate, with a GDP of $1.2 trillion and a GDP per capita of $29,247. According to the study, "Electronics, petroleum, and liquefied natural gas producers would enjoy a significant increase in per capita income. Malaysia's long life expectancy, relatively high level of education, and above-average fertility rate will all contribute to the country's rapid growth." Credit Suisse managing director Viktor Shvets said that "Malaysia has all the essential components to become a developed nation."

Malaysia ranks 6th in the world in the World Bank's Ease of Undertaking Business Index. Malaysia's strengths in the ranking include acquiring credit (ranked first), safeguarding investors (ranked fourth), and doing cross-border commerce (ranked 5th). Dealing with construction permissions is one of the weaknesses (ranked 43rd). Malaysia received a perfect ten for the degree of disclosure, nine for director culpability, and seven for shareholder litigation in the survey's investor protection category. In the survey's investor protection category, Malaysia trails Singapore, Hong Kong, and New Zealand.

Malaysia's industrial sector accounts for 36.8% of the country's GDP. The electronics, automotive, and construction industries all contribute significantly to the industrial sector. Kuala Lumpur has a significant financial industry and is placed 22nd in the Global Financial Centres Index.

The rate of Capital gains on the sale of Malaysian shares, for a seller who is not a Malaysian citizen or permanent resident, is 30% for disposals within 5 years of acquisition and 10% for disposals more than 5 years after acquisition. The Department of Statistics Malaysia website is a great resource for equity research on that market.

Kuala Lumpur, Malaysia

Indonesia

The Indonesia Stock Market is situated in Jakarta. It was originally known as the Jakarta Stock Exchange (JSX), but after combining with the Surabaya Stock Exchange in 2007, it was renamed. The Indonesia Stock Exchange has 656 listed firms, denominated in Indonesian rupiah, with 1.1 million total stock investors.

The Indonesian Stock Exchange is currently housed in the IDX building in Sudirman's Central Business District. Some indices on the exchange reflect compliance with Sharia law.

Indonesia's economy is the largest in Southeast Asia and one of the largest developing market economies. Indonesia is categorized as a recently industrialized nation since it is an upper-middle-income country and a member of the G20. It is the world's 15th biggest economy by nominal GDP and the 7th largest by GDP.

Indonesia's Internet economy is anticipated to reach US$130 billion by 2025, up from US$40 billion in 2019. Indonesia's economy is reliant on the domestic market, government expenditure, and state-owned companies (the central government owns 141 enterprises). In Indonesia's market economy, the management of pricing for a variety of essential products (including rice and electricity) is also subject to government intervention. Individual Indonesians and foreign corporations have, nevertheless, dominated the majority of the economy since the 1990s.

Following the Asian financial crisis of 1997, the government acquired a large percentage of private-sector assets by purchasing nonperforming bank loans and company assets through the debt restructuring process, and the firms in custody were eventually sold for privatization many years later.

Since 1999, the economy has rebounded, and growth has recently increased to around 4–6%. Indonesia surpassed India as the second-fastest-growing G-20 economy in 2012, after only China. Since then, the yearly growth rate has been hovering around 5%. However, owing to the COVID-19 pandemic, Indonesia had a recession in 2020, with economic growth falling to -2.07 percent, the lowest since the 1997 crisis.

Agriculture is a crucial sector, accounting for 14.43 percent of GDP. Agriculture currently occupies roughly 30% of the land area and employs approximately 49 million people. In 2017, the country manufactured almost 1.2 million automobiles, placing it as the world's 18th largest producer. Indonesian automotive firms may now build automobiles with a significant percentage of local material (80–90%).

Indonesia has 50 million small enterprises, with web usage increasing by 48% in 2010. Before the end of 2012, Google stated that it will create a local office in Indonesia. Internet-related activity contributed to 1.6 percent of GDP, according to Deloitte. It is larger than exports of electronic and electrical equipment and liquefied natural gas, which account for 1.51% and 1.45% of total exports, respectively.

The US Trade Representatives opted not to categorize Indonesia as a "developing nation" in 2019 since its participation in world trade only topped 0.5 percent. Indonesia has the greatest anticipated growth rate of high-net-worth people among the ten largest Asian economies, according to Asia Wealth Report. According to Knight Frank's 2015 Wealth Report, there were 24 people with a net worth of more than $1 billion in 2014. The majority of them lived in Jakarta, with the rest dispersed throughout Indonesia's major cities. There are 192 centamillionaires (those with more than $100 million in wealth) and 650 high-net-worth people (those with more than $30 million in wealth).

Unless covered by a tax treaty, the sale of listed shares owned by a foreign shareholder in an Indonesian business is subject to a final tax of 5% of gross proceeds. Equity Research can be done with the Statistics Indonesia website.

Jakarta, Indonesia

Philippines

The Philippine Stock Exchange, Inc. (PSE) is the country's national stock exchange. The Manila Stock Exchange and the Makati Stock Exchange merged in 1992. The exchange has been in operation since 1927.

There are 275 firms listed on the Philippine Stock Exchange as a whole, and they are denominated in Philippine pesos. PSE's primary index is the PSE Composite Index (PSEi), which is made up of thirty publicly traded companies. Six more sector-based indexes are also available. For the fourth time in five years, Alpha Southeast Asia magazine named the PSE as the best stock market in Southeast Asia.

According to the International Monetary Fund for 2021, the Philippines' economy is the world's 27th biggest by nominal GDP and Asia's 10th largest. The Philippines is one of Southeast Asia's growing economies, with the third-biggest GDP nominal behind Thailand and Indonesia.

The Philippines is usually thought of as a recently industrialized country with an economy that is transitioning from agriculture to services and manufacturing. GDP by purchasing power parity was expected to reach $1.47 trillion in 2021, ranking it 18th in the world.

Semiconductors and electronic items, transportation equipment, textiles, copper products, petroleum products, coconut oil, and fruits are also major exports. Japan, China, the United States, Singapore, South Korea, the Netherlands, Hong Kong, Germany, Taiwan, and Thailand are all major commercial partners.

The Philippines, along with Indonesia, Malaysia, Vietnam, and Thailand, has been designated as one of the Tiger Cub

Economies. Its economy is now one of Asia's fastest-growing. However, substantial issues persist, most notably the huge income and growth inequalities across the country's many regions and socioeconomic groups, as well as the need to reduce corruption and invest in the infrastructure required for future growth.

By 2050, the Philippine economy is expected to be the fourth largest in Asia and the thirteenth or sixteenth largest in the world. The Philippines, as a recently industrialized country, still has a substantial agricultural sector, but services have grown to dominate the economy. Processing and assembly processes in the manufacture of electronics and other high-tech components, generally from foreign multinational firms, account for a large portion of the industrial sector.

With shipyards in Subic, Cebu, General Santos City, and Batangas, the Philippines is a key player in the worldwide shipbuilding sector. Because the country is surrounded by water, it offers a plethora of natural deep-sea ports that are excellent for development as production, building, and maintenance locations.

ABS is produced in the Philippines and is used in Mercedes-Benz, BMW, and Volvo vehicles. The most well-known automobile manufacturers in the country are Toyota, Mitsubishi, Nissan, and Honda. Kia and Suzuki are two of the country's compact vehicle manufacturers. Motorcycles are made by Honda and Suzuki. According to a market research report published in Canada, more investments in this industry are projected to increase in the next years.

The Philippines' aerospace goods are mostly for export and include manufacturing parts for both Boeing and Airbus aircrafts. Texas Instruments has a factory in Baguio that has been in operation for 20 years and is the world's largest manufacturer of DSP chips.

The Philippines overtook India as the global leader in business process outsourcing in 2008. The Philippines is home to the bulk of the top 10 BPO companies in the United States. BPO centers may be found at IT parks and centers around the Philippines' Economic Zones. With an average yearly increase rate of 20%, the BPO business continues to demonstrate substantial advances.

The CGT is 15% for individual taxpayers, both resident and non-resident, and domestic companies. Equity Research on the Filipino market can be done through the Philippine Statistics Authority website.

Sunset in Manila, The Philippines

Vietnam

The main stock market in Vietnam is the Ho Chi Minh City Stock Exchange (HOSE or HSX), which is situated in Ho Chi Minh City. The Ho Chi Minh City Securities Trading Center (HoSTC), together with the Hanoi Securities Trading Center, was established in 2000 as an administrative agency of the State Securities Commission.

There are 396 listings on the exchange, and they are denominated in Vietnamese dongs. Vietnam limits foreign ownership of listed companies to 49%. From 4/1/2021, HOSE has officially raised the minimum number of stock transactions from 10 to 100.

Vietnam's economy is a socialist-oriented market economy that is the world's 36th biggest in terms of nominal gross domestic product and the world's 23rd largest in terms of purchasing power parity. Vietnam has been transitioning from a highly centralized command economy to a mixed economy that employs both directive and indicative planning through five-year plans with assistance from an open market-based economy since the mid-1980s, thanks to the I Mi reform era.

During that time, the economy grew at a breakneck pace. Vietnam is undergoing a phase of global economic integration in the twenty-first century. Almost all of Vietnamese businesses are small or medium-sized. Vietnam has established itself as a top agricultural exporter and a desirable investment location in Southeast Asia.

Vietnam's economy currently relies heavily on foreign direct investment to draw funds from abroad in order to maintain its economic stability. To assist the high-end tourism business, foreign investment in luxury hotels and resorts are increasing. According to a February 2017 projection by PricewaterhouseCoopers, Vietnam's economy may be the world's fastest-growing, with a projected annual GDP growth rate of around 5.1 percent, making it the world's 20th-largest by 2050.

Vietnam has also been named to the CIVETS and Next Eleven lists. Despite the country's economic progress since Doi Moi, there are still concerns that have many experts and scholars concerned about the country's current economic downturn. As of March 2018, Vietnam's economy was still growing, with the greatest yearly growth rate in over a decade, prompting media outlets to suggest that it may become one of Asia's tigers in the near future.

Because of its high foreign investment inflow and productivity development, Vietnam's economy might overtake Singapore within the next decade. Vietnam is emerging as a new Asian manufacturing powerhouse, particularly for Korean and Japanese companies. Samsung, for example, manufactures around 40% of its phones in Vietnam. A substantial automobile sector has emerged in the last decade. As of 2019, Samsung employs approximately 200,000 people in the Hanoi region of Vietnam to manufacture smartphones, with some products being outsourced to China and major sections of the phones being manufactured in India.

Gains from the sale of a stake in a Vietnamese firm are frequently subject to a 20% CIT. Although it is not a distinct tax, it is commonly referred to as capital gains tax ("CGT"). Research on Vietnamese equities can be done with the General Statistics Office of Vietnam website.

Ho Chi Minh city, Vietnam

Sri Lanka

The Colombo Stock Exchange is Sri Lanka's primary stock exchange. Since 1995, the CSE has had its headquarters at the World Trade Center Towers in Colombo, and it also has branches in Kandy, Jaffna, Negombo, Matara, Kurunegala, Anuradhapura, and Ratnapura.

As of January 25, 2021, the Colombo Stock Exchange has 296 firms listed (denominated in Sri Lankan rupees), covering 20 economic sectors, with a market capitalization of Rs. 3,699 billion. According to the Colombo Stock Exchange, investment flows from the Scandinavian area to Sri Lankan equities have improved noticeably in recent years, with inbound investments growing at a rate of 39 percent per annum since 2013.

According to a CSE statement, Scandinavian nations

have together invested Rs.8.2 billion in local stocks so far this year, accounting for 23% of total foreign acquisitions. Except for a few firms where specific limitations apply, foreign investment in the stock market is authorized without restriction.

Sri Lanka's free-market economy was valued at $84 billion in nominal GDP in 2019 and $297 billion in purchasing power parity terms. From 2003 to 2012, the country grew at a rate of 6.4 percent per year, outpacing its regional neighbors, owing to the expansion of non-tradable industries, which the World Bank cautioned was both unsustainable and unequal, and which has subsequently slowed.

Sri Lanka was reclassified as a lower middle-income country by the World Bank in 2019 with an income per capita of 13,620 PPP Dollars or 3,852 nominal US dollars, down from an upper-middle-income classification previously. Sri Lanka has achieved the Millennium Development Goal of reducing severe poverty and is on course to achieve the majority of the other MDGs, surpassing other South Asian nations.

In 2016, Sri Lanka's poverty headcount index was 4.1 percent. Sri Lanka has begun focusing on long-term strategic and structural development problems as it seeks to transition to an upper-middle-income country since the conclusion of the three-decade civil conflict. In 2019, services contributed up 58.2 percent of the Sri Lankan economy, up from 54.6 percent in 2010, industry 27.4%, up from 26.4 percent a decade before, and agriculture 7.4 percent.

Though the agricultural export industry is competitive, technical advancements have been sluggish to reach the protected domestic sector. Sri Lanka is the world's largest producer of solid and industrial tires, and its clothing industry is progressing up the value chain. However, the rise in trade protection over the last decade has raised concerns about a return to inward-looking policies.

Ports and airports contribute to the country's status as a maritime and aviation center in terms of services. The Port of Colombo is South Asia's largest transshipment center. The software and information technology sector is expanding, and it is competitive and exposed to worldwide competition. Tourism is a rapidly growing industry. Sri Lanka was voted the greatest location to visit in 2019 by Lonely Planet, and the best island by Travel+Leisure.

The United States, the United Kingdom, and India are Sri Lanka's major export destinations. The primary import partners are China, India, and the United Arab Emirates. The tea business, which is overseen by the Ministry of Public Estate Management and Development, is one of Sri Lanka's most important industries. In 1995, it surpassed Kenya to become the world's largest exporter, with a 23 percent share of worldwide tea exports. Sri Lanka's clothing sector mostly exports to the United States and Europe. Around 900 factories serve brands like Victoria's Secret, Liz Claiborne, and Tommy Hilfiger across the country.

The applicable rate of capital gains tax is 10% in Sri Lanka. Equity research can be done with the Department of Census and Statistics of Sri Lanka website.

Colombo, Sri Lanka

Cambodia

Cambodia's national stock exchange is the Cambodia Securities Exchange (CSX). The goal of the exchange is to promote high economic growth by enabling money flows, investment, and reallocation through capital market mechanisms. The Canadia Tower in Phnom Penh, Cambodia's capital, serves as the exchange's headquarters.

With a total market capitalization of $103.1 million as of 2016, CSX was claimed to have the smallest overall market capitalization of any stock exchange in the world for its listed businesses. The Market Cap hit US$2.4 billion in June 2021. There are 7 companies listed on the exchange, and they are denominated in Cambodian riels.

Cambodia's economy is presently based on an open market

system, and the country has made significant economic growth over the previous decade. In 2018, Cambodia's GDP was $25 billion. Despite its rapid growth, the country's per capita income remains low in comparison to most of its neighbors. Textiles and tourism are Cambodia's two largest industries, but agricultural activities remain the primary source of income for many Cambodians living in rural areas.

Trading operations and catering-related services are largely concentrated in the service sector. Off-shore oil and natural gas deposits have recently been discovered in Cambodia. With a GDP of $3 billion in 1995, the government changed the country's economic structure from a planned to a market-driven system. Following these adjustments, growth was expected to be 7%, with inflation falling from 26% in 1994 to only 6% in 1995.

Imports grew as a result of the flood of international help, and exports increased as well, notably from the country's clothing sector. Despite consistent economic development, the ASEAN economy only grew by 0.71 percent in 2016, compared to 37.62 percent for her neighbor Indonesia. Cambodia's foreign policy is now focused on building amicable borders with its neighbors (such as Thailand and Vietnam) and integrating into regional (ASEAN) and global (WTO) economic systems.

The need for a stronger education system and a trained workforce are some of the challenges that this growing economy faces, particularly in the poverty-stricken countryside, which suffers from inadequate basic infrastructure. Cambodia, despite its low salaries, abundant labor, closeness to Asian raw supplies, and favorable tax treatment, continues to draw investors. Cambodia's garment industry accounts for the majority of the country's manufacturing sector, accounting for 80% of the country's exports.

Non-resident investors may be required to pay the 14 percent withholding tax on capital gains from the sale of direct shares in a Cambodian company as Cambodian-source income. Equity Research on the Cambodian market can be done through the National Institute of Statistics of Cambodia website.

Evening view of Phnom Penh, Cambodia

Myanmar

In December 2015, the Yangon Stock Exchange (abbreviated YSX) opened in the old Myanmar Central Bank and Myawaddy Bank offices in Yangon. There are 6 companies listed on the exchange, and they are denominated in Myanma kyats.

According to the World Bank, Myanmar's economy has a

nominal GDP of USD $76 billion in 2019 and a purchasing power adjusted GDP of USD $328 billion in 2017. Burma began on a significant strategy of changes in 2011, when new President Thein Sein's administration came to power, including anti-corruption, currency exchange rate regulation, foreign investment regulations, and taxes.

Foreign investments grew 6567 percent from US$300 million in 2009–10 to US$20 billion in 2010–11. The kyat, the Burmese currency, has strengthened by roughly 25% as a result of the large inflow of money. The government responded by easing import restrictions and eliminating export tariffs. The United Nations Development Programme issued a study on April 30, 2021, claiming that the COVID-19 virus and the February 2021 Myanmar coup d'état might undo economic achievements gained over the previous sixteen years.

Rice is the most important agricultural product, accounting for around 60% of the country's total cultivated land area. Agriculture, light industry, and transportation are dominated by the private sector, while energy, heavy industrial, and military sectors are controlled by the government.

Despite the fact that foreign investment is welcomed, it has only had a limited impact thus far. This is because the junta government's actions have harmed foreign businesses, and there has been worldwide pressure to boycott the military administration. Public-sector companies are still inefficient, and privatization attempts have come to a halt.

Because of the large number of black market transactions, estimates of Burmese international trade are very unclear. The failure to establish monetary and fiscal stability is a serious ongoing issue. As a result, Burma remains a poor country, with the bulk of the population's living conditions remaining unchanged over the last decade. Poor government planning, domestic instability, little foreign investment, and a significant trade imbalance are the primary drivers of ongoing slow growth.

The tax on non-resident foreigners' disposals or transfers must be paid in the same currency as the transaction. The capital gains tax rate on the transfer of shares is 40%. The Myanmar Central Statistics Organization website is a good place to look when doing equity research on this market.

South Korea's fast-food chain Lotteria (not US Mc Donalds) in Myanmar

Laos

The Lao Securities Exchange (LSX) is the country's major stock exchange, with headquarters in Vientiane. The LSX has raised more than LAK 6.7 trillion in capital (approximately USD 750 million). To help establish the exchange, the Lao government requested technical and financial assistance from South Korea (Korea Exchange owns a 49 percent interest in the LSX) as well as guidance from neighboring Thailand in 2010. There are 11 listings on the exchange and they are denominated in Lao kips.

Laos' economy is a developing economy with a fast-rising lower-middle-income. The Lao economic model parallels that of the Chinese socialist market and Vietnamese socialist-oriented market economies in that it combines high levels of state ownership with openness to foreign direct investment and private ownership in a mostly market-based framework.

Following independence, Laos created a planned economy akin to that of the Soviet Union. Laos undertook changes known as the New Economic Mechanism in 1986 as part of an economic restructuring aimed at integrating Laos into the globalized world market. The reforms decentralized government authority and promoted private industry alongside state-owned firms.

Laos is currently one of the world's fastest-growing economies, with an average annual GDP growth rate of 8%. The government's main objectives are poverty reduction and universal education for all children, as well as its effort to build a "land-linked" country. The current building of the roughly $6 billion high-speed trains from Kunming, China to Vientiane, Laos, exemplifies this.

In its role as a hydroelectric power provider to neighbors such as China, Vietnam, and Thailand, the nation has become a rising regional force. At the current time, Laos' economy is heavily reliant on foreign direct investment to draw funds from abroad and maintain its economic stability. Despite its fast development, Laos remains one of Southeast Asia's poorest countries. It is a landlocked country with poor infrastructure and a workforce that is mostly uneducated.

Laos, due to its integration into the wider ASEAN Economic Community, its abundant young labor, advantageous tax treatment, continues to draw international investment. The economy continues to be dominated by an unproductive agricultural sector that operates primarily outside of the money economy and in which the government retains a dominating position.

Nonetheless, a number of private businesses have sprouted up in areas including handicrafts, beer, coffee, and tourism. The Lao National Chamber of Commerce and Industry, as well as its provincial branches, are working to encourage private enterprise with backing from the United Nations, Japan, and Germany. The most recent wave of state-owned enterprise reform, which began in 2019, intends to guarantee that the surviving SOEs become successful businesses that provide efficient and long-term revenue for the government. Closing unprofitable firms, ensuring that businesses in which the government has invested are transformed into lucrative ones, and reducing corruption are among these methods. The Lao government's State-Owned Enterprise Development and Insurance Department has 183 firms under its control as of 2019.

In Laos, there is no legal definition of residency for tax

reasons. Profits from the selling of shares are taxed at a rate of ten percent. Equity research can be done through the Lao Statistics Bureau website.

Vientiane Center, Laos

8

South America

Brazil

The B3 Brasil, formerly BM&FBOVESPA, is the Brazilian stock exchange located in Sao Paulo, and is the country's second-oldest exchange. It had a market capitalization of R$2.37 trillion, making it the world's 13th largest stock exchange.

There 368 listings on the exchange, and they are denominated in Brazilian Reals. The exchange offers broad indices, sector indices, and corporate governance indices.

Brazil has a developing mixed economy that was the world's twelfth largest by nominal GDP and eighth-largest by purchasing power parity in 2020. Its industrial sector accounts for three-fifths of the Latin American economy's industrial production. The country's scientific and technological development is argued to be attractive to foreign direct investment, which has averaged US$30 billion per year in recent years.

The agricultural sector, locally called the *agronegócio* (agro-business), has also been dynamic: for two decades this sector has kept Brazil among the most highly productive countries in areas related to the rural sector. The service sector, which accounts for 67.0 percent of GDP, is followed by the industrial sector, which accounts for 27.5 percent. Agriculture accounts for 5.5 percent of total GDP.

The Brazilian labor force is expected to be 100 million people, with 10% working in agriculture, 19% in industry, and 71% working in services. In the Americas, Brazil has the second-largest industrial sector. Brazil's industries span from automobiles, steel, and petrochemicals to computers, aviation, and consumer durables, accounting for 28.5 percent of GDP.

With the Plano Real's greater economic stability, Brazilian and global businesses have invested extensively in new equipment and technology, with a substantial amount of it coming from US companies. Brazil is home to Embraer, the world's third-largest aircraft manufacturer, trailing only Boeing and Airbus.

Brazil's services industry is very diversified and sophisticated. The banking sector accounted for as much as 16 percent of GDP in the early 1990s. Despite being in the midst of major reform, Brazil's financial services industry offers a diverse range of products to local businesses and is attracting a slew of new players, including U.S. financial firms. The Forbes Global 2000 list included 20 Brazilian companies in 2017.

Only assets sold within Brazil are subject to capital gains tax for non-residents. Gains from stock sales on the Brazilian stock market will be taxed at a flat 15% rate for common sales and a flat 20% rate for day-trade transactions and will be considered as variable income. Equity research for the Brazilian market can make use of the Brazilian Institute of Geography and Statistics website as a primary resource.

Bovespa traders in Sao Paulo, Brazil

Chile

The Santiago Stock Market (SSE) was established on November 27, 1893, and is Chile's main stock market and Latin America's third-largest stock exchange, after Brazil's B3 and Mexico's Bolsa Mexicana de Valores.

Stocks, bonds, investment funds, stock options, futures, gold, and silver are all traded on the exchange. There are 268 listings on the exchange, and they are denominated in

Chilean Pesos.

Chile's economy is classified as a market economy and a high-income economy by the World Bank, and it is one of South America's most wealthy countries, leading the area in competitiveness, per capita income, globalization, economic freedom, and low corruption perception.

Chile was named the 30th most competitive country in the world and the first in Latin America in the Global Competitiveness Report for 2009–2010, far ahead of Brazil (56th), Mexico (60th), and Argentina (85th); it has subsequently dropped out of the top 30. According to the World Bank's ease of doing business ranking, Chile was ranked 34th in the world in 2014, 41st in 2015, and 48th in 2016.

Pinochet's administration made Chile a leader in implementing neoliberal policies, thanks to the influence of the Chicago Boys. Large businesses were able to cement their control over the Chilean economy as a result of these measures, resulting in long-term economic development. Mining (mostly copper), business services, personal services, manufacturing, and wholesale and retail trade are the major GDP sectors. Mining accounts for 59.5 percent of exports, while the manufacturing sector accounts for 34 percent, with food goods, chemicals, pulp, paper, and other items accounting for the majority of exports.

Chile's mining industry is one of the country's economic cornerstones. The Chilean government is a big supporter of international investment in the sector and has changed its mining industry rules and regulations to make it more attractive to international investors. Chile's service industry has developed rapidly and steadily in recent decades, aided by rapid advances in communication and information technology, more access to education, and a rise in specialized skills and knowledge within the workforce.

Chile's foreign policy has acknowledged the importance of the tertiary or service sector to the economy, resulting in increased international liberalization and the signing of many free trade agreements. Maritime and aeronautical services, tourism, retail (department stores, supermarkets, and shopping malls), engineering and construction services, informatics, health, and education make up the majority of Chilean service exports.

Chile's financial industry has expanded rapidly in recent years, thanks to a 1997 banking reform law that expanded the scope of legal international operations for Chilean banks. In 2001, the Chilean government adopted more capital market liberalization, and other legislation proposing more liberalization is now pending. People in Chile have benefited from the advent of new financial tools such as home equity loans, currency futures and options, factoring, leasing, and debit cards during the previous 10 years.

Non-resident owners who transfer Chilean shares directly are subject to a 35 percent capital gains tax. If the shareholder has a DL 600 contract that is still active, capital gains will be taxed at a rate of 42 percent. If additional requirements are satisfied, there are exclusions for shares purchased before 1984. Information on Chilean equities is pretty accessible. The two main resources for equity research can be found at the Instituto Nacional de Estadística e Informática website, and the Statistics section of the Banco Central de Chile website.

"Sanhattan", the financial district of Santiago, Chile

Colombia

The Colombia Securities Exchange (Bolsa de Valores de Colombia, or BVC) was formed by the merger of three separate stock exchanges: Bogotá (Bolsa de Bogotá, 1928), Medellin (Bolsa de Medellin, 1961), and Occidente (Bolsa de Occidente, 1962).

The exchange is part of MILA, an agreement between the Santiago Stock Exchange, the Colombia Securities Exchange, the Lima Stock Exchange, and the Mexican Stock Exchange. There are 89 listings on the exchange, and they are denominated in Colombian Pesos.

Colombia is the fourth-largest economy in Latin America in terms of gross domestic product. Over the previous decade, Colombia has seen unprecedented economic growth. Colombia was Latin America's 4th and 3rd largest economy by Real GDP during the twentieth century.

Colombia's primary export is petroleum, which accounts for approximately 45 percent of the country's total exports. Manufacturing accounts for over 12% of Colombia's exports and is growing at a pace of more than 10% per year. Colombia boasts the world's fastest-growing information technology industry and Latin America's longest fiber-optic network.

Outside of Asia, Colombia boasts one of the world's major shipbuilding industries. During the 2000s and 2010s, modern businesses like shipbuilding, electronics, automobiles, tourism, construction, and mining developed rapidly, but most of Colombia's exports remain commodity-based.

Only behind Mexico, Colombia is Latin America's second-largest manufacturer of domestically manufactured electronics and appliances. In 2014, Colombia had the second-fastest-growing economy in the world, after only China. Since the early 2010s, the Colombian government has expressed an interest in exporting modern Colombian pop culture to the rest of the world (which includes video games, music, movies, TV shows, fashion, cosmetics, and food) as a means of diversifying the economy and completely changing the image of Colombia; a national campaign akin to the Korean Wave. Colombia is second only to Mexico in cultural exports and already leads the area in cosmetic and beauty exports.

Colombia is one of the top five producers of coffee, avocado, and palm oil in the world, as well as one of the top ten producers of sugarcane, banana, pineapple, and cocoa. HACEB has been producing refrigeration since 1940, making it one of Colombia's leading household appliance manufacturers. Challenger, Kalley, Imusa, and Landers are other domestic firms. Imusa was purchased by Groupe SEB in 2011 as a way to grow into the Latin American market. Colombia also produces for international businesses such as Whirlpool and GE. LG has also expressed interest in establishing a manufacturing facility in Colombia.

Colombia is also the third-biggest manufacturer of appliances in Latin America, after Mexico and Brazil, and is quickly expanding. Colombia is the second biggest high-tech market in South America and a major producer of electronics in Latin America. Colombia is also Latin America's second-largest manufacturer and exporter of domestically produced electronics. Challenger, PcSmart, Compumax, Colcircuirtos, and Kalley are just a few of these firms.

Despite the fact that creativity is still low, the government sees a lot of promise in the high-tech industry and is spending substantially in education and innovation centers all around the country. As a result, Colombia has the potential to become a significant international electronics producer and a key player in the global high-tech sector in the near future.

Construction has recently played an important part in the economy, and it is increasing at a rate of about 20% per year. As a result, construction in Colombia is on the rise. Colombia's government is substantially investing in transportation infrastructure as part of a plan known as the "Fourth Generation Network." The Colombian government wants to build 7,000 kilometers of highways.

The petroleum and natural gas industries, as well as coal mining, chemicals, and manufacturing, are the most attractive to American investors. Colombia's GDP is dominated by the services sector, which contributed 58 percent of GDP and is likely to continue given global trends. Industry is distinguished by its heterogeneity since it employs the most people (61%) in both the official and informal sectors.

The selling of shares in a Colombian corporation is exempt from all taxes, including VAT, stamp duty, and registration fees. The sale of limited liability company social quotas is subject to a 0.7 percent registration tax on the transfer value.

Bogota, Colombia

Argentina

The Buenos Aires Stock Market (BCBA, from Spanish: Bolsa de Comercio de Buenos Aires) is the institution in charge of Argentina's main stock exchange, which is located in the city center of Buenos Aires. It was founded in 1854 as the successor of Bernardino Rivadavia's Banco Mercantil.

The MERVAL (from MERcado de VALores) is the most

important stock market index, which comprises the most important companies. Burcap, Bolsa General, and M.AR. are among the other indices, as are the currency indicators Indol and Wholesale Indol. There are 106 companies listed on the exchange, and they are denominated in Argentine Pesos.

Argentina is a country in the process of development. It is South America's second-largest economy, behind Brazil. Argentina has a diverse industrial base, abundant natural resources, a highly educated population, an export-oriented agriculture sector, and a diverse natural resource base.

Argentina's economic performance has been erratic in the past, with periods of rapid expansion interspersed by deep recessions. Argentina is a prominent agricultural producer, with exports of cattle, citrus fruit, grapes, honey, maize, sorghum, soybeans, squash, sunflower seeds, wheat, and yerba mate.

Mining and other extractive industries, such as gas and petroleum, are expanding sectors, with mining accounting for about 4% of GDP today, up from 2% in 1980. Each year, the World Bank publishes a list of the top generating nations based on the total output value. Argentina has the 31st most valuable industry in the world (57.7 billion dollars), behind Mexico, Brazil, and Venezuela, but ahead of Colombia, Peru, and Chile, according to the 2019 ranking.

Manufacturing is the largest single sector in the economy (15 percent of GDP) and is highly integrated into Argentine agriculture, with agricultural products accounting for half of the country's industrial exports. Argentina's industrial production has grown very diverse, based on food processing and textiles during its early development in the first part of the twentieth century. Food processing and drinks, motor cars and auto parts, refinery products, biodiesel, chemicals and pharmaceuticals, steel and aluminum, industrial and farm machinery, and electronics and home appliances are the leading industries by production value.

The service sector, which accounts for approximately 60% of overall GDP, is the most important contributor. Argentina's service industry is diverse, with well-developed social, corporate, financial, insurance, real estate, transportation, communication, and tourist sectors. The telecommunications industry is booming, and the economy is benefiting from extensive access to communications services. Argentina's banking system grew up on public sector banks but is currently dominated by the private sector, with deposits exceeding US$120 billion. Private sector banks make for the majority of the country's 80 active institutions and control almost 60% of deposits and loans, with foreign-owned banks outnumbering local banks. The public Banco de la Nación Argentina, on the other hand, has long been Argentina's largest bank. This organization, which is not to be confused with the Central Bank, currently accounts for 30% of total deposits and a fifth of the lending portfolio.

Argentina's transportation system is sophisticated, and it outperforms the rest of Latin America. Manufacturing (36 percent), natural resources (34 percent), and services (34 percent) account for roughly equal amounts of foreign direct investment in Argentina. Foreign investment in local production is led by the chemical and plastics industry (10%) and the automobile industry (6%).

Non-residents are liable to a 13.5 percent effective tax rate on gross proceeds when selling Argentine shares, or a 15 percent income tax on the real capital gain if the seller's tax cost basis can be properly proved for Argentine tax purposes. Information on Argentinian equities is relatively easy to obtain. The first stop for equity research on the Argentinian market would be the Argentinian National Institute of Statistics and Censuses website.

High rises of Puerto Madero, financial district of Buenos Aires, Argentina

Peru

The Lima Stock Exchange (BVL, or Bolsa de Valores de Lima) is Peru's stock exchange, based in Lima, the country's capital.

It has a number of indices. The S&P/BVL Peru General Index is a value-weighted index that monitors the performance of the Lima Exchange's largest and most actively traded stocks. There are 261 listed companies on the exchange and the listings are denominated in Peruvian Nuevo Sols.

Peru's economy is listed by the World Bank as a developing, social market economy with a high degree of foreign exchange and an upper-middle-income economy. Peru's economy is the world's 47th largest in terms of total GDP, and the country currently has a high human development index.

With a GDP growth rate of 6.3 percent in 2012, the country was one of the world's fastest-growing economies, with the economy expected to rise 9.3 percent in 2021 even after the COVID-19 pandemic. Peru's economy is reliant on commodity exports, putting it at risk from price fluctuations in foreign markets, though the economy has started to diversify in recent decades.

Copper, gold, zinc, textiles, chemicals, pharmaceuticals, manufacturers, equipment, services, and fish meal are Peru's main exports, with the United States, China, Brazil, the European Union, and Chile as its main trading partners.

Services account for 59.9% of Peruvian GDP, with manufacturing (32.7%) and agriculture (7.6%) accounting for the rest. From legalizing parts of the informal sector to massive privatization in the mining, energy, and telecommunications sectors, Peru's economy has undergone significant free-market reforms. The nuevo sol has a low inflation rate of 2.5 percent right now. Since its inception, the sol's exchange rate against the US dollar has largely remained between 2.80 and 3.30 to 1. The sol is the most stable and reliable of all the currencies in the Latin American region.

Peru appears well-positioned to flourish in the coming years, with expanding ports loading up boats for China on one side and a new superhighway to Brazil on the other, as well as a free trade deal with the United States in its pocket.

Ordinary income is taxed on capital gains. Capital gains from the selling of shares sold by a Peruvian company on the Lima Stock Exchange, on the other hand, are taxed at a 5% rate if the seller is a non-domiciled entity.

San Isidro, financial center of Lima

Ecuador

The Bolsa de Valores de Quito (BVQ) is one of Ecuador's two stock exchanges, along with the Guayaquil Stock Exchange, and lists over 300 Ecuadorian firms. On the BVQ, about 30 financial services companies participate as market participants. The BVQ is a self-regulatory body that is affiliated with the Federación Iberoamericana de Bolsa (FIAB). The

ECU index tracks the performance of key companies listed on the BVQ. The listings are denominated in US Dollars.

Ecuador's economy is the eighth largest in Latin America and the 69th largest globally in terms of total GDP. Ecuador's economy is dependent on oil, bananas, shrimp, gold, and other primary agricultural products, as well as money transfers from Ecuadorian emigrants working in other countries.

Shifts in global market dynamics and technological advancements have resulted in the economic growth of other industries such as textiles, processed foods, metallurgy, and the service sector. The main industries are petroleum, food processing, textiles, wood products, and chemicals. Oil exports account for 40% of total exports, helping to keep the trade balance positive. The industry is primarily concentrated in Guayaquil, the country's largest industrial hub, and Quito, where it has expanded significantly in recent years.

This city is also the country's largest business hub. The majority of industrial production is aimed at the domestic market. Despite this, industrially manufactured or processed goods are only exported in small quantities.

Ecuador taxes non-residents' capital gains on the selling of shares in local companies at a rate of 10%.

World Trade Center Guayaquil

Uruguay

The Montevideo Stock Exchange, or Bolsa de Valores de Montevideo (BVM), is Uruguay's main stock exchange. It is also known as the Bolsa de Montevideo. It was founded in 1867 and is based in Montevideo. The exchange's transactions total almost 3 billion annually.

The economy of Uruguay is characterized by an export-oriented agricultural sector and a well-educated workforce, along with high levels of social spending. The main industries are food processing, electrical machinery, transportation equipment, petroleum products, textiles, chemicals, and beverages. The software industry has grown significantly in recent decades. Many start-ups have been extremely popular, like PedidosYa. Uruguay also exports their software; the country's longitude is close to that of the United States, making it appealing to businesses looking to outsource software production to Uruguayan firms. Genexus, Códigos del Sur, and Overactive are three prominent Uruguayan tech companies.

Specific capital gains (residents or non-residents) on the sale of shares in Uruguayan firms are taxed at a rate of 12 percent.

World trade center, Montevideo

Bolivia

The Bolivian Stock Exchange (also known as the Bolsa Boliviana de Valores, BBV) is a stock exchange located in the Bolivian capital of La Paz. The exchange, which was established in 1976, trades stocks, indexes, gold, and local commodities. Stocks in the following sectors are traded on the exchange: Agro-industry, Cooperative, Banks, Electrical, Trade, Industrial, Oil, Security, Services, Financial Services, Transport, and Municipality. It's important to bear in mind that investing in Bolivia can be difficult. On the 2021 Index of Economic Freedom, the nation is ranked 172nd. The listings are denominated in Bolivianos.

Bolivia's economy is the 95th largest in nominal terms and the 87th largest in terms of purchasing power parity in the world. Bolivia is classed as a lower-middle-income nation by the World Bank. Bolivia's economy has always been dominated by a single commodity. Bolivia has only had brief periods of economic diversity, from silver to tin to coca. Efforts to modernize the agriculture industry have been hampered by political instability and challenging geography.

Similarly, low population growth combined with short life expectancy has kept the labor supply in flux and hampered the expansion of enterprises. Inflation and corruption have also stifled progress, although the fundamentals of Bolivia's economy improved unexpectedly in the early twenty-first century, prompting major credit rating agencies to raise the country's economic rating in 2010.

The manufacturing industry's largest sector is food, beverage, and tobacco processing. This industry has a major position in the manufacturing industry, which is constantly expanding in terms of output as well as the number of firms and employment. Bolivia's service sector is still underdeveloped. Bolivians live in one of the poorest countries in South America, with little purchasing power. The retail industry is beset by low demand and fierce competition from a thriving black market for illegal items.

Bolivian banking has long been plagued by corruption and lax regulation. However, with the 1993 Banking Law and subsequent acts, a series of reforms are progressively strengthening Bolivia's banking industry.

La Paz downtown financial district at dusk

Paraguay

In Asuncion, Paraguay, the Bolsa de Valores y Productos de Asunción (BVPASA) is the only stock exchange of Paraguay. There are 103 listings on the exchange and they are denominated in Paraguayan guaranís.

Paraguay's economy is a market economy that is heavily

reliant on agricultural goods. Increased agricultural exports, particularly soybeans, have boosted Paraguay's economy in recent years. Paraguay benefits from a young population and abundant hydroelectric power, but it lacks natural resources, and political instability has eroded some of the country's economic advantages.

Foreign investment is welcomed by the government. Paraguay was the world's sixth-largest soy producer in 2018. Paraguay is exhibiting indicators of long-term industrial expansion. In order to satisfy the country's medication demands, the pharmaceutical sector is fast displacing international providers. Paraguayan businesses currently provide 70% of domestic demand and have begun to export medicines.

In 2004, the services industry accounted for over half of Paraguay's GDP and employed almost a quarter of the country's working population. Importing products for sale and illegal reexporting, particularly from Argentina and Brazil, generates service industry jobs. The banking and financial services business in Paraguay is currently recuperating from the 1995 liquidity crisis, which saw several major banks close due to rampant corruption. The International Monetary Fund and the World Bank pushed for reforms that helped the banking sector in Paraguay regain some confidence.

Nonetheless, the entire economy is hampered by a lack of financing options. Money laundering has always been a problem in Paraguay. The government has taken measures to address the issue, although anti-money laundering law is inconsistently enforced.

Asunción, Paraguay

Venezuela

The Caracas Stock Market, or Bolsa de Valores de Caracas (BVC), is the Venezuelan stock exchange. BVC was founded in 1947. BVC is a private exchange that conducts operations for the acquisition and permitted selling of securities in accordance with Venezuelan Capital Market Laws.

It is a member of the Latin American Federation of Stock Markets' Executive Committee. Companies issue fixed income and security instruments at the exchange using methods approved by the regulatory authorities in order to raise money from public investors. BVC is also a place where Bonds and other debt products may be traded. There are 60 listings on the exchange, and they are denominated in Venezuelan Bolivars.

Venezuela's economy is mainly reliant on petroleum, and the country has been in a state of utter economic collapse since the mid-2010s. Venezuela is OPEC's sixth-largest producer of crude oil. Venezuela has been a rentier state since the 1920s, with oil as its major export. Since 2015, the country has been experiencing hyperinflation.

Total commerce accounted for 48.1 percent of the country's GDP in 2014. Exports amounted to 16.7% of GDP, with petroleum products accounting for over 95% of all exports. During the 1980s oil prices dropped, the economy shrank, the currency began to depreciate, and inflation surged, reaching a high of 84 percent in 1989 and 99 percent in 1996.

Steel, aluminum, and cement are among the heavy industrial items that Venezuela produces and exports. Production is focused at Ciudad Guayana, near the Guri Dam, which is one of the world's largest dams and provides almost three-quarters of Venezuela's power. Electronics and vehicles, as well as drinks and consumables, are examples of significant manufacturing.

Despite their poor relations, the United States has long been Venezuela's most significant commercial partner. Machinery, agricultural items, medical instruments, and automobiles have all been sent from the United States to Venezuela. Venezuela is one of the top four international oil suppliers to the United States.

In Venezuela, over 500 American firms are represented. In its Doing Business report, the International Finance Corporation classified Venezuela as one of the worst nations to do business with, rating it 180th out of 185 nations, with its worst rankings being safeguarding investors and taxation.

Many firms left Venezuela under the reigns of Hugo Chávez and his successor, Nicolás Maduro. There were 13,000 businesses in the nation in 1999. By 2016, just 4,000 businesses remained in Venezuela, representing less than a third of the country's total.

Night view of Caracas, Venezuela

9

Central America

Mexico

The Mexican Stock Exchange (Spanish: Bolsa Mexicana de Valores), also known as Mexican Bolsa, Mexbol, or BMV, is one of Mexico's two stock exchanges. The other is BIVA, or Bolsa Institucional de Valores. It is Latin America's second-largest stock exchange, trailing only Brazil's B3 in So Paulo. It is also the Americas' fifth-largest stock exchange. BMV Group owns the exchange.

There are 140 listings available and they are denominated in Mexican Pesos. MILA, which includes the stock markets of Santiago, Lima, and Colombia, is Latin America's second-largest financial market by total capitalization. Stocks, debentures, mutual fund shares, and warrants are available on the exchange.

Mexico's economy is a developing consumer economy. According to the International Monetary Fund, it is the 15th largest in nominal terms and the 11th largest by purchasing power parity. Administrations have strengthened the country's macroeconomic fundamentals since the 1994 crisis. After a brief period of recession in 2001, Mexico was unaffected by the 2002 South American crisis and retained positive, although low, growth rates.

Mexico, on the other hand, was one of the Latin American countries hardest hit by the 2008 recession, with its GDP falling by more than 6% that year. The Main industries of Mexico are Food and beverages, tobacco, chemicals, iron and steel, petroleum, mining, textiles, clothing, motor vehicles, consumer durables, and tourism.

The Mexican economy has experienced unparalleled macroeconomic stability, resulting in lower inflation and interest rates, as well as higher per capita income. With growing private ownership, the economy is rapidly evolving into new manufacturing and service sectors. With the aim of improving infrastructure, recent administrations have increased competition in ports, railroads, telecommunications, power generation, natural gas distribution, and airports.

More than 90 percent of Mexican trade is covered by free trade agreements (FTAs) with more than 40 nations, including the European Union, Japan, Israel, and most of Central and South America, owing to the country's export-oriented economy. The automotive industry is one of Mexico's most important industrial producers, with globally recognized quality standards. Mexico's automotive industry is distinct from that of other Latin American and developing countries in that it is not merely an assembly plant. The industry manufactures technologically advanced components and conducts some research and development.

Food manufacturing, which involves many world-class

firms, is a greater sector of Mexico's industrial economy than it is in the United States or Western Europe. Mexico's electronics industry has expanded dramatically in the last decade. After China, the United States, Japan, South Korea, and Taiwan, Mexico has the world's sixth-largest electronics industry. Mexico is the United States' second-largest electronic exporter. Mexico is the third-largest manufacturers of computers in the world. While foreign companies dominate most of Mexico's electronics industry, the country also has a sizable domestic electronics industry and a number of electronics companies, including Mabe, a major appliance manufacturer and OEM that has been in operation since the 1950s and has expanded into the global market, Meebox, a designer and manufacturer of desktop and tablet computers, and solar power.

Mexico's tertiary sector is projected to account for 59.8% of GDP. Tourism is one of Mexico's most critical sectors. It is the country's fourth-largest source of foreign exchange. According to the IMF, the Mexican banking system is powerful, with profitable and well-capitalized private banks. The stock market in Mexico is closely tied to events in the United States. As a result, the output of Mexican equities can be influenced by the volatility of the New York stock exchange. This is due to both Mexico's economic reliance on the United States and the high volume of ADR trade in Mexican stocks.

Non-residents who sell stock of a Mexican business face a 25 percent gross proceeds tax or a 35 percent net proceeds tax if the non-resident has a representative in Mexico. The Mexican National Institute of Statistics and Geography publishes a great deal of data that helps in researching

Mexican equities.

Mexico city

Panama

Panama's stock market is known as the Bolsa de Valores de Panama. During Panama's political and economic crisis in 1989, it was a private-sector effort.

There are 26 listings on the exchange. The majority of the trades are for government bonds. The exchange is the region's only US dollar-based securities market. Many Central American and northern South American enterprises with good balance sheets but too small to issue shares in New York are the prime contenders for listing.

Panama's economy is primarily dependent on the services

sector, which accounts for approximately 80% of its GDP and the majority of its foreign earnings. The Panama Canal, banking, trade, the Colón Free Trade Zone, insurance, container ports, and flagship registry, as well as medical and health services, are all available.

Aircraft spare parts, cement, beverages, adhesives, and textiles are among the country's industries. Bananas, shrimp, sugar, coffee, and clothes are among Panama's other exports. Panama's economy is completely dollarized, with the US dollar serving as legal money. Panama is a high-income country with a low-inflation history. Panama has a sizable financial services sector but no central bank to act as a lender of last resort for troubled banks. As a result, Panamanian banks are run cautiously.

Panama's taxation system, which is overseen by the Fiscal Code, is territorial, meaning that taxes only apply to income or gains produced from Panama-based businesses. If the underlying transactions take place outside Panama, the establishment of a sales or administrative office in Panama, or the profit-making re-invoicing of external transactions, does not automatically result in taxation. Dividends received from such profits are tax-free.

Panama city

Dominican republic

The Bolsa de Valores de la Republica Dominicana (BVRD) is the Dominican Republic's only stock exchange, primarily serving as a transaction regulator. It commenced operations in 1991 and is regarded as a key component of the country's globalization and domestic growth. It is also one of Latin America's most active stock exchanges.

The Dominican Republic's economy is the largest in the Caribbean and Central America area, and the ninth biggest in Latin America. The Dominican Republic is a developing country with an upper-middle income that is mostly reliant on mining, agriculture, commerce, and services.

The Dominican Republic is on track to meet its 2030 target of becoming a high-income country, with a growth of 79 percent predicted in this decade. The nation is home to Latin America's single largest gold mine. Although the service sector has lately surpassed agriculture as the Dominican Republic's largest employer (due principally to growth in tourism and free-trade zones).

In the Dominican Republic, over 500 enterprises produce items primarily for the North American market. These primarily foreign-owned enterprises, which are located in 50 industrial-free zones around the nation, benefit from the government's significant tax and other financial incentives for enterprises operating within the zones.

Non-residents pay a higher capital gains tax rate of 27 percent than residents, who pay a lower rate of 25 percent. In the Dominican Republic, sellers are required to withhold 1% of their capital gains tax.

San Domingo, Dominican Republic

El Salvador

The Salvadoran Stock Exchange, or Bolsa de Valores de El Salvador (BVES), is the country's stock exchange. Various government infrastructure projects are securitized through the exchange. In 1992, the exchange was founded. The Central Securities Depository is in charge of it (CEDEVAL). The market rose from $600 million in transactions to more than $3 billion in 2006 and about $6 billion by the end of 2011.

The exchange now has 34 firms listed, the great majority of which are in the financial or insurance industries.

In comparison to other emerging countries, El Salvador's economy has grown at a very slow pace. Rates have not climbed above the low single digits in almost two decades, reflecting a larger context of macroeconomic insecurity that the US dollar's integration has done nothing to alleviate.

El Salvador was once the most industrialized country in Central America, but that status was undermined by a decade of conflict. Manufacturing contributes to about 22 percent of GDP.

World Trade Center, San Salvador

Jamaica

The Jamaica Stock Exchange, or JSE, is the country's primary stock exchange. The Jamaica Stock Exchange (JSE) first opened its doors in 1969 in Kingston, Jamaica. By size and market capitalization, the JSE is now one of the major stock exchanges in the Caribbean.

There are a total of 85 firms and 120 securities listed on the JSE as of September 30, 2019. There are four markets on the Jamaica Stock Exchange: the Main Market, Junior Market, USD Market, and Bond Market. The JSE is also regarded as one of the Caribbean's most sector-diverse exchanges. Banking and finance, retail, manufacturing, insurance, leisure, communications, conglomerates, and services and real estate are among the most important industries.

Jamaica's economy is primarily based on services, which account for 70% of the country's GDP. Jamaica has abundant natural resources, particularly bauxite, as well as a climate that is perfect for agriculture and tourism. Financial sector weakness, speculation, and reduced investment levels diminish trust in the productive sector.

In order to satisfy its U.S. dollar debt commitments, the government continues to seek fresh sovereign debt in local and international financial markets. Foreign enterprises have increased their investment in garment assembly, light manufacturing, and data input in free trade zones. However, the clothing sector has seen a decline in export revenues during the previous five years. Through a mixture of privatization and restructuring, the Jamaican government wants to boost economic activity. The governments of Jamaica and China inked preliminary agreements for the first phase of the Jamaican Logistics Hub (JLH), with the goal of positioning Kingston as the fourth node in the global logistics network, servicing the Americas, alongside Rotterdam, Dubai, and Singapore.

In Jamaica, capital gains are not taxed. However, there is a transfer tax on the market value of some assets transferred, as well as stamp duty on the transfer and disposal of shares.

Bahamas

In the Bahamas, the Bahamas International Securities Exchange (BISX) is a stock exchange. It is based in Nassau and was created in 1999. There are currently 47 listings on the exchange, and they are denominated in Bahamian Dollars.

The Bahamas' economy is reliant on tourism and offshore finance. The Bahamas is the wealthiest country in the West Indies and has the 14th highest nominal GDP in North America. It is a stable and growing country. Financial services are the second-largest sector of the Bahamas' economy, accounting for around 15% of GDP.

Many foreign corporations have fled the Bahamas after the government adopted new banking sector restrictions in December 2000. Despite government incentives, manufacturing and agriculture combined account for only around 10% of GDP and show minimal growth. Overall growth prospects in the short term are primarily reliant on the fortunes of the tourism industry, which is primarily reliant on growth in the United States, which accounts for more than 80% of all visitors. Aside from tourism and banking, the government encourages the growth of a "second pillar," e-commerce.

Citizens of the Bahamas do not pay taxes on income, inheritance, gifts, or capital gains.

Nicaragua

The Nicaraguan Stock Exchange (Bolsa de Valores) is the product of private-sector activities supporting the country's market liberalization programs. The solely organized stock exchange in the nation is BVDN. BVDN provides a platform for domestic and foreign investors to conduct business within the context of an open market economy. The following are the market's primary characteristics: (1) Fixed income financial instruments denominated in US dollars and local currency indexes; (2) complete exemption from income and capital gains taxes for traded securities; (3) no limits on foreign direct investment (FDI); and (4) an efficient regulatory framework.

Nicaragua's economy is mostly based on the agriculture sector. Nicaragua is the poorest country in Central America and the second poorest country in the Americas in terms of nominal GDP. Production for export has been one of the most important engines of economic expansion. Although traditional Nicaraguan exports such as coffee, pork, and sugar continue to lead the way, atypical exports such as textiles and clothing, gold, seafood, and new agricultural goods like peanuts, sesame, melons, and onions are currently seeing the most rapid development.

The service industry is thought to account for 56.8% of the country's GDP and employs 52% of the working population. Transportation, trade, warehousing, restaurant and hotel operations, arts and entertainment, health, education, financial and banking services, telecommunications, and public administration and defense are all included in this sector.

Barbados

Barbados' major stock exchange is the Barbados Stock Exchange (BSE). Its headquarters are in Bridgetown, the country's capital. The Barbados Stock Exchange is one of the four major regional stock markets in the Caribbean. The Jamaica Stock Exchange, the Eastern Caribbean Securities Exchange, and the Trinidad and Tobago Stock Exchange are the other three.

In the Caribbean, the BSE is the third-largest stock market. The BSE is collaborating with authorities from Jamaica and Trinidad and Tobago to merge these stock exchanges into a single entity called the Caribbean Exchange Network. There are currently 21 listings on the exchange, and they are denominated in Barbados Dollars.

Barbados' economy has progressed from a low-income economy centered on sugar production to an upper-middle-income one centered on tourism and offshore business. In 1993, the economy began to expand again after a tough re-adjustment period.

Since then, growth has averaged between 3% and 5% every year. Tourism, international business, and foreign direct investment are the country's three key economic drivers. Barbados' role as a service-driven economy and international business hub helps to promote these goals.

Non-residents are subject to tax on income derived from Barbados only.

Caribbean islands

There are two main exchanges in the Caribbean islands. The Eastern Caribbean Securities Exchange and the Trinidad and Tobago Stock Exchange. The Eastern Caribbean Securities Exchange (ECSE) was founded by the Eastern Caribbean Central Bank (ECCB) to serve the eight-member territories of Anguilla, Antigua and Barbuda, Dominica, Grenada,

Montserrat, Saint Kitts and Nevis, Saint Lucia, and Saint Vincent and the Grenadines as the first regional securities market and regional stock exchange in the Western Hemisphere. Its headquarters are in Basseterre, St. Kitts, in the city of Basseterre. The Trinidad and Tobago Stock Exchange (TTSE) is the Republic of Trinidad and Tobago's principal stock exchange and the Caribbean region's largest stock exchange by market capitalization. Several firms from Barbados, Jamaica, Saint Vincent and the Grenadines, and the Eastern Caribbean Securities Exchange cross-list their equities on the Trinidad and Tobago Stock Exchange, which is a member of CARICOM.

Honorable mentions

Costa Rica Stock exchange

10

Middle East

The Middle East's economy is extremely varied, ranging from hydrocarbon-exporting rentiers to centralized communist regimes to free-market economies. The region is well known for oil production and export, which has a huge influence on the entire region in terms of income and labor usage. Many nations in the area have made attempts to diversify their economies in recent years.

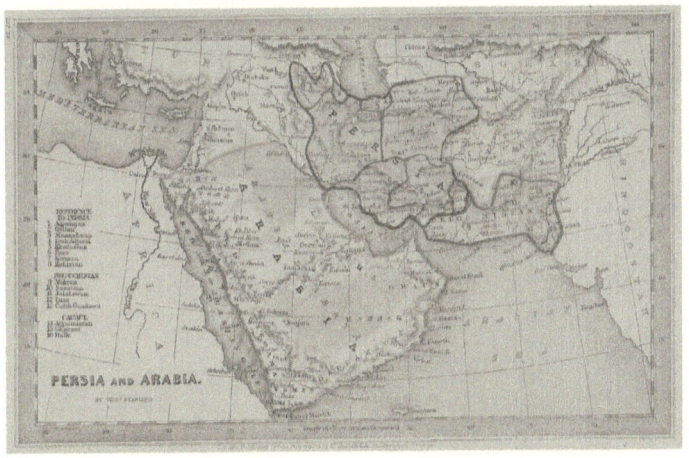

A map of the middle east by Thomas Starling, 1832

United Arab Emirates

There are three main exchanges in the UAE, the Dubai Financial Market, the Abu Dhabi Securities Exchange, and the Nasdaq Dubai. The Dubai Financial Market (DFM) was established in 2000 and there are 178 listings on the exchange, denominated in UAE dirhams.

The majority of them are UAE-based businesses, with a few dual listings for businesses headquartered in other MENA nations. Kuwait, Bahrain, Oman, and Sudan are among the foreign countries represented. Many businesses enable foreigners to invest in their stock.

There are 73 listings on the Abu Dhabi Securities Exchange, also denominated in UAE dirhams. On the other hand, Nasdaq Dubai serves as a facilitator for locals to access international markets that cover regional and worldwide Middle East stocks. Local issuers can access regional and worldwide investment through the exchange.

The United Arab Emirates and the remainder of the Gulf Cooperation Council (GCC), the wider Middle East and North Africa, Turkey, and the Indian subcontinent are all part of the NASDAQ Dubai exchange listings.

DFM, which bought two-thirds of NASDAQ Dubai's shares from Borse Dubai and NASDAQ OMX Group, is the company's dominant stakeholder. One-third of the shares are still owned by Borse Dubai.

The Securities and Commodities Authority (SCA) oversees and regulates both DFM and ADX. NASDAQ Dubai, on the other hand, is controlled by an independent regulator known as the Dubai Financial Services Authority, which is similar to the Securities and Exchange Commission in the United States.

NASDAQ Dubai, unlike DFM and ADX, is an electronic exchange with no trading floor. It is located in the Dubai International Financial Centre (DIFC).

With a gross domestic product of US$421 billion (AED 1.5 trillion) in 2020, the United Arab Emirates, or UAE, is the fourth biggest economy in the Middle East (after Turkey, Saudi Arabia, and Iran). The UAE has been successful in diversifying its economy, notably in Dubai, but it remains largely reliant on petroleum and natural gas earnings, which continue to play a major role in its economy, particularly in Abu Dhabi.

In 2009, oil exports accounted for more than 85% of the UAE's economy. While Abu Dhabi and the other UAE emirates have taken a cautious approach to diversification,

Dubai, which has considerably fewer oil reserves, has taken a more aggressive strategy.

Oil exports accounted for 77% of the UAE's national budget in 2011. Tourism is one of the UAE's largest non-oil revenue streams, with some of the world's most expensive hotels situated there. The UAE's economy is diversifying thanks to a major building boom, a growing manufacturing base, and a booming services sector. There are at present $350 billion in ongoing building projects around the country.

Dubai's diversification in the 1980s was focused on trade and the development of shipping and logistics hubs, particularly Port Rashid and the port and Free Zone of Jebel Ali, as well as Dubai International Airport, resulting in a number of major global shipping, transportation, and logistics companies (DP World, Emirates, DNATA).

The worldwide financial crisis of 2007–8, when Dubai was bailed out by Abu Dhabi, temporarily slowed the growth of Dubai's thriving real estate market. The recovery from the overheated market resulted in stricter regulation and monitoring, as well as a more realistic real estate market in the UAE, with many stalled projects resuming.

With a gross domestic product (GDP) of US$414 billion (AED 1.52 trillion) in 2018, the UAE had the second-largest economy in the Arab world (behind Saudi Arabia). Oil earnings account for a third of the country's GDP.

The UAE's GDP has risen by over 231 times since 1971. From 1981 to 2012, the non-oil trade increased by about 28 times to AED1.2 trillion. The UAE's economy is one of the most open in the world, and its economic history dates back to the days when ships traveled from India to Mozambique along the Swahili coast.

In its World Economic Outlook Report, the IMF attributed the UAE's potentially high economic development to the growing contribution of non-petroleum industries, which grew at a rate of more than 6% on average. Banking, tourism, trade, and real estate are examples of such contributions.

The growth in Emirati buying power has resulted in a significant increase in government spending on infrastructure projects. According to AT Kearney, the UAE is in the top 20 nations for a global service business, among the top 30 on the WEF's "most-networked countries," and in the top quarter of the TI's corruption index.

In an effort to deal with and recover from the economic shocks caused by the months-long coronavirus lockdown, the government of the United Arab Emirates announced a wide reorganization and merging of more than half of its federal institutions, including ministries and departments.

There is no capital gains tax in the UAE, but you may be liable in your home country. Equity Research on the UAE market can be done with the Dubai Federal Competitiveness and Statistics Center website.

Skyline of Dubai, United Arab Emirates

Saudi Arabia

Tadawul, or Saudi Stock Exchange, is the stock exchange in Saudi Arabia. Tadawul was established in 2007, however, trading began in 1954 as an informal financial market.

Through the 1970s, it remained as such, with just 14 listed firms, before gaining formal status as the Saudi Company for Share Registration in 1980. After being controlled by a Special Ministerial Committee, the Saudi Company for Share Registration was formally created. It is governed by the Capital Market Authority, although since 2018, it has been largely self-regulatory.

There are 203 publicly listed businesses on the exchange,

and they are denominated in Saudi riyals. Tadawul is the Middle East's and North Africa's most important stock exchange. Tadawul is the world's ninth-largest stock exchange as of December 2019. The Saudi Parallel Exchange (Nomu) was established as a parallel stock market with fewer listing criteria to give firms another option for going public.

There are two main restrictions on buying Saudi shares as a foreigner, a foreign investor may possess no more than 5% of a company's shares, and all foreign investors (resident or non-resident) may own no more than 49% of a company's shares. Also, it is important to note that the individual companies themselves can restrict foreigners from buying their shares, like Aramco for example.

Saudi Arabia's economy is one of the top twenty economies in the world, as well as the largest in the Arab world and the Middle East. Saudi Arabia belongs to the G20 group of nations. Saudi Arabia possesses the world's second most valuable natural resources, with a total value of $34.4 trillion. The country possesses the world's second-biggest proven petroleum reserves and is the world's largest oil exporter.

It is also an "Energy Superpower" with the fifth-largest known natural gas reserves. Saudi Arabia's economy is highly reliant on oil, and the country is a member of OPEC. Saudi Vision 2030 was announced in 2016 by the Saudi government to lessen the country's reliance on oil and diversify its economic resources. Saudi Arabia had a budget surplus for the first time since 2014 in the first quarter of 2019. The rise in oil and non-oil income has resulted in this $10.40 billion surplus.

According to Saudi government statistics, proven reserves are estimated to be 260 billion barrels (41 km3), or approximately a fifth of global oil reserves. Saudi Arabia's petroleum is not only abundant but also under pressure and near to the surface. As a result, extracting petroleum in Saudi Arabia is considerably cheaper and hence far more profitable than in many other countries.

Saudi Aramco, the state-owned oil company of Saudi Arabia, is in charge of the country's oil reserves and production. The private sector accounts for another 40% of GDP. In 2013, an estimated 7.5 million foreigners worked lawfully in Saudi Arabia, contributing significantly to the Saudi economy, particularly in the oil and service industries.

For many years, the government has supported private sector growth in order to reduce the kingdom's reliance on oil and create job possibilities for the growing Saudi population. In recent decades, the government has begun to allow private sector and foreign investor engagement in areas including electricity generation and telecommunications, as well as joining the World Trade Organization.

High oil prices allowed the government to have budget surpluses throughout much of the 2000s, allowing it to increase spending on job training and education, infrastructure development, and government pay.

The Saudi economy has been described as a befuddling (at least to foreigners) mix of a feudal loyalty system and a more contemporary political patronage system, thanks to its absolute monarchy style of governance, huge public sector, and generous social benefits. Saudis manipulate individual advantages, favors, duties, and connections at every level and in every field of endeavor. Similarly, the government bureaucracy is a tangle of overlapping or conflicting power centers, all of which are patronized by numerous royal princes, each with their own goals, ambitions, and dependents to satisfy.

Saudi Arabia's gross domestic output and real gross domestic income vary substantially in response to oil prices. Saudi Arabia's foreign direct investment was only $1.4 billion in 2017, down from $7.5 billion the year before, according to a UNCTAD study issued in June 2018. Negative intra-company loans by overseas corporations and different divestments are blamed for the drop in investment. Net capital outflows were over 5% of GDP in the first quarter of 2018, compared to less than 2% in late 2016.

According to a study published in Trading Economics, foreign direct investment in the nation increased by $882 million in the second quarter of 2018. Furthermore, according to SAGIA data, foreign investment permits were raised by 130 percent in 2018.

Capital gains earned by a foreigner from the sale of shares in a local firm are taxed at a rate of 20%. Equity research can be done with the Saudi Arabia General Authority for Statistics website.

Riyad, Saudi Arabia

Qatar

Qatar's main stock exchange is the Qatar Stock Exchange. The QSE is a full member of the World Federation of Exchanges, and the MSCI and S&P Dow Jones Indices recently upgraded it. There are 47 listed companies on the exchange, and they are denominated in Qatari riyals.

The Qatar Stock Exchange's major goal is to assist Qatar's economy by offering a venue for Qatari firms to raise money as part of their corporate plan and providing investors with a platform to trade a range of products in a transparent and efficient way.

Qatar's economy is one of the world's richest in terms of GDP per capita, consistently placing among the top ten richest nations according to World Bank, United Nations, and IMF data. Despite restrictions imposed by Saudi Arabia and the United Arab Emirates, the country's economy has risen.

Petroleum and natural gas are the backbones of Qatar's economy, accounting for more than 70% of total government revenue, 60% of GDP, and about 85% of export profits. Qatar has the world's third-largest known natural gas reserves and is the world's second-largest natural gas exporter. Qatar was a poor pearl diving country before the advent of the petroleum-based economy.

In 1939, oil and gas resources were first explored. Oil output and earnings skyrocketed in 1973, propelling Qatar from the ranks of the world's poorest countries to one of the greatest per capita incomes on the planet.

The industry is an important element of the government's effort to diversify the economy and make the most of the country's vast natural gas reserves, which serve as the sector's major feedstock. As a result, industrial development has been meticulously planned. Development has been concentrated on the ports of Ras Laffan Industrial City and Mesaieed Industrial Area, which are important energy hubs, with an eye toward exports.

Over time, the outcome has grown significantly. Industries Qatar, a regional powerhouse that produces petrochemicals, fertilizers, and steel, is second only to Saudi Basic Industries Corporation, the Middle East's biggest chemical manufacturer, in terms of scale.

Manufacturing was the third-largest contributor to GDP among non-oil and gas industries in 2007, accounting for roughly 7.5 percent of total GDP.

The Qatari banking industry escaped the direct effects of the global subprime meltdown, but it was not immune to its aftershocks. Overall, the Gulf Cooperation Council markets performed well in the fourth quarter of 2008, with most banks reporting significant profits. However, the sector is beset by liquidity difficulties, waning consumer trust, and a forced reluctance to lend.

In its spring 2019 review, the International Monetary Fund stated that Qatar had "effectively absorbed the shocks" of the 2017 blockade and the decline in oil prices from 2014 to 2016. Qatar's outlook had been assessed as negative by S&P Global in 2017, however, it was revised to stable in 2019. The Qatar Central Bank indicated in August 2019 that the country's economic development will accelerate over the next two years as oil prices remain steady and exports remain robust.

Foreign individuals that sell shares in Qatar-based enterprises are subject to a 10% gain tax. The Ministry of Development Planning and Statistics is a great resource for equity research on Qatari stocks.

Doha skyline, Qatar

Israel

Israel's only public stock market is the Tel Aviv Stock Exchange (TASE). The Israel Securities Authority is in charge of overseeing the exchange.

TASE has 544 businesses listed, 56 of which are also listed on other stock exchanges. TASE also has over 1000 mutual funds, 180 exchange-traded funds, 60 government bonds, 500 corporate bonds, and 591 exchange-traded notes. These are all denominated in Israeli shekels.

Israel's economy is a well-developed free-market economy. On the World Bank's ease of doing business index, Israel is ranked 35th. After the United States, it boasts the world's second-largest number of startup businesses and the third-largest number of NASDAQ-listed companies after the United States and China (Israeli stocks listed in the US through ADRs).

Intel, Microsoft, and Apple established their first foreign research and development facilities in Israel, and other high-tech multinational businesses such as IBM, Google, HP, Cisco Systems, Facebook, and Motorola all established R&D centers there.

The country's main economic sectors are technology and industrial production; the Israeli diamond industry, which accounts for 23.2 percent of all exports, is one of the world's leading centers for diamond cutting and polishing.

With a scarcity of natural resources, Israel relies on imports of petroleum, raw materials, wheat, automobiles, uncut diamonds, and production inputs. However, recent discoveries of natural gas reserves off its coast, on the one hand, and the leading role of Israel's solar energy industry, on the other, may change the country's near-total reliance on energy imports in the future.

Quality university education and the creation of a highly motivated and educated population are responsible for Israel's high-tech boom and fast economic development by regional standards. With its strong educational infrastructure and high-quality incubation system for new cutting-edge ideas to create value-driven goods and services, the country has been able to develop a high concentration of high-tech companies across the country, with a strong venture capital industry to back them up.

Its primary high-tech district, "Silicon Wadi," is second only to its Californian equivalent in prominence. International corporate heavyweights such as Microsoft founder Bill Gates, investor Warren Buffett, real estate developer and former US President Donald Trump, and telecoms behemoth Carlos Slim have all shown interest in Israel's economic vibrancy. Beyond their typical commercial operations and investments in their home countries, each entrepreneur has made significant investments in a variety of Israeli sectors. Berkshire Hathaway, the holding company of American billionaire Warren Buffett, purchased ISCAR Metalworking, an Israeli firm, for $4 billion in 2006. This was Berkshire Hathaway's first acquisition outside of the United States.

Israel was asked to join the OECD in September 2010. Israel has also signed free trade agreements with the European Union, the United States, the European Free Trading Association, Turkey, Mexico, Canada, Ukraine, Jordan, and Egypt, and was the first non-Latin American country to do so with the Mercosur trade group in 2007. With 4.55 million international visitors visiting Israel in 2019, it is a popular tourist destination, particularly for people of Jewish heritage (about 1 tourist per 2 Israelis).

Capital gains from the sale of shares of an Israeli firm sold on the Israeli stock exchange or on a foreign stock exchange are tax-free for non-residents. You may be liable to capital gains tax in your home country though. The Israel Central Bureau of Statistics website is a great resource for equity research on the Israeli market.

Diamond exchange center, Tel Aviv, Israel

Lebanon

The Beirut Stock Market (BSE) is Lebanon's sole and primary stock exchange. Holding corporations and offshore firms are among the members. There are 15 listings on the exchange, and they are denominated in Lebanese pounds.

Lebanon's economy is classed as a developing country with a lower-middle-income. In 2020, the nominal GDP was $19 billion, with a per capita GDP of $2,500. Government spending was $15.9 billion in 2018, accounting for 23% of GDP.

After the 2006 war, the Lebanese economy grew rapidly, with an average annual growth rate of 9.1% between 2007 and 2010. The Syrian civil war impacted the local economy after 2011, with an annual average growth of 1.7 percent from 2011 to 2016 and 1.5 percent in 2017.

In terms of the debt-to-GDP ratio, Lebanon is the world's third most indebted country. As a result, interest payments accounted for 48% of domestic government income in 2016, restricting the government's capacity to invest in critical infrastructure and other public goods.

The Lebanese economy is based on service. The constitution of Lebanon states that "the economic system is free and safeguards individual initiative and the right to private property."

Metal goods, finance, agriculture, chemicals, and transportation equipment are among the key economic sectors. Banking and tourism are two of the fastest-growing industries. Foreign exchange and capital mobility are both unrestricted.

A 10% withholding tax is levied on income derived from movable capital generated in Lebanon. The Central Administration of Statistics website is a great resource for equity research on the Lebanese market.

Beirut, Lebanon

Jordan

The Amman Stock Exchange (ASE) is a private stock exchange headquartered in Amman, Jordan. The members of ASE are Jordan's 68 brokerage firms. It is regulated by the Jordan Securities Commission. There are 237 listings on the exchange, and they are denominated in Jordanian dinars.

Jordan's economy is classed as a developing market economy. Jordan's GDP per capita increased by 351% in the 1970s, fell by 30% in the 1980s, and increased by 36% in the 1990s. Liberal economic policies were implemented after King Abdullah II's ascension to the throne in 1999.

Between 1999 and 2008, Jordan's GDP grew at an annual pace of 8% each year. Following the Arab Spring in 2011, however, growth fell to 2%. Poverty and unemployment in the country have worsened as a result of the country's growing population, slower economic development, and mounting public debt.

Jordan has a GDP of $44.4 billion, which places it 89th in the world. Jordan has FTAs with the United States, Canada, Singapore, Malaysia, the European Union, Tunisia, Algeria, Libya, Turkey, and Syria, among others. Iraq, the Palestinian Authority, the Gulf Cooperation Council, Lebanon, and Pakistan are all set to sign more FTAs.

Jordan is a member of the GAFTA, the Euro-Mediterranean Free Trade Area, and the Agadir Agreement, as well as having advanced status with the EU. Jordan's economy is based on phosphates, potash, and fertilizer derivatives, tourism, remittances from abroad, and international aid.

Jordan relies on natural gas for 93 percent of its domestic energy needs due to a lack of coal reserves, hydroelectric power, huge expanses of forest, and economically viable oil discoveries. Jordan used to rely on Iraq for oil until the 2003 invasion of Iraq by the United States. Jordan also boasts a slew of industrial zones dedicated to the textile, aerospace, defense, ICT, pharmaceutical, and cosmetics industries. Jordan is a knowledge-based economy that is only getting started.

Jordan's economy is hampered by a lack of water, full reliance on oil imports for energy, and regional instability. Only around 10% of the land is arable, and the water supply is scarce. Rainfall is scarce and unpredictable, and much of Jordan's groundwater is nonrenewable.

Jordan's economy has declined in recent years, averaging approximately 2% each year. Jordan's total foreign debt was $19 billion in 2011, accounting for 60% of its GDP. In 2016, the debt totaled $35.1 billion, accounting for 93.4 percent of the country's GDP.

The effects of regional instability are attributed to a decrease in tourist activity, a decrease in foreign investments, an increase in military expenditure, attacks on the Egyptian pipeline supplying the Kingdom with gas, the collapse of trade with Iraq and Syria, expenses from hosting Syrian refugees, and accumulated interest from loans. Syrian refugees cost Jordan more than $2.5 billion a year, according to the World Bank, accounting for 6% of GDP and 25% of the government's annual revenue.

As a result of the increased rivalry for jobs between Syrian migrants and Jordanians, wage growth has slowed significantly in Jordan. The slump, which began in 2011, has lasted till now. The Syrian civil war has had a significant impact on the country's top five contributing sectors to GDP: government services, finance, manufacturing, transportation, and tourism and hospitality. Only a tiny portion of these expenditures is funded by foreign aid; Jordan bears 63 percent of the overall costs.

The government has implemented an austerity program with the goal of reducing Jordan's debt-to-GDP ratio to 77 percent by 2021. The initiative was successful in avoiding the debt from exceeding 95% in 2018.

Tax in Jordan is dependent on the sector in which the equity shares are. Rates are variable. Equity research on Jordanian stocks can be done with the Department of Statistics of Jordan website.

Amman, the capital city of Jordan

Kuwait

The Kuwait Stock Exchange (KSE), originally known as Boursa Kuwait, is Kuwait's national stock exchange. There are 166 companies listed on the exchange, and they are denominated in Kuwaiti dinars.

Kuwait's economy is a prosperous petroleum-based economy. Kuwait is one of the world's wealthiest countries. The Kuwaiti dinar is the world's most valuable currency. Kuwait is the fifth-richest country in the world in terms of gross national income per capita, according to the World Bank. Kuwait's economy ranks twenty-first in the world in terms of GDP per capita. Petroleum currently accounts for 43 percent of overall GDP and 70 percent of export profits as a result of different diversification initiatives.

Kuwait's second-largest industry is steel production. Mineral fuels, including oil (89.1% of total exports), aircraft and spacecraft (4.3%), organic chemicals (3.2%), plastics (1.2%), iron and steel (0.2%), gems and precious metals (0.1%), machinery, including computers (0.1%), aluminum (0.1%), copper (0.1%), and salt, sulphur, stone and sand (0.1%) were Kuwait's main export products in 2019.

In the 2019 Economic Complexity Index, Kuwait was rated 63rd out of 157 nations (ECI). Kuwait Petroleum Corporation (KPC), an integrated worldwide oil business, is the holding company for the government's petroleum activities, which comprises Kuwait Oil Company, which produces oil and gas. Kuwait wants to become a worldwide center for the petrochemical sector as part of Kuwait Vision 2035. The Al Zour Refinery is the Middle East's biggest refinery. The Al Zour LNG Facility is the largest liquefied natural gas import terminal in the Middle East. A total of $3 billion has been invested in the project. Biofuel and clean fuels are two more megaprojects.

Kuwait's second-largest industry is steel production. Kuwait's primary steel production firm, United Steel Industrial Company (KWT Steel), meets all of Kuwait's domestic market demands (particularly construction) making Kuwait self-sufficient in steel.

Kuwait is the Gulf Cooperation Council's (GCC) finance industry leader. In terms of economic growth, the Emir has advocated for Kuwait to concentrate its efforts on the banking sector. Kuwait's historical financial dominance (among Gulf monarchs) extends back to the establishment of the National Bank of Kuwait in 1952. The bank was the Gulf's first local publicly listed company. The Souk Al-Manakh, an alternative stock market in Kuwait that traded shares of Gulf firms in the late 1970s and early 1980s, arose in the late 1970s and early 1980s. Its market capitalization was the third biggest in the world at the time, after only the United States and Japan, but ahead of the United Kingdom and France.

Kuwait has a thriving wealth management business that sets it apart from the rest of the region. Kuwaiti investment firms manage more assets than any other GCC country save Saudi Arabia, which is significantly larger. In a preliminary assessment, Kuwaiti businesses accounted for almost one-third of all assets under management in the GCC, according to the Kuwait Financial Centre. Kuwait's relative strength in the financial industry is reflected in its stock market. For many years, the total value of all businesses listed on the Kuwaiti market, with the exception of Saudi Arabia, significantly surpassed the value of those listed on any other GCC bourse.

Foreign shareholders' capital gains on the sale of assets and shares are considered ordinary company earnings and are taxed at a rate of 15%. The Kuwait Central Statistical Bureau website is a great resource for equity research on Kuwaiti stocks.

Skyline of Kuwait city

Oman

Oman's main stock market is the Muscat Securities Market (MSM). It was created by the Royal Decree in 1988, to oversee and control the Omani securities market and to effectively collaborate with other organizations in the development of the Sultanate's financial infrastructure.

After 10 years of uninterrupted development, the market required improved functionality. Since then, two Royal Decrees have reorganized MSM. There are 111 listings on the exchange, and they are denominated in Omani riyals.

Oman's economy is agricultural and rural. In the last fifty years, Oman's GDP per capita has steadily increased. It increased 339 percent in the 1960s, peaked at 1,370 percent in the 1970s, then slowed to a modest 13 percent in the 1980s before increasing to 34 percent in the 1990s.

Oman liberalized its markets in order to become a member of the World Trade Organization, which it did in 2000. In addition, the US Congress ratified the US-Oman Free Trade Agreement on July 20, 2006. This went into effect on January 1, 2009, and eliminated tariffs on all consumer and industrial goods. It also offers significant safeguards to international companies looking to invest in Oman.

In order to improve the business and investment climate and promote private sector-led growth in the Sultanate, the government implemented a number of important policy measures in 2018, including the establishment of a commercial arbitration center, the adoption of a new commercial companies' law, and the further streamlining of licensing processes through Invest Easy.

Oman's economy and petroleum income have permitted the country's rapid expansion during the last 50 years. Oman is not a member of OPEC, despite cooperating with the organization in recent years. In 1964, oil was discovered in the heart of the country at Fahud in the western desert. In August 1967, the Petroleum Development Oman commenced production. PDO is 60% owned by the Omani government and 40% by foreign investors (Royal Dutch Shell owns 34 percent; the remaining 6 percent is owned by Compagnie Francaise des Petroles [Total] and Partex).

Oman's tenth five-year plan (2020–2025) is the first step in putting Vision 2040 into action, and it will focus on economic diversification. The economic diversification strategy intends to wean Oman away from oil and gas-based revenue streams, and it has identified five sectors with significant development potential and economic rewards. Agriculture and fisheries, manufacturing, logistics and transportation, energy and mining, and tourism are the industries in question. According to the World Bank, growth in 2020–21 will be boosted by a substantial rise in gas output from the new Khazzan gas project, as well as infrastructure investment plans in both the oil and non-oil sectors.

Exemptions do not apply to the disposal of shares for non-Omani individuals (tax rates ranging from 5 percent to 50 percent). The National Center for Statistics and Information of Oman website is a great resource for equity research on Omani stocks.

Ruwi, Business district of Muscat, Oman

Bahrain

Bahrain Bourse, often known as the Bahrain Stock Exchange (BSE), is the country's stock exchange. The exchange currently has 42 firms listed, and they are denominated in Bahraini dinars. The Bahrain Bourse is represented by three indices: Bahrain All Share Index, the Dow Jones Bahrain Index, and the Estirad Index. Foreigners can buy, sell, and hold bonds, mutual fund units, and warrants of domestic joint-stock corporations.

Foreigners who have lived in Bahrain for at least a year are allowed to buy, own, and/or sell up to 49 percent of a domestic joint-stock company's shares. An individual foreigner, on the other hand, cannot possess more than 1% of a company's issued capital.

Bahrain's economy is highly reliant on oil and gas. The Bahraini currency is the world's second most valuable currency. Bahrain has made significant investments in the banking and tourist industries since the late twentieth century. Manama, the country's capital, is home to a number of significant financial institutions.

Bahrain's financial industry is thriving. The City of London's Global Financial Centres Index ranked Bahrain the world's fastest expanding financial center in 2008. The banking and financial services business in Bahrain, notably Islamic banking, has profited from the regional growth fueled by oil demand.

Bahrain's biggest exported product is petroleum, which accounts for 60 percent of export receipts, 70 percent of government income, and 11 percent of GDP. The second-largest exported product is aluminum, which is followed by finance and building materials.

Bahrain is the fourth freest economy in the Middle East and North Africa area, and the 63rd freest economy in the world, according to the 2020 Index of Economic Freedom. Bahrain is ranked 70th on an alternative ranking issued by the Fraser Institute. Bahrain was recognized by the World Bank as a high-income economy.

Despite efforts to diversify the economy, oil still accounts for 85 percent of Bahraini budget income, according to the CIA World Fact Book, implying that decreased global energy prices have resulted in large budget deficits in recent years - roughly 10% of GDP in 2017. The Kingdom is the Persian Gulf's primary financial hub and a center for Islamic finance, which has been attracted by the industry's robust regulatory environment.

Both foreigners and Bahrainis are exempt from capital gains and dividend taxes. The Bahrain Open Data Portal website is a great resource for equity research on the Bahraini market.

Manama skyline, Bahrain

11

Africa

Africa's economy is made up of commerce, industry, agriculture, and labor resources. In 2019, over 1.3 billion people lived in 54 African nations. Africa is a continent with abundant natural resources. Commodity, service, and manufacturing sales have all increased in recent years. By 2050, the economies of West Africa, East Africa, Central Africa, and Southern Africa are anticipated to total $29 trillion.

Africa was named the world's poorest inhabited continent, however, the World Bank predicts that if present development rates continue, most African nations would attain "middle income" status (defined as at least US$1,000 per person per year) by 2025. Africa's poor economy has a number of causes: historically, Africa had a number of empires trading with many parts of the world; however, European colonization and the subsequent challenges posed by decolonization, exacerbated by the Cold War, created an environment of economic and social instability.

However, Africa was the world's fastest-growing continent,

expanding at 5.6 percent per year, and GDP is anticipated to grow at a rate of more than 6% per year in the future. Several business analysts have identified Africa as the world's future economic development engine.

Map of Trans-African Highways

South Africa

The Johannesburg Stock Exchange (JSE) is Africa's most important stock exchange. The JSE has 442 firms listed, and they are denominated in South African rands. The JSE had a market capitalization of US$1,005 billion as of August 2020.

South Africa's economy is the continent's second-biggest. It is, nevertheless, the continent's most industrialized, technologically advanced, and diverse economy. South Africa is one of just eight nations in Africa with an upper-middle-income economy. In 1996, when international sanctions were lifted after more than a decade, South Africa's Gross Domestic Product has nearly quadrupled, peaking at $400 billion in 2011, but has since fallen to below $283 billion in 2020.

Within two decades following the end of apartheid, foreign exchange reserves rose from $3 billion to over $50 billion, resulting in a diversified economy with a rising and large middle class. State-owned companies (SOEs) play a major part in the South African economy, with the government having a stake in roughly 700 SOEs in a variety of industries.

In 2016, inefficient government bureaucracy, restrictive labour regulations, a shortage of skilled workers for some high-tech industries, political instability, and corruption were the top five challenges to doing business in the country, while the country's banking sector was rated as a strong positive feature of the economy.

The country is a member of the G20 and the only African country in the organization. The arrival of Dutch immigrants in 1652, originally dispatched by the Dutch East India Company to construct a provisioning station for passing ships, marked the start of South Africa's official economy. With the advent of French Huguenots and German immigrants, the colony grew in size, and certain colonists were given the freedom to pursue commercial farming, resulting in agriculture's domination of the economy. The colony was acquired by the British at the end of the 18th century. This resulted in the Great Trek, which pushed farming farther onto the continent while also establishing the Transvaal and Orange Free States as autonomous Boer republics. Diamonds were discovered in Kimberley in 1870, and some of the world's biggest gold reserves were discovered in the Witwatersrand region of Transvaal in 1886, rapidly changing the economy into one dominated by natural resources.

As a result of the Boer War, which saw Boer women and children imprisoned in British-built concentration camps, the British seized the territory. During this time, the country began to industrialize, which included the formation of the first South African labor unions. The government avoided using economic populism as a strategy.

Inflation has been reduced, governmental finances have been stabilized, and some foreign money has been recruited. However, the rate of increase remained low. President Thabo Mbeki pledged at the start of 2000 to stimulate economic development and foreign investment by loosening restrictive labor regulations, speeding up privatization, increasing government expenditure, and slashing interest rates significantly.

Organized labor was a vocal opponent of his policies. From 2004 onwards, economic growth accelerated substantially, with increases in both employment and capital formation. In

April 2009, amid fears that South Africa would soon join the rest of the world in the late-2000s recession, Reserve Bank Governor Tito Mboweni and Minister of Finance Trevor Manuel disagreed: whereas Manuel predicted a quarter of economic growth, Mboweni predicted further decline: "technically," he said, "that's a recession."

During the global financial crisis of 2007–2009, Nobel Laureate economist Joseph Stiglitz advised South Africa that inflation control should be a secondary priority. Unlike other developing economies, South Africa has struggled to recover from the late-2000s recession, with private and public consumption growth driving the recovery, but export volumes and private investment have yet to completely return.

Under the present policy framework, South Africa's long-term potential growth rate is predicted to be 3.5 percent. Per capita GDP growth has been poor. The government and the majority of South Africans regard high unemployment (over 25%) and inequality to be the most pressing economic issues confronting the country. These problems, as well as those related to them, such as crime, have harmed investment and growth, resulting in a negative feedback impact on employment.

Crime is cited as a serious or very severe barrier on investment by 30% of businesses in South Africa, making it one of the top four most commonly cited restraints. In 2017, political tensions in the country erupted after President Jacob Zuma fired nine cabinet members, including Finance Minister Pravin Gordhan. The finance minister was viewed as a key figure in efforts to re-establish trust in South Africa. S&P Global downgraded South Africa's credit rating to junk status in April 2017, as a result of the tensions. Fitch Ratings followed suit, downgrading the country's credit rating to BBB-, a sub-investment grade. In the week after the government reshuffle, the South African rand fell by more than 11%.

Non-residents are subject to capital gains tax (CGT) only on capital gains from the disposal of certain South African property, but a tax on the sale of shares can be subject to tax in your home country. Equity Research on the South African market can be done with the Statistics South Africa website.

Johannesburg, South Africa

Egypt

Egypt's stock market, the Egyptian Exchange (EGX), is made up of two exchanges: Cairo and Alexandria, both of which are overseen by the same board of directors and use the same trading, clearing, and settlement processes. There are 176 listings on the exchange, and they are denominated in Egyptian pounds.

Under President Gamal Abdel Nasser (1954–1970), Egypt's economy was a highly controlled economy centered on import substitution. Following President Abdelfattah el Sisi's (2014–present) 2030 Vision, which aims to diversify Egypt's economy, the country's economy grew to be the second biggest in Africa after Nigeria in nominal GDP and the 34th in the world as of 2021.

Since the early 2000s, the speed with which Egypt has implemented fundamental reforms, such as fiscal and monetary policies, taxes, privatization, and new business laws, has aided the country's transition to a more market-oriented economy and spurred greater international investment. The macroeconomic yearly growth outcomes have been reinforced as a result of the changes and initiatives.

As Egypt's economy recovered, more pressing concerns such as unemployment and poverty began to fade. Political stability and closeness to Europe benefit the country, as do growing exports and a strong currency. Egypt is stable and well-supported by foreign parties, according to investors. Egypt has had a very stable mixed economy, with an average growth of 3–5% during the last quarter-century. The economy went through several periods of growth, with the public and private sectors playing varying degrees of prominence.

Following the 2011 revolution, the Egyptian economy experienced a severe slump, and the administration faced significant problems in restoring growth, market confidence, and investor trust. As a result of propping up the Egyptian pound against the dollar, Egypt's foreign exchange reserves plummeted from $36 billion in 2010 to barely $16.3 billion in 2012. Rating agencies have lowered the country's credit rating multiple times due to concerns about civil instability and the country's ability to fulfill its financial objectives.

In order to restore macroeconomic stability and prosperity, Egypt floated its currency and started on a domestic economic reform program funded by a $12 billion IMF loan in 2016. The Egyptian Central Bank is the country's central bank, and it oversees and supervises the financial sector as well as the Egyptian pound. In Egypt, state-owned or nationalized banks still account for 85% of bank accounts and about 60% of total deposits. In rural regions, just 57 percent of families have access to financial services.

Egypt has traditionally served as the Arab world's cultural and information hub, with Cairo serving as the region's main publishing and broadcasting hub. Since being split from the transportation industry, Egypt's information and communications technology sector has grown substantially. According to the WTO agreement, the telecommunications sector has been deregulated since the beginning of 2006. In the past, private equity has not been frequently employed in Egypt as a form of company finance. The government, on the other hand, has implemented a number of legislative adjustments and reforms aimed at developing domestic private equity funds and attracting private equity financing from abroad. Textiles, hydrocarbon and chemical manufacturing, and generic pharmaceutical production are among the key industries.

Capital gains tax does not apply to transactions made on the stock exchange. Dividends paid to shareholders by firms listed on the stock market are not taxed. The exchange, however, was hit with a ten percent capital gain tax on mergers and acquisitions in 2013. Today, capital gains earned by foreign individuals and corporations through the sale of securities listed on the Egyptian Stock Exchange or from the sale of Treasury bills are tax-free. You may be liable to capital gains tax in your home country. The Central Agency for Public Mobilization and Statistics of Egypt is a great resource for equity research on the Egyptian market.

Central business district, Egypt's new administrative capital

Nigeria

The Nigerian Exchange Group (NGX Group) is one of Africa's largest stock market. The Group provides services to Africa's largest countries and works to improve African economies' competitiveness in order to attain global prosperity. There are 328 listings on the exchange, and they are denominated in Nigerian Nairas.

Nigeria's economy is a mixed-income, rising market with growing manufacturing, finance, services, communications, technology, and entertainment industries. In terms of nominal GDP, it is the world's 27th biggest economy, while in terms of purchasing power parity, it is the 24th largest.

Nigeria boasts Africa's largest economy; its resurgent manufacturing sector became the continent's largest in 2013, and it generates a significant amount of products and services for the West African peninsula. Furthermore, as of 2019, the debt-to-GDP ratio is 16 percent. Nigeria's GDP has nearly quadrupled in purchasing power parity from $170 billion in 2000 to $451 billion in 2012, however, estimates of the size of the informal sector (which is not included in official calculations) put the true amounts closer to $630 billion.

Following that, GDP per capita increased from $1400 per person in 2000 to an estimated $2,800 per person in 2012 (with the informal sector included, GDP per capita is projected to be about $3,900 per person).

When measures were to be reassessed following the rebasing of its economy in 2014, these values were to be revised higher by as much as 80% (percent). Despite accounting for two-thirds of governmental income, oil only accounts for around 9% of GDP. Only around 2.7 percent of the world's oil is produced in Nigeria. Despite its importance, as government revenues are still highly reliant on it, the petroleum industry remains a tiny component of the country's total economy.

Nigeria, formerly a significant net exporter of food, now imports part of its food items, despite the fact that automation has led to a renaissance in food manufacturing and exporting, as well as a drive toward food sufficiency.

Nigeria will have the greatest average GDP growth in the world between 2010 and 2050, according to Citigroup research. Nigeria is one of two African countries among the 11 Global Growth Generators.

Nigeria's economic analysis was altered to account for fast-growing contributions to the country's GDP, such as telecommunications, banking, and the film sector.

Nigeria and the Paris Club reached a deal in 2006 to purchase back the majority of its debts owing to them in exchange for a cash payment of around US$12 billion.

Furthermore, Nigeria's human capital is underdeveloped (it was rated 151st among nations in the United Nations Development Index), and non-energy infrastructure is inadequate. Nigeria sought to execute an economic reform program known as the National Economic Empowerment Development Strategy (NEEDS). NEEDS aimed to improve the country's standard of living by implementing a number of reforms, including macroeconomic stability, deregulation, liberalization, privatization, transparency, and accountability. The NEEDS initiative tackled fundamental issues such as a lack of fresh water for domestic use and irrigation, unstable power supply, deteriorating infrastructure, barriers to private industry, and corruption. NEEDS was created with the goal of creating 7 million new jobs, diversifying the economy, increasing non-energy exports, increasing industrial capacity utilization, and improving agricultural production.

The State Economic Empowerment Development Strategy is a related program at the state level (SEEDS). The National Millennium Goals for Nigeria, supported by the United Nations, are a longer-term economic development initiative. Nigeria is dedicated to accomplishing a wide variety of ambitious targets encompassing poverty reduction, education, gender equality, health, the environment, and international development cooperation throughout the program.

Nigeria was making progress in achieving many goals, but fell short on others, according to a UN report. Nigeria, in particular, had progressed in its attempts to offer universal basic education and safeguard the environment. Reduced chronic corruption, which obstructs growth and tarnishes Nigeria's economic climate, is a prerequisite for attaining many of these worthy goals.

The World Bank has praised President Olusegun Obasanjo's anti-corruption effort, which includes the arrest of officials suspected of wrongdoing and the recovery of stolen monies. Nigeria began recovering US$458 million in illegal cash placed in Swiss banks by the late military dictator Sani Abacha, who governed Nigeria from 1993 to 1998, with the help of the World Bank.

While broad-based success has been gradual, these initiatives are beginning to show up in international corruption surveys. Nigeria's rating in Transparency International's Corruption Perceptions Index has steadily improved from

2001 when it was ranked 147th out of 180 nations.

In the future decades, two-thirds of Nigerians anticipate their living standards to improve.

Any gains made by a non-resident through the sale of stocks in a Nigerian company are tax-free in Nigeria. This is due to the fact that any gains realized from the sale of shares are tax-free for both resident and non-resident owners. The National Bureau of Statistics of Nigeria is a great resource to do equity research on the Nigerian market.

Lagos, Nigeria

Morocco

The Casablanca Stock Exchange (French: La Bourse de Casablanca) is a Moroccan stock exchange. After the Johannesburg Stock Exchange in South Africa and the Nigerian Stock Exchange in Lagos, the Casablanca Stock Exchange

(CSE) is Africa's third-biggest Bourse.

It has one of the best performances in the Middle East and North Africa area. It was founded in 1929 and now has 19 members and 81 listed securities (denominated in Moroccan dirhams), with a market capitalization of $71.1 billion in 2018.

Morocco's economy is regarded to be a reasonably free economy driven by supply and demand. Morocco has been privatizing various economic sectors that were formerly controlled by the government since 1993. Morocco has emerged as a key participant in African economic affairs, ranking fifth in terms of GDP. In its African Competitiveness Report, the World Economic Forum ranked Morocco as the most competitive economy in North Africa.

The services sector contributes for slightly over half of GDP, with industry (mine, building, and manufacturing) accounting for the remaining quarter. Tourism, telecoms, and textiles are the industries that have seen the most development. Morocco, however, remains too reliant on agriculture, which accounts for approximately 14% of GDP but employs 40–45% of the Moroccan population. With a semi-arid environment, ensuring adequate rainfall is difficult, and Morocco's GDP fluctuates depending on the weather.

Fiscal restraint has enabled consolidation, with the budget deficit and debt as a proportion of GDP both dropping. The country's economic structure is marked by a significant degree of openness to the outside world. Morocco has the second-largest non-oil GDP in the Arab world, after Egypt. With the assistance of the International Monetary Fund, the World Bank, and the Paris Club of creditors, the Moroccan government has followed an economic program aimed at increasing economic growth from the early 1980s.

The country's currency, the dirham, has been completely convertible for current account transactions since 2018, and banking sector reforms and state-owned companies have been enacted.

Agriculture, phosphate minerals, and tourism are the mainstays of the Moroccan economy. Fish and seafood sales are also important. Morocco is the world's third-largest phosphate producer (after the United States and China), and phosphate price changes on the international market have a significant impact on the Moroccan economy. Since independence, tourism and remittances from workers have been vital. Textile and apparel manufacture is part of a developing manufacturing sector that employs 40% of the industrial workers and accounts for roughly 34% of total exports.

In 2017, the youth unemployment rate was at 42.8 percent. Morocco was rated 121st out of 189 nations on the Human Development Index in 2018, behind Algeria (82nd) and Tunisia (91st). According to the NGO Oxfam, it is the most unequal country in North Africa.

Non-residents are solely taxed on income earned in Morocco. Expats are not subject to any particular rules (unless a double taxation treaty applies). Capital gains on the sale of a Moroccan asset are typically taxed at 20% as part of regular income, with a minimum of 3% of the selling price being taxed.

Casablanca Morocco

Kenya

The Nairobi Securities Exchange (NSE) was founded in 1954 as the Nairobi Stock Exchange and is headquartered in Nairobi, Kenya's capital. There are 65 listings on the exchange, and they are denominated in Kenya shillings.

Kenya's economy is market-based, with a government-run private trade system and a few state-owned companies. Agriculture, forestry, fishing, mining, manufacturing, energy, tourism, and financial services are all important sectors.

Kenya has the third-largest economy in Sub-Saharan Africa as of 2020, after only Nigeria and South Africa. Kenya's government is usually pro-investment, and it has adopted a number of regulatory changes to facilitate both international and domestic investment, including the establishment of an export processing zone. Remittances from non-resident Kenyans working in the United States, the Middle East, Europe, and Asia are becoming a larger part of Kenya's foreign financial inflows.

Economic prospects were good as of September 2018, with GDP growth anticipated to exceed 6%, owing to gains in the telecommunications, transportation, and construction sectors, as well as a rebound in agriculture. A vast pool of highly educated professional employees is supporting these advancements.

Kenyans, particularly young Kenyans, have a high degree of IT knowledge and creativity. Kenya rose to 56th place in the World Bank's ease of doing business ranking in 2020, from 61st place in 2019. Kenya has a well-developed social and physical infrastructure in comparison to its neighbors. GDP growth averaged over 5% between 2013 and 2018 under the Jubilee Party government of Uhuru Kenyatta. Some of the progress can be attributed to the growth of small companies.

Despite this strong growth, Kenya's debt sustainability, current account deficit, fiscal consolidation, and revenue growth remain issues. Kenya's current economic growth strategy is called Vision 2030. By 2030, it aims to build an affluent, internationally competitive nation with a good quality of life. It intends to accomplish this by transforming Kenyan trade while also ensuring a safe and secure environment. There are three pillars to the vision: economic, social, and political.

Kenya's foreign investment policies have been largely restrictive. Despite these limitations, between 60% and 70% of the industry is still controlled by foreign investors. During the transition to independence, British colonialists engaged in fraudulent asset transfers, which accounted for a large amount of this. This exacerbated poverty and aided the development of conditions that would lead to reliance on foreign help.

Kenyans, on the other hand, have fared better economically and in terms of improving their own quality of life than many of their Sub-Saharan African neighbors. Despite the fact that Kenya is the most industrialized country in East Africa, manufacturing contributes to just 14% of GDP. The sector's fast development following independence stalled in the 1980s, plagued by hydroelectric power shortages, high energy prices, deteriorating transportation infrastructure, and the dumping of low-cost imports.

Capital gains on the sale of Kenyan stocks are subject to tax at 5%. The Kenya National Bureau of Statistics website is a great resource for equity research on the Kenyan market.

EXOTIC MARKETS

The economic capital of Africa, Nairobi, Kenya

Zimbabwe

The Zimbabwe Stock Exchange (ZSE) is the country's official stock exchange. Its history stretches back to 1896, although international investment has only been allowed since 1993. There are roughly a dozen participants on the exchange, and there are now 63 stocks listed (denominated in US dollars). The ZSE All Share and the ZSE Top 10 are the two main indexes.

Zimbabwe's economy is mostly based on the tertiary sector, which accounts for 60% of the country's overall GDP. With a score of 60.6 percent, Zimbabwe has the second-largest informal economy as a percentage of its economy.

Agriculture and mining both contribute significantly to exports. Zimbabwe's economy expanded at a rate of 12 percent on average from 2009 to 2013, making it one of the world's fastest-growing economies after a period of negative growth from 1998 to 2008, before slowing to 0.7 percent growth in 2016.

The country possesses metallurgical-grade chromite deposits. Coal, asbestos, copper, nickel, gold, platinum, and iron ore are some of the other commercial mineral resources. Zimbabwe proposed a land redistribution act in 2000 to gather white-owned commercial farms acquired via colonialism and restore them to the black majority. The new occupiers, mostly indigenous residents and a few important members of the ruling ZANU-PF administration, were unskilled or disinterested in farming, thus they were unable to maintain the old landowners' labor-intensive, highly efficient management.

Selling the land or equipment resulted in short-term gains. The current lack of agricultural knowledge resulted in significant export losses and harmed market trust. The country's food output has plummeted, and empty land is increasingly being used by rural populations that practice subsistence farming.

Unlike traditional export products such as tobacco and coffee, the production of basic foods such as maize has recovered as a result. Zimbabwe has also seen its 30th instance of hyperinflation in recorded history. Government spending accounts for 29.7% of GDP. State-owned businesses are heavily supported.

Taxes and tariffs are high, and governmental regulation is too expensive for companies. It takes a long time and money to start or end a business. Hiring and firing employees is a time-consuming procedure due to labor market rules. Unemployment had climbed to 94 percent by 2008. According to a 2014 analysis by the Africa Progress Panel, Zimbabwe performed the lowest of all the African nations studied when estimating how long it will take to double per capita GDP, taking 190 years at its present rate of progress.

Uncertainty surrounding the indigenization program (forced acquisition), the perceived lack of a free press, the possibility of abandoning the US dollar as the official currency, and political uncertainty following the end of the government of national unity with the MDC, as well as power struggles within ZANU-PF, have raised fears that the country's economic situation will worsen.

The finance minister highlighted "low levels of output and the accompanying trade imbalance, negligible foreign direct investment, and lack of access to international credit due to enormous arrears" as major reasons for the economy's dismal performance in September 2016.

Zimbabwe ranked 140th out of 190 countries in the World Bank Group's ease of doing business report. They received good marks for their capacity to obtain loans (rank 85) and for protecting minority investors (rank 86).

Capital Gains tax on Zimbabwe stocks will be liable at a rate of 20%. The Zimbabwe National Statistics Agency website is a great resource for equity research on that market.

Harare, capital of Zimbabwe

Tunisia

The Bourse des Valeurs Mobilières de Tunis (BVMT), often known as the Bourse de Tunis, is the Tunisian stock market. It was launched in 1969 and now has about 50 equities on its platform, denominated in Tunisian dinars. The Financial Market Council, which is controlled by the government, is in charge of the exchange. The government has offered tax advantages to encourage more firms to go public, but corporations have been hesitant to do so.

Tunisia's economy is undergoing liberalization following decades of significant governmental guidance and engagement in the country's economy. For more than a decade, prudent economic and budgetary planning has resulted in moderate but consistent growth.

Oil, phosphates, agri-food products, auto parts manufacture, and tourism have all contributed to Tunisia's economic prosperity in the past. Tunisia was ranked 92nd in the World

Economic Forum's Global Competitiveness Report in 2015 and 2016.

On September 2, 2020, a new administration was sworn in. Hichem Mechichi, the country's Prime Minister, has stated that his top priorities are to solve the country's economic and social problems, rebalance public finances (via discussions with lenders), and initiate reforms to reduce subsidies and programs that support state-owned enterprises.

Tunisia presented draft reform programs to international partners in April 2021, but the government has yet to present a comprehensive, detailed strategy to address the country's deep economic and financial challenges, which are now manifested in unprecedented levels of the budget deficit and public debt.

For non-resident individuals, the capital gains tax on the sale of Tunisian shares will be 2.5%.

Tunis, Tunisia

Namibia

The Namibian Stock Exchange (NSX) is the country's only stock exchange. It is one of the major stock exchanges on the African continent, with its headquarters in Windhoek. In neighboring South Africa, it has a cooperation with the JSE. There are 44 listings on the exchange, and they are denominated in Namibian dollars.

Namibia's economy is divided into two parts: a contemporary market sector that generates the majority of the country's wealth, and a traditional subsistence sector. Namibia boasts over 200,000 skilled employees and a significant number of well-trained professionals, despite the fact that the bulk of the population is engaged in subsistence agriculture and herding.

Namibia is a higher-middle-income nation, with an estimated yearly GDP per capita of US$5,828. However, income distribution and living standards are extremely unequal. With a Gini coefficient of 59.7 (CIA) and 74.3 (UN), it tops the list of nations with the most income disparity. The Namibian government has embraced free-market economic ideas since independence in order to encourage commercial growth and job creation in order to integrate disadvantaged Namibians into the economy.

The administration has actively sought donor aid and international investment to help achieve this aim. The liberal Foreign Investment Act of 1990 offers protection against nationalization, flexibility to transfer money and earnings, currency convertibility, and an equitable dispute resolution mechanism.

Namibia is likewise taking a pragmatic approach to the delicate subject of agricultural land reform. The government, on the other hand, manages and owns a number of companies, including Transnamib and NamPost. The sophisticated formal economy of the country is based on capital-intensive industry and agriculture. Namibia's real economy, on the other hand, is highly reliant on revenue produced from primary commodity exports in a few key industries, such as minerals, particularly diamonds, cattle, and fish.

Furthermore, because the majority of Namibia's imports originate from South Africa, the Namibian economy remains intertwined with that of South Africa. Namibia is a member of the International Monetary Fund and the World Bank, as well as the Lomé Convention of the European Union.

Namibia has no capital gains tax but gains on shares can be

liable to income tax. The Namibia Statistics Agency website is a great resource for equity research on the Namibian market.

Windhoek, the capital and economic center of Namibia

Botswana

The Botswana Stock Exchange (BSE) is located in Gaborone, Botswana. The BSE was founded in 1994, and there are 36 market listings on the BSE, as well as three stock indexes, all denominated in Botswana pulas.

Botswana's economy has grown at a rate of around 5% per year over the last decade, making it one of the world's fastest-growing economies. During the first 30 years of the country's independence, private sector employment grew at a rate of around 10% per year. Botswana's economy saw substantial growth after a period of stagnation around the turn of the century, with GDP exceeding 6-7 percent targets.

The African Development Bank has lauded Botswana for enduring one of the world's longest economic booms. Since the late 1960s, the country's economy has grown at a rate comparable to that of some of Asia's major economies. The government has routinely run budget surpluses and has substantial foreign exchange reserves. Diamond mining, conservative fiscal policies, international financial and technical support, and a cautious foreign policy have all contributed to Botswana's strong economic performance in comparison to some of its neighbors.

Diamond mining is the mainstay of Botswana's economy. Diamond mining provides 50% of the government's revenue, mostly through Debswana Diamond Company, a 50:50 joint venture with De Beers. Transparency International's Corruption Perceptions Index ranks it as the least corrupt country in Africa.

It boasts Africa's fourth highest gross national income per capita in terms of buying power and is above the global average. In Botswana, trade unions represent a small percentage of the workforce. Although the Botswana Federation of Trade Unions is solidifying its role as the country's sole national trade union center, they are often loosely organized "in-house" unions.

Although Botswana's economy is seen as a model for the area, the country's significant reliance on mining and unemployment may jeopardize its future prosperity.

Capital gains tax is applicable on Botswana shares and dependent on the non-resident individual. The Statistics

Botswana website is a great resource for equity research on stocks in Botswana.

iTowers of Masa Square CBD, Gaborone, Botswana

Sudan

Sudan's main stock market is the Khartoum Stock Exchange. It is shortened to KSE and is located in Khartoum. The Khartoum Index is the KSE's primary stock index. The KSE has grown substantially in recent years, with 53 listed firms valued at around US$5 billion. The listings on the exchange are denominated in Sudanese pounds.

Sudan's economy grew rapidly until the second half of 2002, thanks to increased oil output, high oil prices, and substantial inflows of foreign direct investment. In 2006 and 2007, the economy grew at a rate of more than 10%

each year. Sudan has worked with the IMF since 1997 to pursue macroeconomic reforms, including a controlled float of the currency. In the fourth quarter of 1999, Sudan began exporting crude oil.

Agriculture continues to be significant since it employs 80% of the workforce and accounts for a third of GDP. Despite rapid increases in average per capita income, the Darfur conflict, the aftermath of two decades of civil war in the south, a lack of basic infrastructure in large areas, and a reliance by much of the population on subsistence agriculture ensure that much of the population will remain at or below the poverty line for years.

The government established the Sudanese Pound as a new currency in January 2007, with an initial exchange rate of $1.00 equaling 2 Sudanese Pounds. Cotton, peanuts, gum arabic, and sesame seeds are examples of agricultural primary resources. Cotton and peanuts remain the country's principal agricultural exports, despite efforts to diversify its agriculture crops. Agricultural processing, electronics assembly, plastics manufacture, furniture, tanning, sugar production, meat processing, and other light industries are among Sudan's rapidly developing companies, which may be found in any of Khartoum's industrial zones.

Sudan is concentrating on becoming a hub for the medical industry in East Africa, providing facilities and concessions for medical investments, and succeeding in covering about 70% of needs and exporting to many neighboring countries due to the many countries relying on Sudan for medicines and medical services.

In recent years, the Giad Industrial Complex in Al Jazirah state has begun producing small cars and trucks, as well as some heavy military equipment like armored personnel carriers and main battle tanks like the "Bashir" and "Zubair," as well as handguns, light and heavy machineguns and howitzers, and, most recently, drones.

Sudan is known to have abundant natural resources, and substantial gold exploration has begun, with about 30 tons of gold produced annually, providing a significant boost to the country's foreign exchange reserves, and with the participation of numerous international investment firms. Asbestos, chromium, mica, kaolin, and copper are currently mined in large quantities.

Under Executive Order, the United States placed a trade embargo on Sudan and a complete asset freeze on the Sudanese government in 1997. The United States felt Sudan's government-supported international terrorism, destabilized neighboring countries, and allowed human rights violations. Because U.S. businesses are unable to engage in Sudan's oil industry as a result of the embargo, China, Malaysia, and India are the primary investors.

In Sudan, the Capital gains from the sale of shares and bonds and capital assets are subject to a 15% tax rate.

development in Khartoum, the capital city of Sudan

Ivory Coast

The Bourse Régionale des Valeurs Mobilières SA ("Regional Securities Exchange SA"), often known as the BRVM, is a regional stock exchange in West Africa that serves the following countries: Benin, Burkina Faso, Guinea, Ivory Coast, Mali, Nigeria, Senegal, and Togo. There are 76 listings on the exchange, and they are denominated in CFA francs.

In the aftermath of political turmoil in recent decades, the Ivory Coast's economy has remained stable and is now rising. The Ivory Coast is mainly market-driven and strongly reliant on agriculture. Almost 70% of the population of the Ivory Coast is involved in some sort of agricultural activity.

In the 1960s, GDP per capita increased by 82 percent, reaching a high of 360 percent in the 1970s. However, this was not sustainable, and it shrank by 28% in the 1980s and another 22% in the 1990s. The combination of this and rapid population expansion resulted in a gradual decline in living standards. In 1996, the gross national product per capita was at US$727, and it is presently growing again. The Ivorian economy began to recover in 1994, thanks to a depreciation of the CFA franc and improved cocoa and coffee prices, as well as growth in non-traditional primary exports such as pineapples and rubber, limited trade and banking liberalization, offshore oil and gas discoveries, and generous external financing and debt rescheduling by multilateral lenders. The devaluation of the CFA franc by 50% in1994, resulted in a one-time spike in inflation of 26%, although the rate decreased dramatically in 1996–1999. Furthermore, the government's compliance with donor-mandated reforms resulted in yearly growth of 5% in the same period.

Small farming crop cultivation continues to be the primary source of income for the bulk of the population. Cocoa, coffee, and tropical woods are the main exports. Ivory Coast's infrastructure is very good by developing-country standards. There are more than 13,000 kilometers (8,000 miles) of paved roads; modern telecommunications services, including a public data communications network; cellular phones and Internet access; two active ports, one of which, Abidjan, is the most modern in West Africa; rail links, both within the country and to Burkina Faso, which are in the process of being upgraded; and regular air service within the region.

Capital gains tax on the sale of shares is dependent on a

number of factors from the non-resident individual. Equity research can be done through the Institut National de la Statistique de Côte d'Ivoire website.

Abidjan, Ivory Coast

Tanzania

The Dar es Salaam Stock Exchange (DSE) is a stock exchange in Dar es Salaam, Tanzania's commercial capital and largest city. It was founded in 1996, and there are 29 listings on the exchange, denominated in Tanzanian shillings.

Tanzania's economy is a lower-middle-income economy that is mostly reliant on agriculture. Since 1985, Tanzania's economy has been shifting from a command to a market economy. Although overall GDP has grown since the reforms began, GDP per capita has fallen substantially initially and has just recently surpassed the pre-transition level in 2007. The GDP rose by a third to $41.33 billion with the rebasing of the economy in 2014. Tanzania's economy increased by 5.8% in 2019, hitting $55.5 billion in GDP, making it the second biggest in East Africa after Kenya and the seventh-largest in Sub-Saharan Africa.

It has maintained relatively strong economic growth in comparison to global trends, as is typical of African countries, although it is worth mentioning that the last five years have witnessed the weakest growth since 2000, according to World Bank data. So far, the medium-term picture is encouraging, with a growth forecast at 6% in 2020/21, bolstered by substantial infrastructure spending. Tanzania's economic growth dropped to 2.5 percent in 2020 owing to the Covid-19 epidemic, which has impacted the labor market, manufacturing capacity, and productivity. Tourism has ceased, and industrial and agricultural exports have plummeted. Tanzania's economy is expected to recover in 2021 with a GDP growth of 3.6 percent.

Capital gains on the sale of shares listed in Tanzania will be exempt from tax if the individual owns less than 25% of the shares outstanding of the company. The National Bureau of Statistics of Tanzania is a great resource for research on Tanzanian stocks.

Dar es Salaam, the financial center of Tanzania

Zambia

Zambia's main stock market is the Lusaka Stock Exchange (LuSE). It is based in Lusaka and was founded in 1993. There are 22 listings on the exchange, and they are denominated in Zambian kwachas.

Zambia is a developing country that is classified as a middle-income economy. Zambia's economy was one of the fastest-growing in Africa during the first decade of the twenty-first century, and its capital, Lusaka, was the fastest growing city in the Southern African Development Community.

Zambia's economy has stagnated in recent years as a result

of falling copper prices, large budget deficits, and energy shortages. Zambia is still one of Africa's poorest countries, with 58 percent of the population living on less than $1.90 per day and a life expectancy of 62 years. Although the government has succeeded in lowering the cost of doing business, other crucial measures of the business climate have deteriorated, such as trade barriers and government and judicial integrity.

Zambia is one of the most urbanized countries in Sub-Saharan Africa. About half of the country's 16 million inhabitants live in a few metropolitan regions scattered along key transit routes, while rural parts are sparsely inhabited.

National GDP has more than quadrupled since independence, but per capita earnings are now roughly two-thirds of what they were at independence, owing in large part to high birth rates. Zambia's GDP per capita is $1,305 as of 2019. Zambia's economic growth surpassed the 6 percent -7 percent level for the first time since 1989, which is required to considerably decrease poverty.

Because of rising copper prices and the construction of new mines, copper output has consistently grown since 2004. Cooperation with international agencies on poverty reduction initiatives continues, with a new loan arrangement with the IMF announced. Although tighter monetary policy would assist to reduce inflation, Zambia's state debt remains a major concern.

There is no capital gains tax in Zambia, although you may be liable in your home country. The Zambia Statistics Agency is a great resource for research on Zambian stocks.

Lusaka is the capital and largest financial district in Zambia

Uganda

Uganda's main stock exchange is the Uganda Securities Exchange (USE). Established in 1997, The USE is governed by Uganda's Capital Markets Authority, which reports to Uganda's central bank, the Bank of Uganda. There are 17 listings on the exchange, and they are denominated in Ugandan shillings.

Uganda's economy has a lot of potentials and appears to be on the verge of significant expansion and development. Uganda has abundant natural resources, including fertile terrain, consistent rainfall, and mineral reserves.

Since the introduction of self-rule, Uganda has had chronic political instability and unpredictable economic management, resulting in a record of sustained economic deterioration, placing it among the world's poorest and least-developed countries. The informal economy, which is dominated by women, is widely characterized as a group of disadvantaged people who labor without any safeguards.

Though substantial petroleum reserves have been discovered in the country's west, national energy requirements have consistently been greater than domestic energy output. Following the turbulence of the Amin era, the nation embarked on an economic rebuilding program in 1981, with significant foreign aid.

Overly expansionary fiscal and monetary policies, as well as a resurgence of civil unrest, resulted in a drop in economic performance from mid-1984 onward. Since the 1990s, the economy has expanded; real gross domestic product increased at an annual rate of 6.7 percent on average from 1990 to 2015, while real GDP per capita increased at a rate of 3.3 percent.

In Uganda, Capital gains are taxed at the standard corporate tax rate of 30%. The Uganda Bureau of Statistics is a great resource for equity research on the Ugandan market.

Kampala, the financial center of Uganda

Rwanda

The Rwanda Stock Exchange Limited was established in 2005 with the goal of conducting stock market activities in Rwanda. Because it was established as a business limited by shares, the Stock Exchange was demutualized from the outset. There are now 10 companies listed on the exchange, and they are denominated in Rwandan francs.

Rwanda's economy has rapidly industrialized as a result of effective government policies. Rwanda has seen an economic boom since the early 2000s, which has improved the living conditions of many Rwandans.

The government's progressive ideals have acted as a catalyst for the economy's rapid transformation. Rwandan President Paul Kagame has stated his desire to turn Rwanda into the "Singapore of Africa." In 2006, the country had a high period of economic growth, and the following year, it achieved an annual growth rate of 8%, which it has maintained since, making it one of Africa's fastest-growing economies.

This continuous economic development has reduced poverty and reduced fertility rates, with the percentage of the country's population living in poverty falling from 57 percent to 45 percent.

The country's infrastructure has developed quickly as well, with power connections increasing from 91,000 to 215,000. Commercial institutions, mining, tea, coffee, and tourism are all areas where foreign investment is now focused.

The four prewar autonomous trade unions are back in existence, as are minimum wage and social security rules. CESTRAR, the largest union, was founded as a government agency but became entirely autonomous after the 1991 constitution's political changes.

As Rwanda's security improves, the country's fledgling tourist industry offers enormous promise as a source of foreign money. Rwanda was placed 42nd in the Global Entrepreneurship Index study in 2016, and the second best country in Africa to do business.

However, according to a recent study published in the Review of African Political Economy, a UK-based political science magazine, economic development may be slower than official numbers show.

Capital gains in Rwanda is usually 5% in most cases on shares listed on the exchange. The National Institute of Statistics of Rwanda is a great resource for equity research in the region.

Kigali, the financial center of Rwanda

III

Part Three

The Handyman's toolbox
While Part 2 of this book is only a picture at a moment in time, this section is pretty timeless. Part 2 may experience evolutions and revolutions, available markets will come and go, and taxes may change overnight. Part III is nothing of that sort, you can read this book tomorrow or in 20 years, and the same principles laid out forward will be relevant still. It's all about having a toolbox, that you can reach out to, in any situation and know where to pick things up, know where to start.

12

Timeframe and broker

If you made it this far, I commend you. The previous section is quite dense, dry and boring, but if you have come this far, you are probably quite the geek as I am, and enjoy anything business & trading related. This section will be quite different, so far we have discovered the what, now let's dig into the how.

Choosing a timeframe

There are 4 main timeframes you can take when trading not only exotic securities but any security, the same way you would in your home market. You can either be day-trading, swing-trading, position trading, or investing. These 4 main categories very remote from each other, but the main differentiator is the timeframe.

The most well-known active trading style is day-trading. It's frequently used as a euphemism for aggressive trading. Day-trading is the practice of purchasing and selling securities on the same day, as the name suggests. Positions are filled and closed on the same day, and no position is kept overnight. Professional traders, such as experts or market makers, have traditionally done day trading. Electronic trading, on the other hand, has made this activity more accessible to newcomers. For retail traders, day-trading strategy usually lacks a fundamental base and relies heavily on technicals. In the context of this book, day trading refers to positions held no longer than a week.

Swing trades are often held for more than a day, but not as long as position trading. Swing traders frequently use a mix of technical and fundamental research to construct a set of positions. Swing-trading is usually a position held for a few days and no more than a few weeks.

Position trading, on the other hand, is a type of trading that uses longer timeframes. Position trading relies less on technical analysis, and more on fundamental analysis, which is the style of trading we recommend. A position can be held for longer, from a couple of weeks to a couple of months.

Finally, Investing is any position that goes over the one-year threshold. Technicals are almost absent, and heavy fundamental work is done on selection, Value-investing books and gurus such as Benjamin Graham or Warren Buffet are referred to as champions in this style, but you will be surprised to know that it is not necessarily the style we recommend.

As you can see by now, you have on one extreme day-trading, and on the other extreme investing, with many timeframes possible in between. The shorter the timeframe, the harder it is to get returns. Active day trading requires lots of time, is too reliant on technicals which can become very abstract, nebulous, speculative, and without a strong fundamental base. I would rather trade in the style of position trading where I can hold the position for longer and give time to the market to price in the underlying fundamentals of a company or market.

Selecting a broker overseas

Agatha Christie once said, "Where large sums of money are concerned, it is advisable to trust nobody." This is particularly relevant when it comes to choosing a broker to deal with international shares. It will come with no surprise that our industry is filled with unscrupulous opportunists ready to jump on the next oblivious victim. When choosing a broker, a couple of important things to look for will give you the best chances to avoid all the traps laid out.

There are so many stockbrokers out there that separating the excellent from the poor can be difficult. Unregulated and/or offshore brokers are a particularly prevalent concern in the brokerage sector. Brokers who aren't regulated aren't usually completely dishonest. Working with them, on the other hand, has a high chance of disaster. Dealing with an unlicensed broker may be like playing with fire because there are so many frauds in the brokerage sector. You have limited, if any, remedy if you are a victim of fraud. Regulations are in place for a purpose in every business sphere, particularly in the financial services industry.

Using an unlicensed broker is frequently less expensive. This is due to the cheaper start-up and operating expenses required once again. These fees are often passed on to the consumer by regulated brokers. They may accomplish this in a variety of ways, but it generally begins with larger commissions.

Unregulated brokers also provide considerably higher trading leverage. This is by far the most beneficial service provided by an unregulated broker. While restrictions are in place for a purpose, it's understandable that disgruntled traders find limitations annoying.

Another major determining factor for choosing a broker is availability. This is why you need a broker. You need a piano to become a maestro. The piano will not write the masterpiece for you, but it is the primary tool to do so. A brokerage account is no different. You will need a brokerage account that gives you access to the exchange. You need to be actively seeking a broker that gives you the most access possible to each market around the globe. Look for the list of available instruments on the broker's website before opening an account.

For smaller accounts, start with a single household broker that will cover most developed regions. As your account grows, multiply your brokerage accounts in order to increase your access to more emerging markets.

For Emerging and frontier market access, you will have to find a broker located in that region and open an account with them, making the process quite difficult and not for the faint-hearted.

On the same note, financial instrument choice is the next determining factor for opening an account. Does the broker allow you to trade stocks on margin? to trade CFDs? to trade options? The more choice you have the better. Spend a little bit of time making sure that the broker gives you as many options as possible.

Brokerage accounts are not free, there is a price to pay for access. It can be in various formats such as commissions, financing fees, or wide spreads. Make sure that the broker fees are reasonable, and that they will not impede on your trading style. If spreads are too wide, and commissions too high, you will need to increase your timeframe in order to recoup the costs.

Lastly, make sure that the broker enforces KYC, as in Know Your Customer. This is regulation red tape that prevents in some parts money laundering. If the broker does not verify your identity with a utility bill and a copy of your passport, they show a lack of professionalism. That lack of professionalism will show up whenever you need them to do their part.

EXOTIC MARKETS

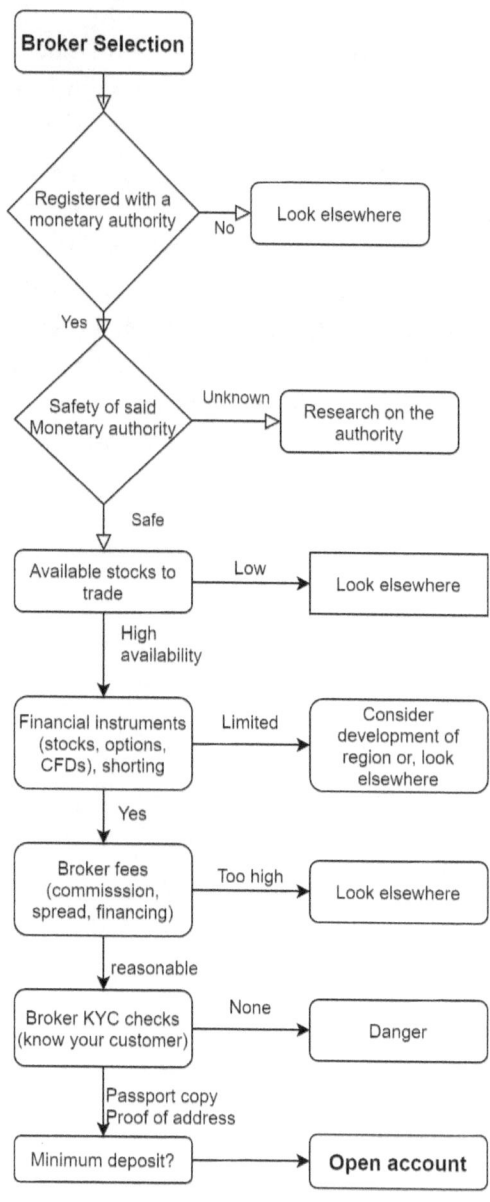

Flowchart for broker selection

Broker Diversification

A brokerage account is no different than a stock position. Most retail investors and traders will go to great lengths in diversifying their stock portfolio to protect them from country risk, industry risk, or stock risk. But most of them fail to see the obvious mistake of not doing the same with their brokerage account.

When you open a brokerage account with broker X, and subsequently open various diversified positions in stocks, you are still not diversified enough. You see, you deposited 100% of your investing/trading capital with broker X. Therefore, you have 100% *exposure* to broker X. If broker X goes bankrupt, or the CEO runs with the secretary, or the new government in the country of residence of Broker X decides to freeze all brokerage activity, your money is tied up, and most likely inaccessible for a while, if not gone.

The simple remedy to protect yourself against that is to take the same diversification approach you take with stocks, with brokerage accounts. For access to markets, you will have to use multiple brokers anyway, especially if you make dealings in emerging overseas markets and it's a great opportunity for you to plan ahead and make it part of your broker diversification process.

A good setup would be to have one or two big accounts with US or European brokers with the majority of your capital tied to, and then much smaller brokerage accounts, specific to certain emerging geographies. The current landscape of the international brokerage industry is set up like that anyway.

13

Macro selection

So the big question is, which country do I invest in then? Or even better, how do I pick countries to invest in?

This chapter will cover the macro selection process, as in picking which countries to select. The selection process can be divided into two main parts: the quantitative selection (Country Quant selection) and the Qualitative selection (Country Quality scorecard). They are broken down in such a manner to differentiate the Quant part, which is more numerical and easily automated, from the Quality part, which is the part that takes more time and focus.

GDP growth

When looking at the Quant metrics, the first and most obvious one would be GDP growth. If you just start comparing countries based on GDP growth, you will be able to shortlist some countries straight away. It is not hard to determine which regions of the world are growing or contracting just by looking at the GDP growth. It is not bulletproof though, some developing countries have informal economies (not counted in GDP figures), some countries make the numbers up, and GDP is only published quarterly, therefore it is usually published long after the market moves. Nevertheless, it would be foolish not to start from there and then dig deeper after a first screener made of GDP growth rates.

MACRO SELECTION

Country	Last	Previous	Reference	Unit
China	18.3	6.5	Mar/21	%
Turkey	7	5.9	Mar/21	%
Argentina	2.5	-4.3	Mar/21	%
South Korea	1.9	-1.1	Mar/21	%
India	1.6	0.5	Mar/21	%
Singapore	1.3	-2.4	Mar/21	%
France	1.2	-4.6	Mar/21	%
Australia	1.1	-1	Mar/21	%
Brazil	1	-1.1	Mar/21	%
United States	0.4	-2.4	Mar/21	%
Canada	0.3	-3.1	Mar/21	%
Switzerland	-0.5	-1.6	Mar/21	%
Russia	-0.7	-1.8	Mar/21	%
Indonesia	-0.74	-2.19	Mar/21	%
Italy	-0.8	-6.6	Mar/21	%
Euro Area	-1.3	-4.7	Mar/21	%
Japan	-1.6	-1.1	Mar/21	%
Netherlands	-2.4	-2.9	Mar/21	%
Saudi Arabia	-3	-3.9	Mar/21	%
Germany	-3.1	-3.3	Mar/21	%
South Africa	-3.2	-4.2	Mar/21	%
Mexico	-3.6	-4.5	Mar/21	%
Spain	-4.2	-8.9	Mar/21	%
United Kingdom	-6.1	-7.3	Mar/21	%

Quarterly GDP growth rate table for G20 countries. (source: tradingeconomics.com)

Services PMI

Next, the Purchasing Manager's index needs some particular attention. It is available in most countries, and measures economic activity, on a monthly basis (figures are published at the beginning of the next month). The reading is usually on a scale of 50, whereby above 50 the economy is expanding, and below 50 the economy is contracting. It comes in two flavors, the manufacturing PMI, and the services PMI. In more developed regions like Europe, services make up a bigger portion of the economy, while in developing countries, manufacturing is far more important.

If we look at the chart below, we can see a comparison between the services PMI of Italy and Sweden over the last three years. You can obviously see the dip in the middle due to the COVID 19 pandemic. You should really pay attention to what's happened after the pandemic. We can clearly see Sweden's economic activity outperforming Italy's with a reading of 71.20 compared to 53.10 respectively, in the latest data points.

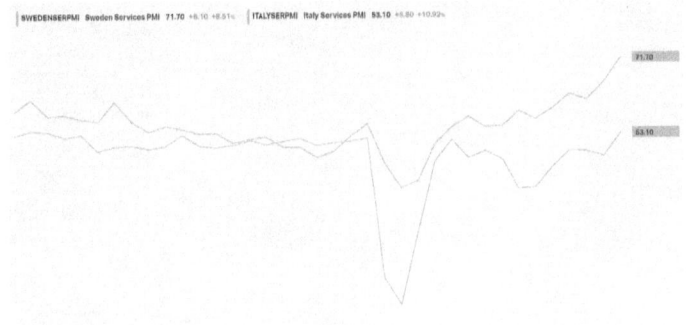

Services PMI of Italy and Sweden over the last 3 years (source: koyfin.com)

Now turn your attention to the next chart, where we compare Sweden's and Italy's country ETFs performance. Over a 3 year period, Sweden has returned +66.73% against +25.29% for Italy. The outperformance is clearly identified to have started at the same time as the Services PMI. This is no coincidence.

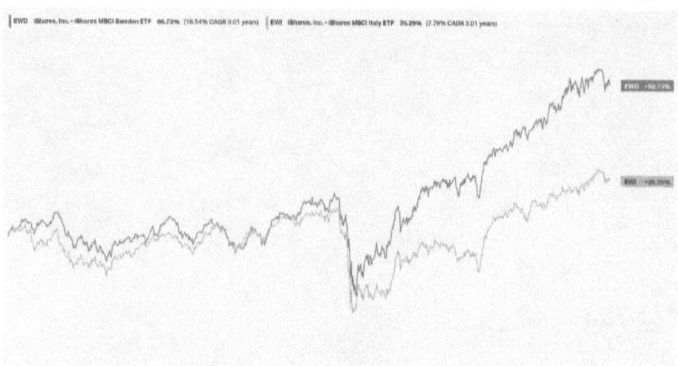

Performance of Italy and Sweden country ETFs over the last 3 years (source: koyfin.com)

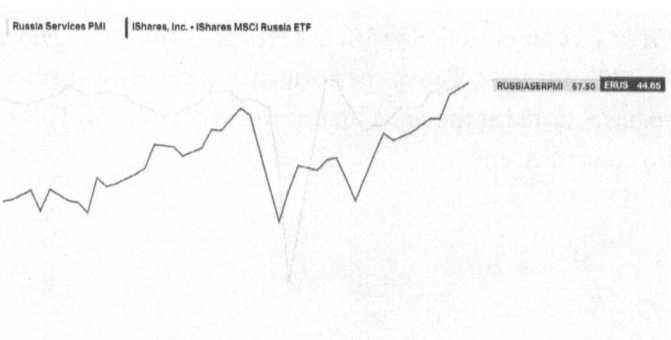

The Russia Service PMI indicator against the Russia country ETF performance over the past 3 years. (source: koyfin.com)

Manufacturing PMI

The next flavor of PMI is Manufacturing. Just like its Services counterpart, an index of more than 50 indicates an expansion in the manufacturing segment of the economy in comparison with the previous month while a reading of 50 indicates no change and a reading below 50 suggests a contraction of the manufacturing sector.

Investors can gain a better understanding of national economic trends and circumstances by tracking the manufacturing PMI. Investors predict a positive stock market in response to increased corporate earnings while the index is rising. Bond markets, on the other hand, may decrease when the PMI increases, due to the susceptibility of bonds to inflation.

The PMI, which is released monthly, has a significant impact on investor and company confidence. This is due to the fact that the index is based on a poll of buying and supply management executives who are in charge of their firms' supply chains. The finest people to analyze the ebb and flow of company situations are purchasing managers. The manufacturers for whom they work must be able to react rapidly to changes in demand, ramping up or cutting back material purchases in anticipation of demand for their completed goods.

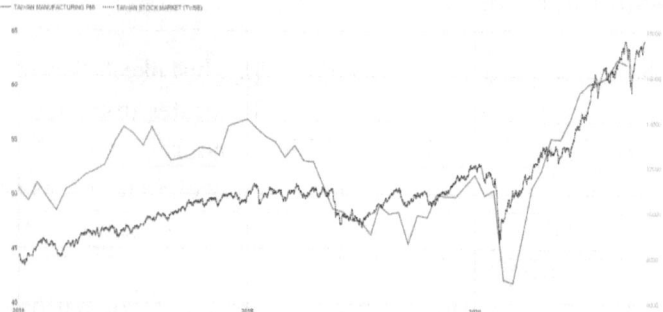

The Taiwan Manufacturing PMI indicator against the Taiwan stock market (TWSE) performance over the past 5 years. (source: tradingeconomics.com)

The South Korea Manufacturing PMI indicator against the South Korea stock market (KOSPI) performance over the past 5 years. (source: tradingeconomics.com)

Consumer Confidence

The Consumer Confidence Index (CCI) is a study that determines how hopeful or pessimistic consumers are about their future financial conditions. The CCI is founded on the idea that if consumers are optimistic, they would spend more and help to boost the economy, but if they are pessimistic, their purchasing habits may lead to a recession.

While some economists regard the CCI as a trailing indicator, the Organisation for Economic Co-operation and Development (OECD) regards consumer confidence as a leading indicator for the economy. Leading indicators give qualitative data that may be used to track the present state of the economy and predict economic turning points.

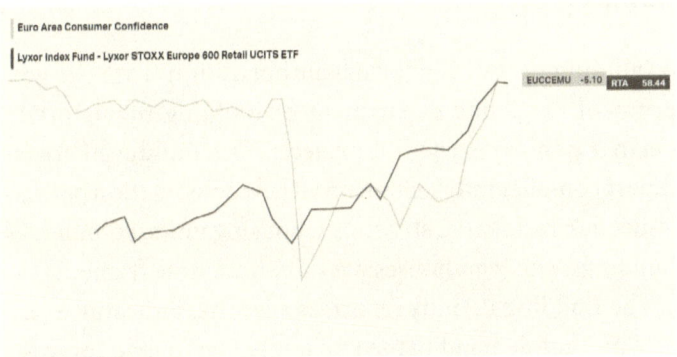

The Euro Area Consumer Confidence indicator against the Europe 600 retail ETF over the past 3 years. (source: koyfin.com)

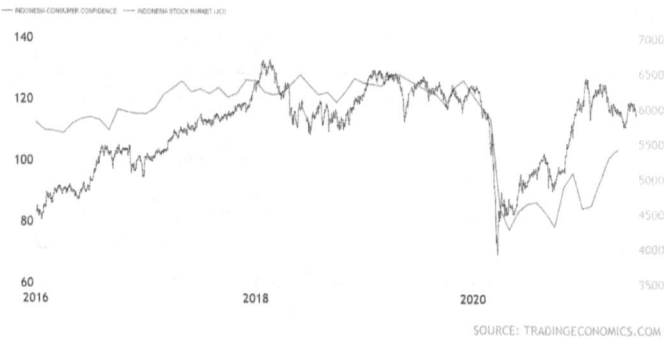

The Indonesia Consumer Confidence indicator against the Indonesia stock market performance (JCI) over the past 3 years. (source: tradingeconomics.com)

Building permits

A building permit is a formal authorization from the government's building department or building regulators to begin a new construction project. The Building Permits report compiles information on all new construction permits issued for residential structures, housing units, commercial buildings, and warehouses over a certain time frame.

The Building Permits report, as a leading indicator, evaluates present demand in the real estate market and forecasts the construction industry's future performance. Its purpose is to assess the strength of the national housing market as well as the overall condition of the economy. A housing market is a useful tool for determining where large-scale investments should be made. Because the report includes both national and local data, it may be used to determine which local areas are boosting the economy and which are pulling it down.

The government can use this information to spread the expansion to nearby areas or other locales or to support local economies by rerouting government spending as required. The Fed and analysts can also deduce the progress of the private sector due to the building industry's broad scope. For example, in 2006, the number of construction permits issued in the United States began to decline sharply, indicating an impending economic slowdown. It started as a subprime mortgage issue and grew into a full-blown disaster that will be remembered as the Great Recession. This pattern persisted until 2009 when the global economy began to recover from the 2008 financial crisis.

The housing market is seen as a leading indicator of consumer and corporate confidence. When consumers feel financially comfortable and have faith in the economy, they are more likely to take out loans and buy homes, either as a primary residence or as an investment. They would choose detached houses, which are often more expensive than normal residential units if they are not only safe but also prosperous. Consumer confidence is high, indicating a downward trend in unemployment and rising economic demand, both of which might speed up inflation.

The building sector is one of the most important economic drivers in the country. Construction projects often require a huge number of employees, both skilled and unskilled. It also consumes a lot of raw resources, such as concrete, bricks, and sand, in the industrial sector. As a result, every building project stimulates activity in a variety of businesses, including mining, excavation, transportation, utilities, and others.

Construction projects are by their nature enormous. They contribute in huge numbers and for extended periods of time to national employment, lowering the unemployment rate considerably. Furthermore, they encourage the expansion of industrial production sectors by creating a large demand for them. Building permits, on the other hand, do not always imply that work will begin right away. The majority of projects obtain approval ahead of schedule, and new projects that begin development are recorded in the Housing Starts statistics.

The Philippines Building Permits indicator against the Philippines stock market performance (PSEI) over the past 3 years. (source: tradingeconomics.com)

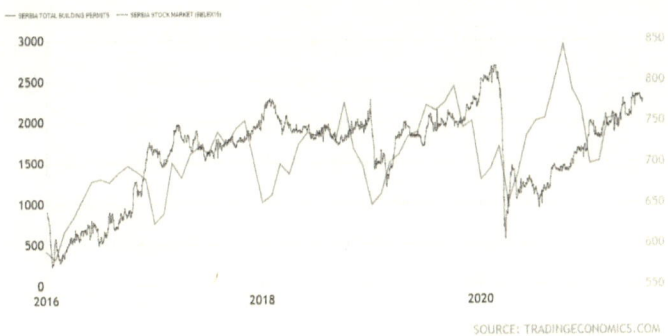

The Serbia Building Permits indicator against the Serbia stock market performance (BELEX15) over the past 3 years. (source: tradingeconomics.com)

From the two charts above on the Philippines and Serbia, we can clearly state that building permits are correlated with the economy, and therefore the stock market of each region. This is because emerging and developing countries are heavy on real estate and property, as the culture is to invest in tangible assets rather than intangible assets.

Business Confidence

This business confidence indicator provides information on future developments, based upon opinion surveys on developments in production, orders, and stocks of finished goods in the industry sector. It can be used to monitor output growth and to anticipate turning points in economic activity.

The BCI gives an indication of how people think about their capacity to get work and how they spend their money.

Consumers will refrain from making significant and expensive purchases such as luxury products and vehicles if the indicator shows negative results. Reduced confidence has an impact on both banks and governments. Lending will likely decline, as will the number of mortgage applications. To boost economic development, central banks may try to lower benchmark interest rates, and governments may be pushed to decrease taxes.

Brazil monthly business confidence indicator against Brazil stock market (BOVESPA) performance, last 5 years. (source: tradingeconomics.com)

MACRO SELECTION

Chile monthly business confidence indicator against Chile stock market (IGPA) performance, last 5 years. (source: tradingeconomics.com)

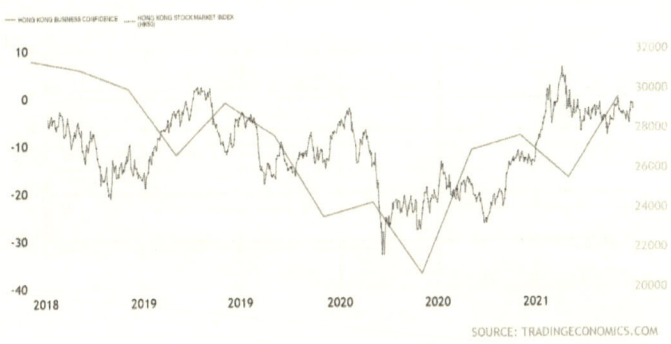

Hong Kong monthly business confidence indicator against Hong Kong stock market (HK50) performance, last 5 years. (source: tradingeconomics.com)

Industrial Production

The industrial production indicator (IPI) is a monthly economic statistic that compares real output in manufacturing, mining, electricity, and gas to a base year. The industrial production indicator monitors output in the manufacturing, mining (which includes oil and gas field drilling services), and electricity and gas utility industries. It also calculates capacity, which is an estimate of the maximum output that can be sustained, and capacity utilization, which is the ratio of actual output to capacity.

The composite index is an important macroeconomic indicator for economists and investors because fluctuations in the industrial sector account for the majority of the variation in overall economic growth. Industry-level data are useful for managers and investors within specific lines of business, whereas the composite index is an important macroeconomic indicator for economists and investors.

Capacity utilization is a good measure of demand strength. Low capacity utilization, often known as overcapacity, indicates a lack of demand. This might be seen by policymakers as a signal that fiscal or monetary stimulus is required. Investors, on the other hand, may see it as a precursor to a slump or a hint of impending stimulus. On the other side, high capacity utilization might signal that the economy is overheating, raising the danger of price hikes and asset bubbles. Interest rate hikes or fiscal austerity might be used by policymakers in response to these risks. Alternatively, they may let the business cycle run its course, which would almost certainly result in a recession.

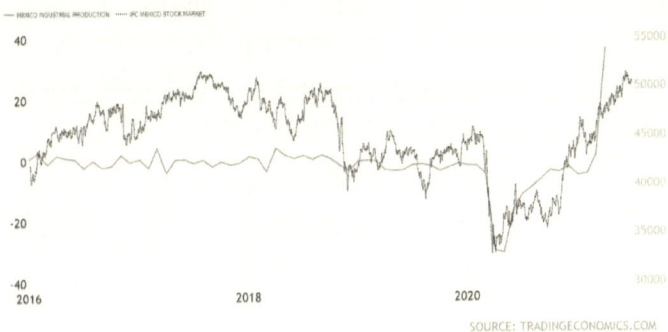

The Mexico Industrial Production indicator against the Mexico stock market (IPC) performance over the past 5 years. (source: tradingeconomics.com)

Front the chart above, Mexico's economy is in large part a manufacturing center for its neighbor, the US.

Manufacturing Production

The Manufacturing production indicator is a coincident indicator (tells you what happens at present in the economy) therefore it has less weight than the leading indicators previously mentioned.

Nonetheless, it is quite useful in emerging geographies where less data is prevalent and can give a good picture of the current state of the economy. It is also published on a monthly basis, giving you a preliminary reading on the economy before the GDP figures come out, and potentially put you a few steps in front of people you don't consult the Manufacturing activity of the region. From the chart below on Armenia, you can see the more agile Manufacturing Production data, being in front of the GDP growth rate figures, therefore telling you in advance on the state of the economy, before the GDP numbers come out.

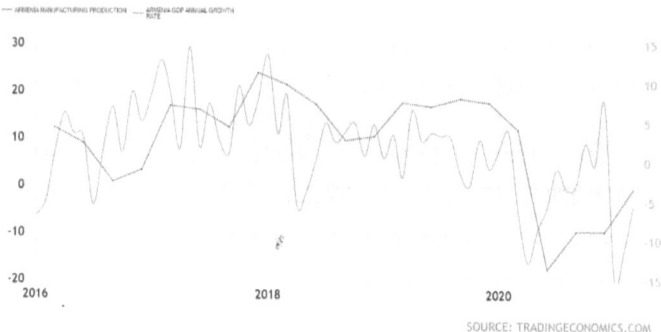

The Armenia Manufacturing Production indicator against the Armenia annual GDP growth rate over the past 5 years. (source: tradingeconomics.com)

More economic indicators can be looked out when choosing regions to invest in, but these should work well as a starting point. When you are doing research on a particular market, you can refer to the flowchart below to conduct your due diligence process.

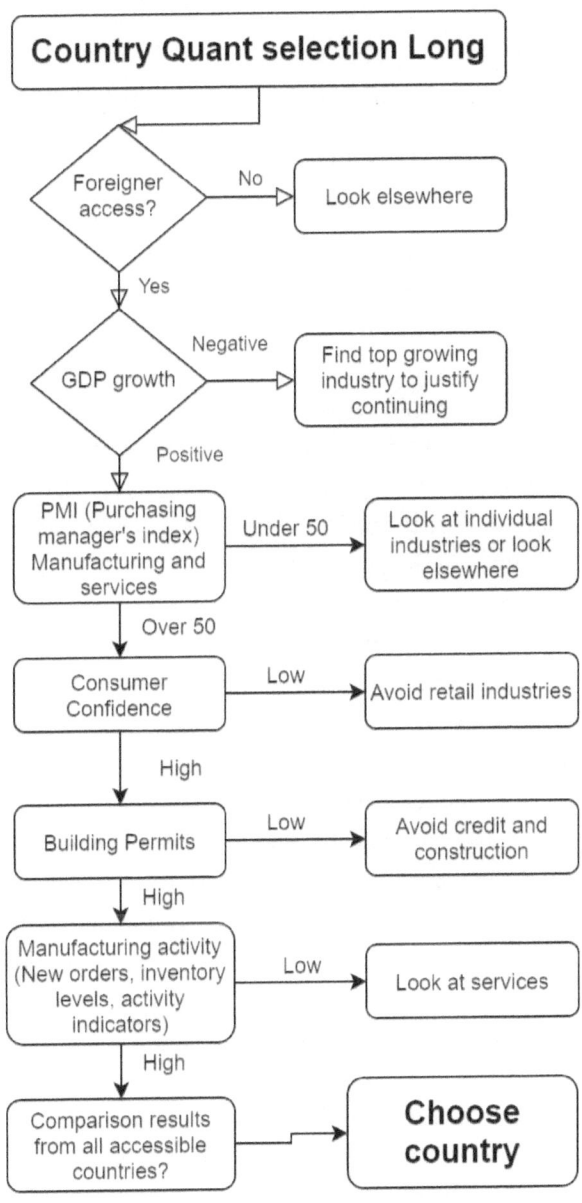

Country Quantitative Selection flowchart

Country Quality scorecard

After having gone through the Country Quantitative selection process, you should have shortlisted a couple of good candidates. You can now evaluate each country on its own merits in order to pick the best one. The second part of the selection is called quality because it does just that, it focuses on quality. Therefore, you will no longer rely on numerical values and comparators, but on the actual facts about each country in order to determine which one is best.

Economic dangers posed by events such as terrorism, war, sanctions, and other conflicts between the leaders of two or more nations are the most significant international political hazards for corporations.

To put it another way, there is a danger of losing money as a result of unstable governments, economies, or threatened countries. This notion appears to apply to a wide range of issues. Some of the hazards that international politics poses to companies are constant, while others arise solely in response to certain events and only on a rare occurrence. Whatever the scenario, nearly every political event has two significant implications for international business players: currency fluctuations and tightened/weakened international trade regulations.

The first step in properly handling the effects of any political climate shift is to identify them.

Despite the fact that modern media is biased and conflict-oriented, it is nevertheless a useful source of information that may help you identify possible hazards for your portfolio. If a concerning occurrence or political dispute occurs in the area where your investments operate, you will be able to begin taking preventive actions before the situation worsens. Not all political developments have the ability to hurt your portfolio. The fact is that only around half of them are. Some events would have major societal ramifications but just minimal commercial ramifications. Make a list of the many sorts of political risks that might affect you, such as capital controls, increased taxes, labor strikes, and protests.

Not only risks can come to fruition from your research, sometimes investment ideas can come too. As each passing president is only there temporarily in most cases, it is important to check which administration is in power at the time of your investment research. Presidents get elected by their people usually on promises they made. Whether they follow up or not is not the main issue, but rather which industries will likely be impacted the most. Sometimes it is just a case of a clear investment program, in education, for example, therefore investment ideas can be generated quickly and easily in that fashion. But sometimes, a little bit more digging may be involved but it is usually straightforward enough by looking at the administration's elective program.

The culture of a country is also a major determining factor. It is my reason to believe that most developed countries like the US and Europe have a deteriorating culture, and are headed in the wrong direction in that front. It is no coincidence that the countries that have experienced the longest a free market-driven democratic society, are the ones slowly parting away from it. And on the other hand, the countries having recently faced adversity, lack of freedom, and no free market, are now moving towards it. The culture of a country can be measured through various rankings such as the ease of doing business ranking (from the Doing Business report), the global competitiveness index, and the Index of economic freedom.

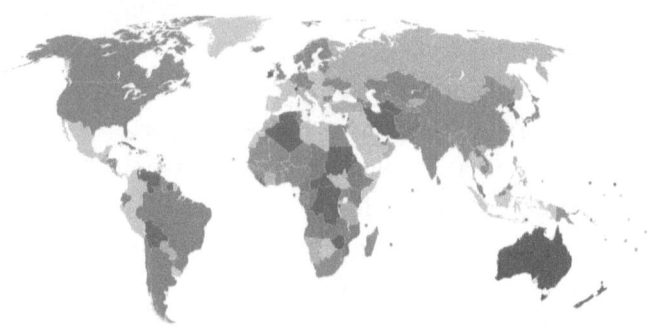

The 2021 heatmap of the Index of Economic Freedom

The World Bank Group established an indicator called the ease of doing business index. Higher rankings (lower number values) reflect better, typically simpler business regulations and greater property rights safeguards. To support its efforts, the World Bank financed empirical research that shows that changing these regulations has a significant economic growth benefit.

The ease of doing business index is designed to assess rules that directly influence firms, rather than more general circumstances such as a country's proximity to big markets, infrastructure quality, inflation, or crime.

The Doing Business Report (DB) is a report that is issued once a year. It has been developed by the World Bank Group every year since 2003 with the goal of measuring the costs to businesses of business regulation in 190 countries. The research has become one of the World Bank Group's hallmark knowledge products in the subject of private sector development, and it is credited for inspiring the creation of numerous regulatory changes in developing countries.

The Global Competitiveness Report is a yearly report published by the World Economic Forum. The study "evaluates a country's potential to offer high levels of prosperity to its inhabitants." This, in turn, is dependent on how efficiently a country utilizes its resources. As a result, the Global Competitiveness Index assesses the collection of institutions, policies, and variables that determine economic prosperity in the short and medium term.

On the basis of the most up-to-date theoretical and empirical research over 110 variables make up the model, two-thirds of which originate from the Executive Opinion Survey and one-third from publicly available sources like the United Nations. Each pillar represents an area believed to be a significant factor of competitiveness, and the variables are arranged into twelve pillars.

According to the research, when a country grows, salaries tend to rise, and in order to maintain this greater income, worker productivity must rise in order for the country to remain competitive. Furthermore, the factors that drive productivity in Sweden are unavoidably different from those that drive productivity in Ghana. As a result, the GCI divides nations into three distinct stages: factor-driven, efficiency-driven, and innovation-driven, each indicating a rising level of economic complexity.

The Heritage Foundation and The Wall Street Journal established the Index of Economic Freedom in 1995 as an annual index and ranking to evaluate the degree of economic freedom in the world's countries. The index's designers claim to follow Adam Smith's philosophy in The Wealth of Nations, which states that "fundamental institutions that safeguard individuals' liberty to pursue their own economic interests result in greater prosperity for the wider community."

According to the Heritage Foundation's website, "Every person's fundamental right to govern his or her own labor and property is known as economic freedom. Individuals in an economically free society are free to work, create, consume, and invest as they see fit. Governments in economically free societies let labor, capital, and products to travel freely and refrain from coercion or restriction of liberty beyond what is required to preserve and sustain liberty." The organization seeks to identify where such freedoms exist and do not exist by producing annual reports.

According to the Heritage Foundation, the top 20% of the index had twice the per capita income of the second quintile and five times that of the lowest 20%. According to Carl Schramm, who published the first chapter of the 2008 Index, cities in Medieval Italy and mid-nineteenth-century Midwestern America prospered to the extent that they had economic flexibility and institutional adaptability produced by economic freedom.

The rankings mentioned previously tend to give the impression that they belong in the Quantitative selection process, as the results are in a number ranking format. But in reality, these rankings are useful in giving you qualitative information about each country. Do not aim to only invest in top-ranking countries for each index, but rather use the rankings to interpret the facts about each country, and find the best candidate from the first batch filtered from the Quant selection process.

Lastly, the remaining thing to check about a country's quality in terms of investment, is Foreign direct investment. Before you do something, it would be sensible to check if others have done it in the past as well.

Foreign Direct investment does not mean foreign investors buying stocks in a country. Foreign direct investment is a financial investment made by a company or individual from one nation into a company in another one. In general, FDI occurs when a foreign firm develops overseas business activities or buys foreign business assets. FDIs, on the other hand, are distinct from portfolio investments, in which an investor simply buys stocks in foreign-based firms.

In contrast to heavily controlled nations, foreign direct investments are most often made in open economies with a competent workforce and above-average growth potential for the investor. Foreign direct investment usually entails more than simply a cash outlay. It may also contain management or technological provisions. The main characteristic of foreign direct investment is that it creates either effective control over or at least significant influence over a foreign company's decision-making.

You can refer to the subsequent flowchart whenever you are at the Qualitative selection of a country in your investment research.

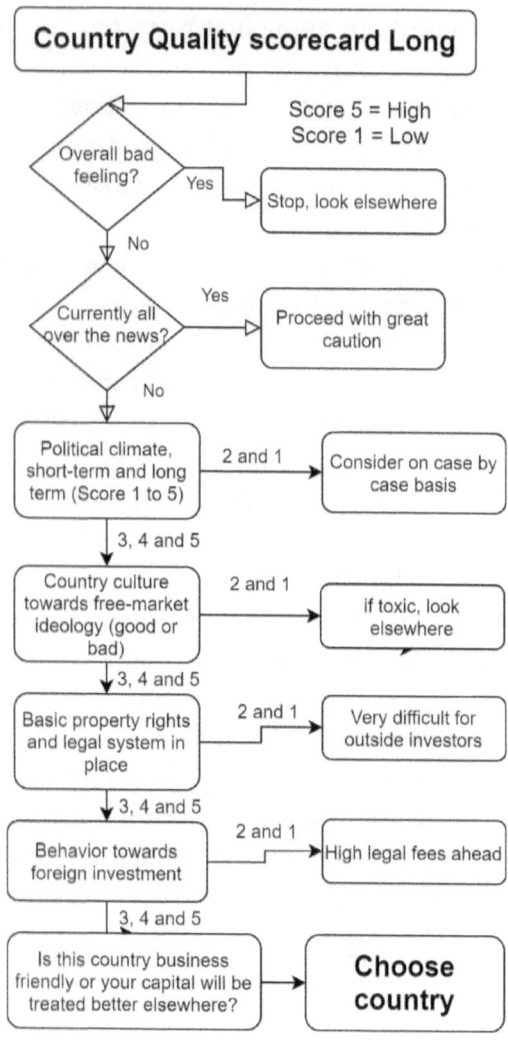

Country Qualitative selection scorecard

14

Industry selection

After having to select a potential country to trade in, the next logical step would be to look at the industries in that region. This is where Pervasives can come in.

Pervasives collects statistical data published by local authorities. Because the data is very unorganized and messy, Pervasives processes that data and publishes it in a digestible and interactive format. The end result is a collection of sector and industry intelligence in real-time, as the data is updated every month.

So far, we still have not even mentioned the United States. Let's finally use the United States as an example of how you can start researching sectors and industries.

Producer Price Index

The first tool in analyzing industries in the US would be the Producer Price Index.

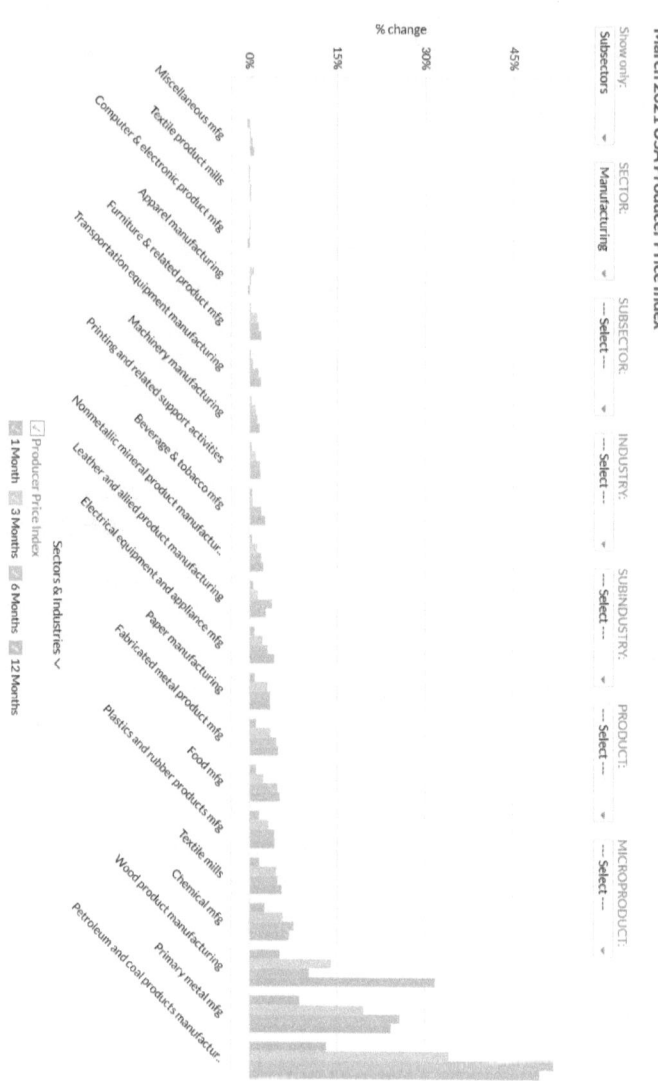

Producer Price Index in the US, broken by major industry groups, within the Manufacturing Sector (look at the filter SECTOR: Manufacturing) (source: pervasives.com)

INDUSTRY SELECTION

The Producer Price Index (PPI) is a collection of indices that track the average change in selling prices received by domestic goods and service providers over time. PPIs are used to track price changes from the seller's perspective. Other indices, such as the Consumer Price Index (CPI), measure price change from the perspective of the customer. Due to government subsidies, sales and excise taxes, and distribution expenses, the prices of sellers and buyers may differ.

Each month, around 10,000 PPIs for individual goods and groups of products are issued. PPIs are available for almost all goods-producing businesses, including mining, manufacturing, agriculture, fishing, and forestry, as well as natural gas, energy, construction, trash, and scrap materials. The PPI program covers around 72 percent of the output of the service sector. Wholesale and retail commerce; transportation and warehousing; information; finance and insurance; real estate brokering, renting, and leasing; professional, scientific, and technical services; administrative, support, and waste management are among the industries represented in the data.

Purchase and sales contracts are frequently adjusted using PPI data. These contracts usually include financial sums that must be paid at a later date.

It is a producer-level indicator of total price change. PPIs measure price changes before they reach the retail level. As a result, they may signal future pricing adjustments for businesses and consumers. These data are used by the President, Congress, and the Federal Reserve in developing budgetary and monetary policy.

From the perspective of a trader/investor, the PPI is a great tool to show us the change in potential nominal revenue companies receives. When it is going up, in simple terms the companies are charging more for their goods and services. Sometimes, that is just a reflection of price movements going down the value chain, therefore having little impact on the company. But in most cases, this is reflecting of a demand or supply shock that moves prices and therefore sales of these companies. Having followed the PPI data closely for a while, it is no coincidence when companies do well in line with increases in prices from PPI data, and conversely, companies do poorly in line with decreasing PPI data.

INDUSTRY SELECTION

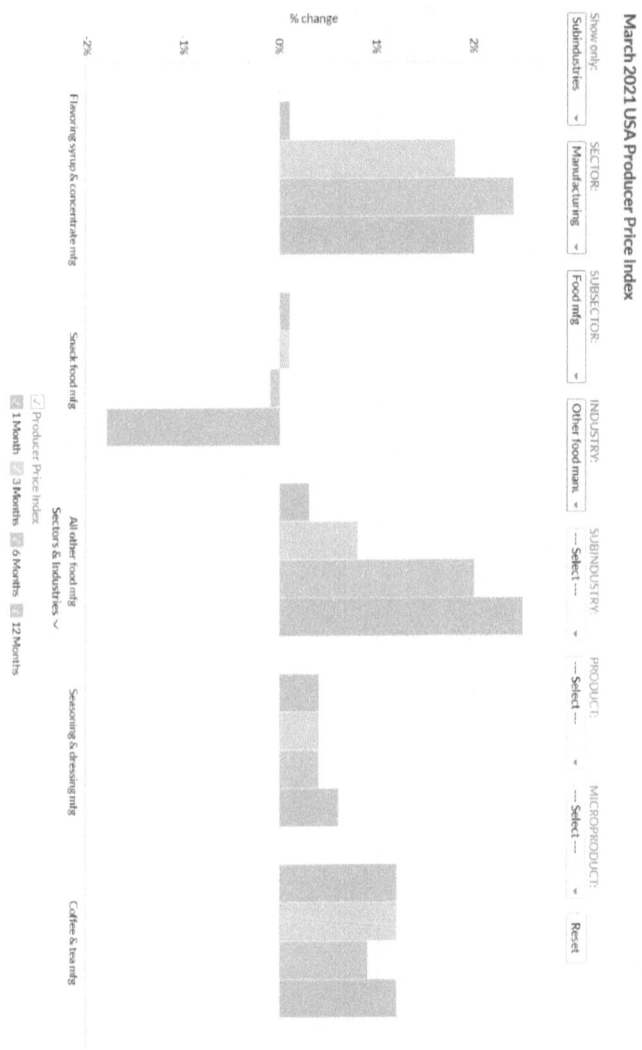

US PPI filtering on the other foods manufactured industry, within the Food Manufacturing subsector. (source: pervasives.com)

EXOTIC MARKETS

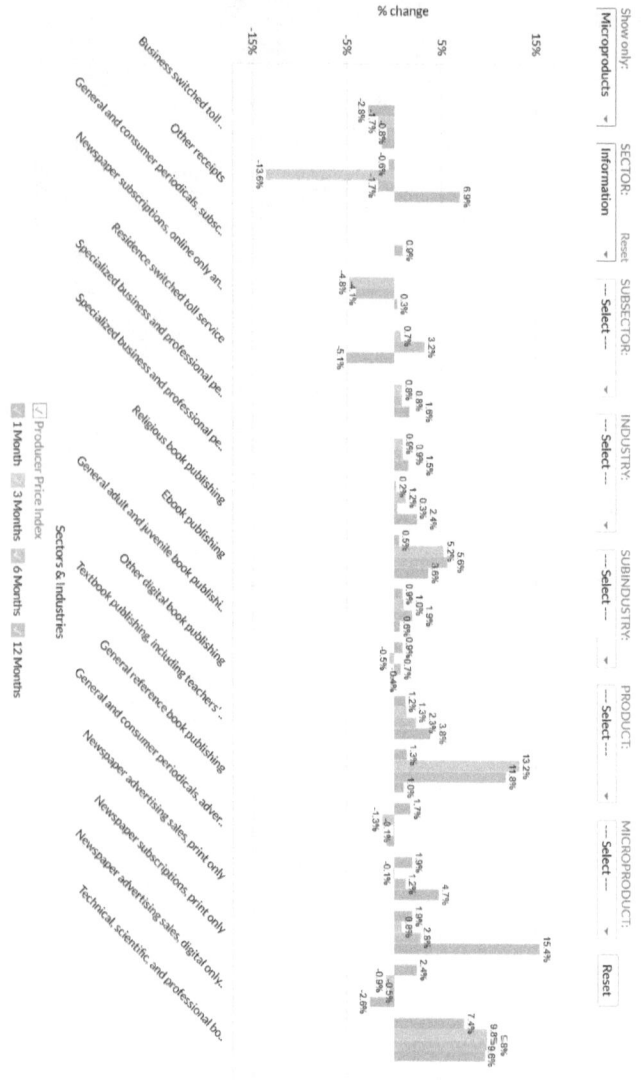

A look at PPI filtered by the Information sector (source: pervasives.com)

INDUSTRY SELECTION

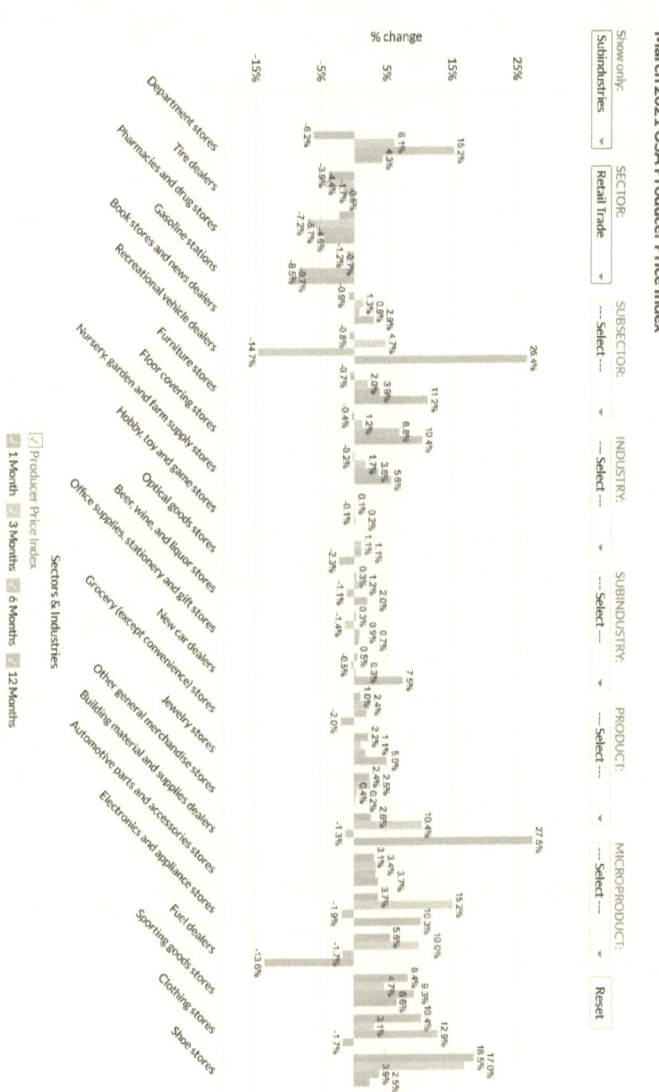

A look at PPI filtered by the Retail Trade Sector (source: pervasives.com)

Employment

The monthly employment data series is the first economic indicator of current economic trends each month, together with the unemployment rate, and input to many gauges of the economy including, the overall health of the economy, earnings trends, wage-push inflation (average hourly earnings), and short-term fluctuations in demand (average weekly hours).

Because businesses will lay off workers in a downturn of the industry and increase in an upturn of the industry, employment data gives a wealth of information on the health of an industry. Usually, businesses take action as preventive measures before the downturn/upturn occurs.

Thankfully for us investors and traders, employment data is usually pretty accessible in a lot of regions, through the labor department of each region.

Even better sometimes, the data is broken down into each subindustry, giving us more information on the state of each industry. You can see from the next examples covering employment in the US, you can drill down the employment data from supersectors to subsectors.

This becomes quite powerful when you then match your findings with your consultation of the PPI for industries and sectors.

INDUSTRY SELECTION

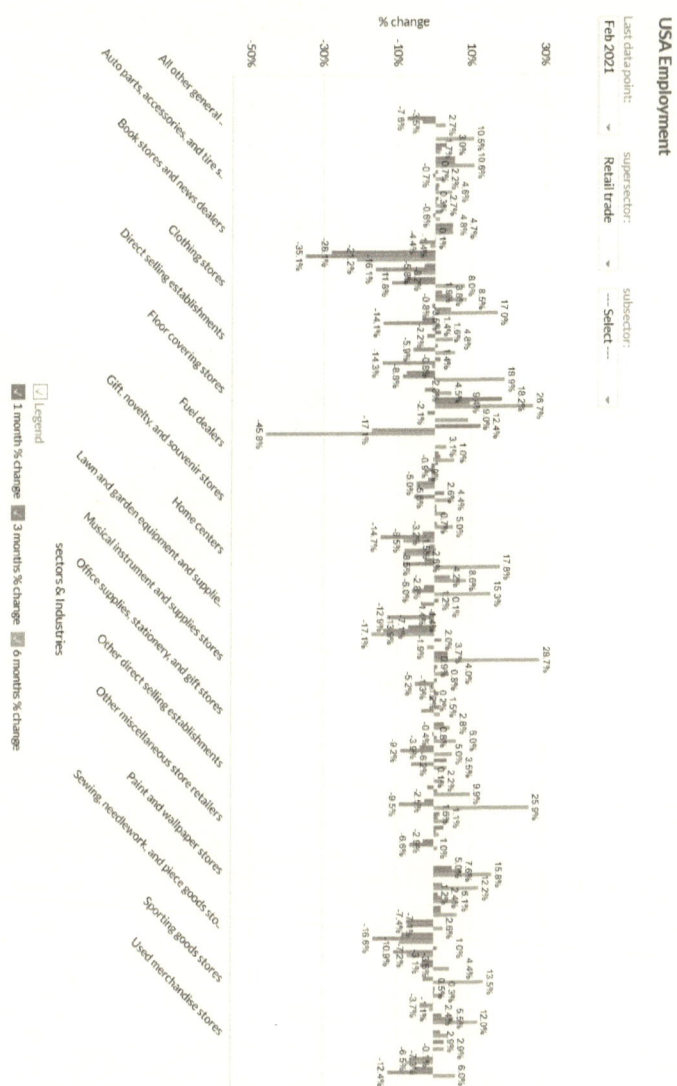

US employment data % change broken down by industries, filtered for the retail trade supersector (source: pervasives.com)

EXOTIC MARKETS

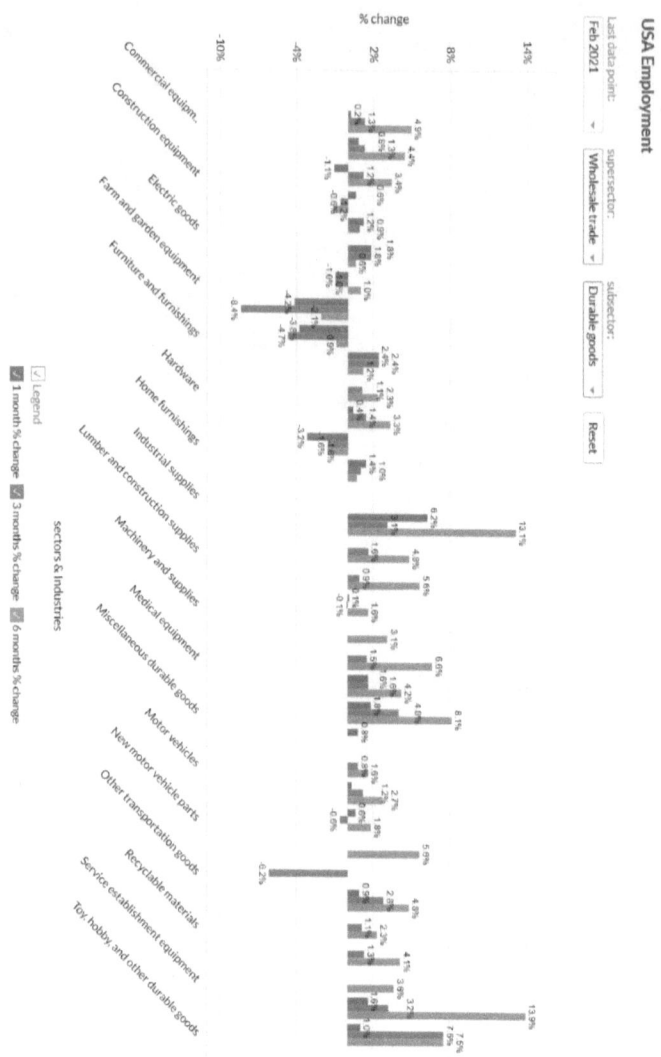

US employment data % change broken down by industries, filtered for the wholesale trade supersector, and durable goods subsector (source: pervasives.com)

US employment data % change broken down by industries, filtered for the construction supersector and specialty trade subsector (source: pervasives.com)

European Manufacturing & Services

The European Union is a big mess for a lot of things. But they are quite efficient at one thing, publishing clean data. The best data set they provide is the economic sentiment indicator.

The economic sentiment indicator is a composite statistic developed by the European Commission's Directorate-General for Economic and Financial Affairs. Its goal is to track GDP growth at the national, EU, and eurozone levels. The ESI is a weighted average of balances of responses to chosen questions posed to businesses and consumers in five sectors covered by the EU Business and Consumer Surveys. Industry (40 percent), services (30 percent), consumers (20 percent), retail (5 percent), and construction (5 percent) are the sectors covered.

The discrepancy between the percentages of respondents who gave positive and negative responses is used to create balances. Seasonally adjusted EU and euro-area aggregates are calculated based on national findings. The ESI has a long-term average of 100 and a standard deviation of 10. As a result, numbers greater than 100 imply higher-than-average economic mood, and vice versa. The data has been seasonally adjusted.

Pervasives publishes both Manufacturing and Services data of the ESI, Europe is a very developed region, therefore more weight should be given to services, as they make up a greater part of the economy.

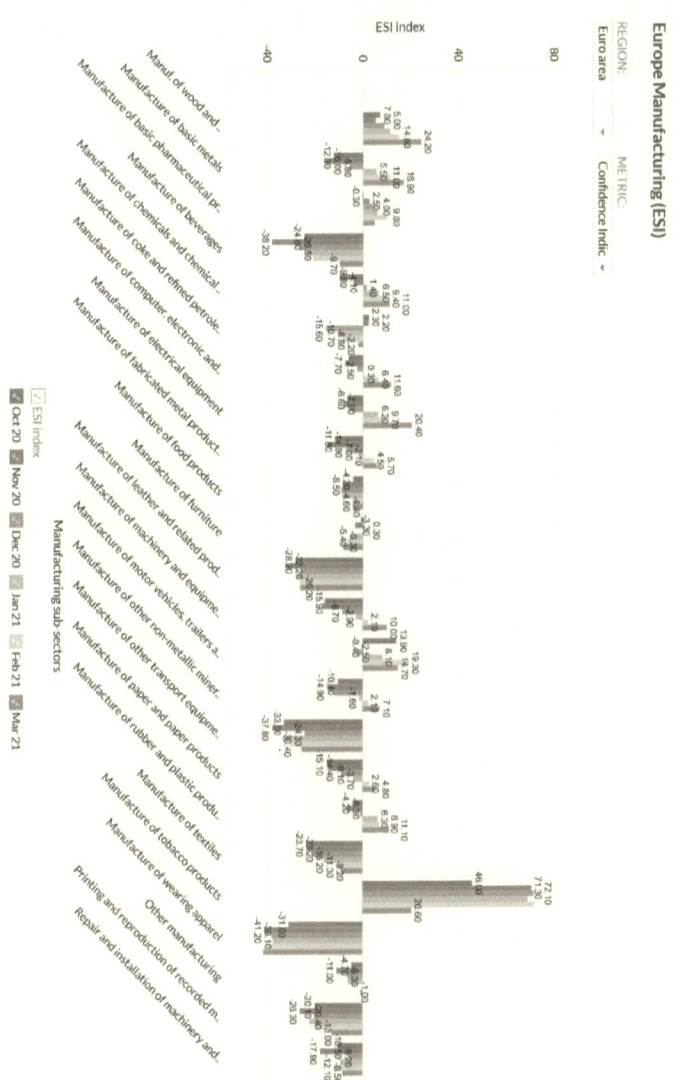

*Europe Manufacturing ESI, Euro area, Confidence indicator
(source: pervasives.com)*

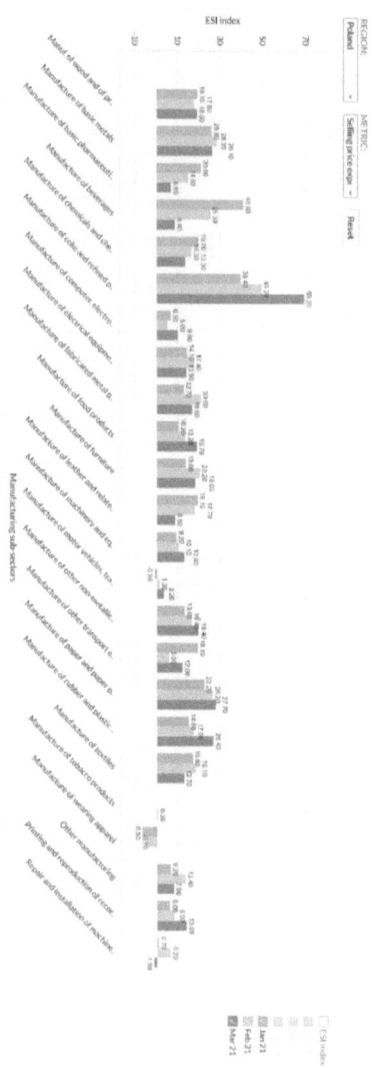

Europe Manufacturing ESI, Poland, Selling price expectations for the next 3 months (source: pervasives.com)

INDUSTRY SELECTION

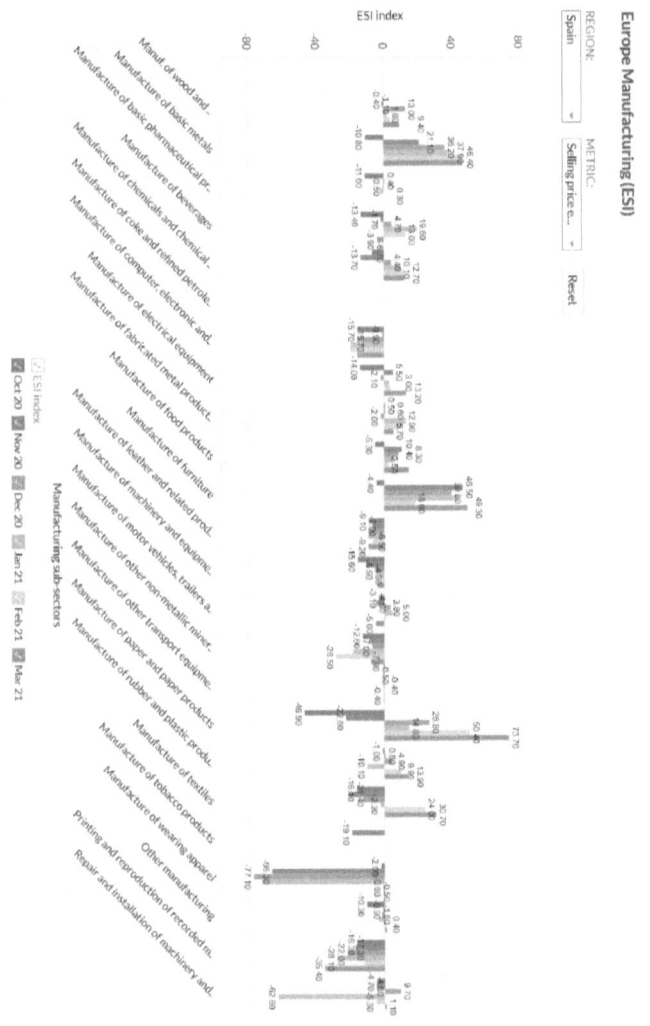

Europe Manufacturing ESI, Spain, Selling price expectations for the next 3 months (source: pervasives.com)

EXOTIC MARKETS

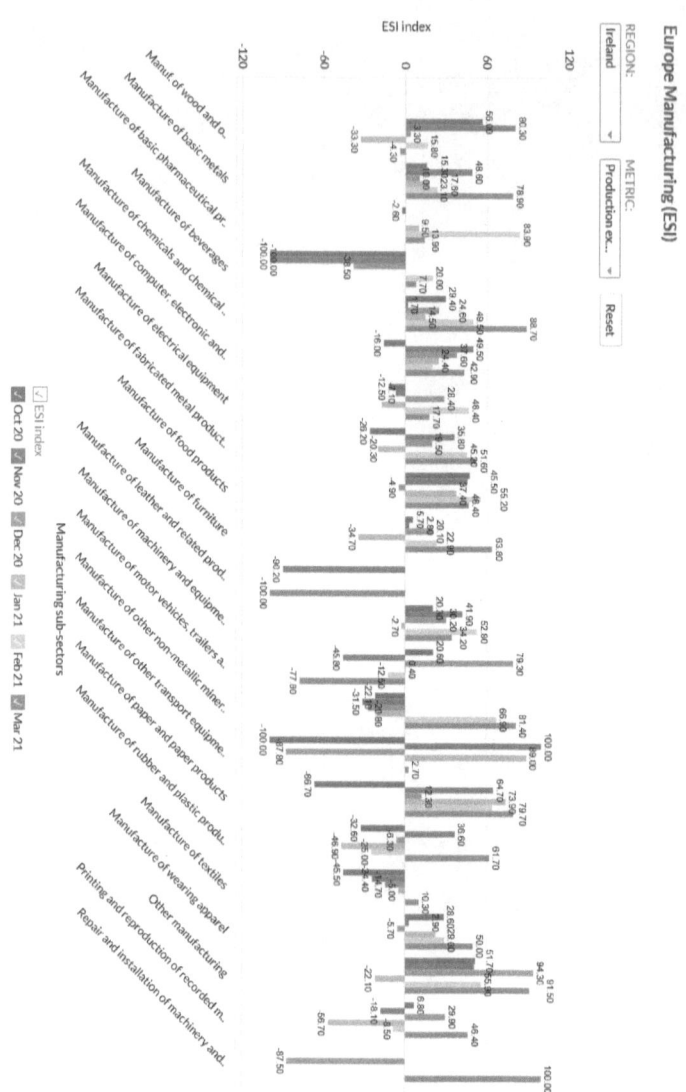

Europe Manufacturing ESI, Ireland, Production expectation for the next 3 months (source: pervasives.com)

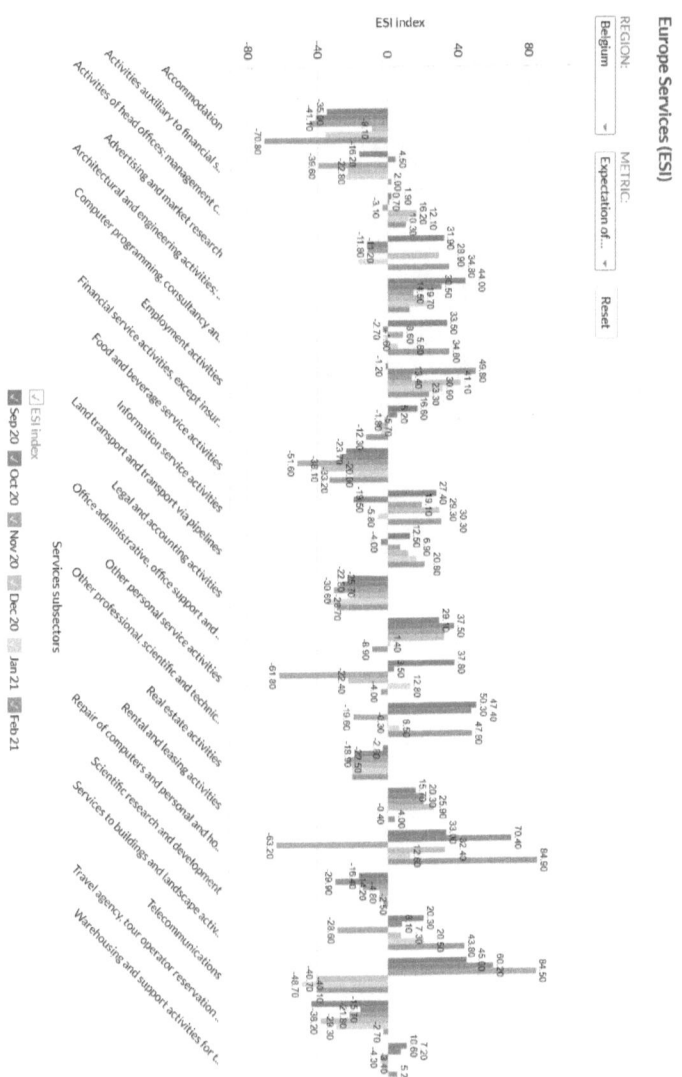

Europe Services ESI, Belgium, Expectation of demand over the next 3 months (source: pervasives.com)

EXOTIC MARKETS

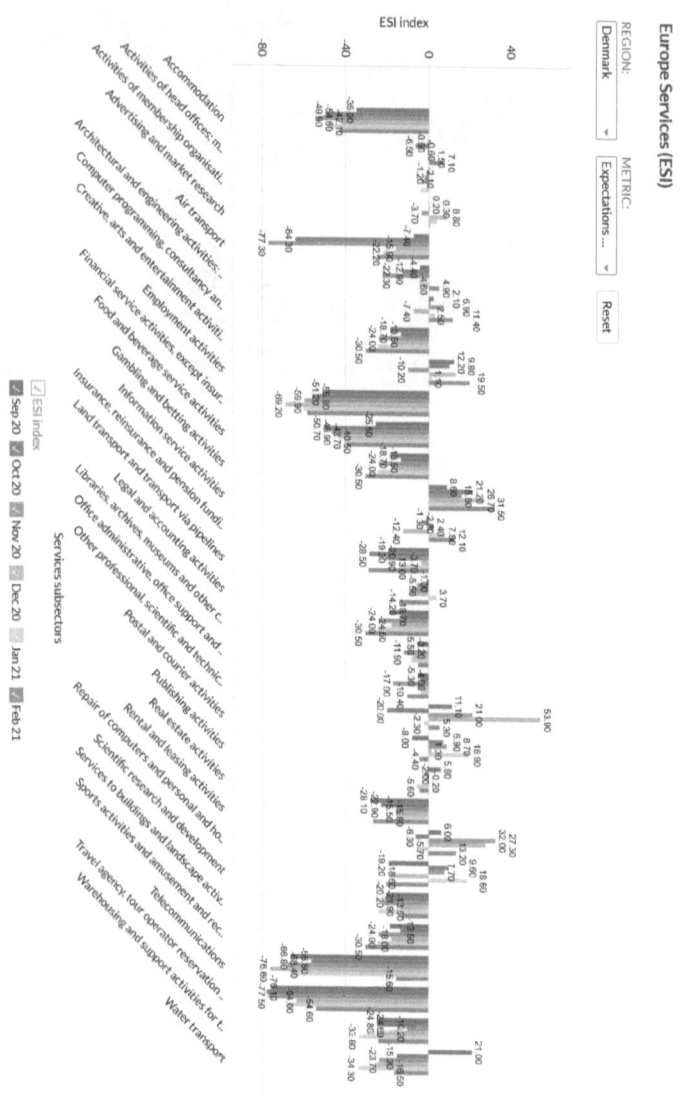

Europe Services ESI, Denmark, Expectation of the employment over the next 3 months (source: pervasives.com)

INDUSTRY SELECTION

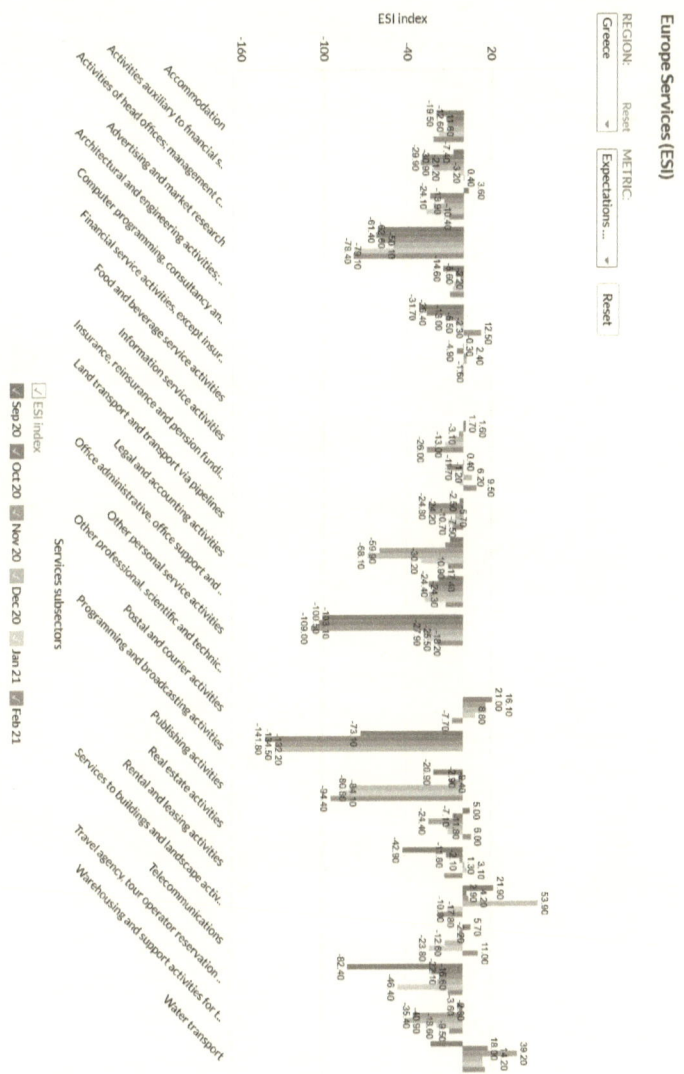

Europe Services ESI, Greece, Expectation of the prices over the next 3 months (source: pervasives.com)

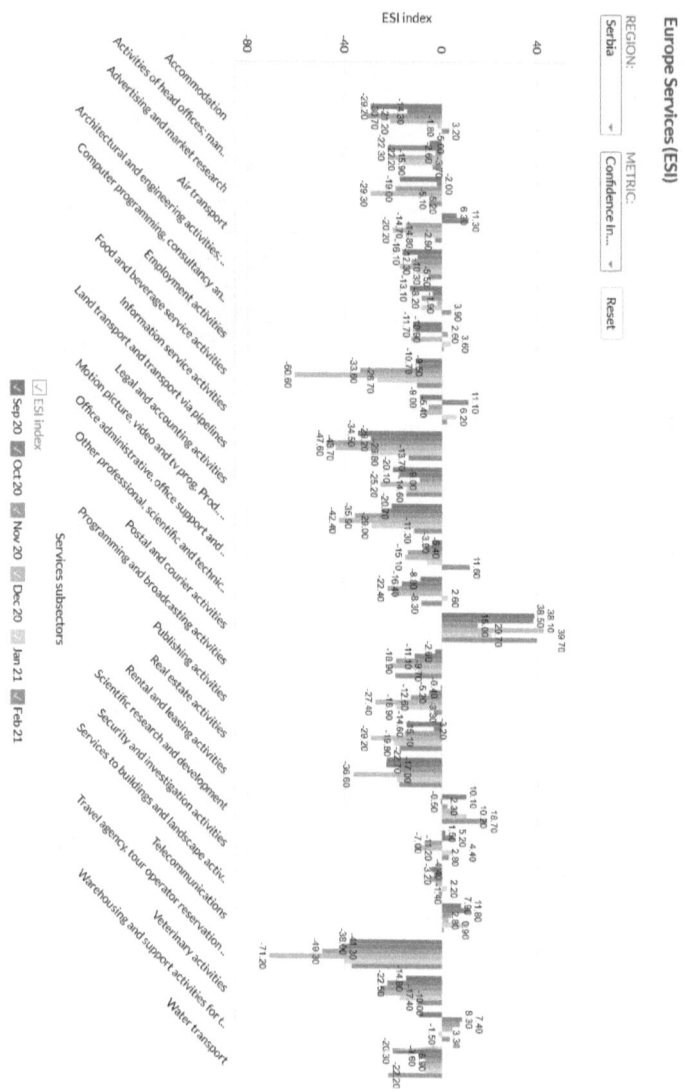

Europe Services ESI, Serbia, Confidence Indicator (source: pervasives.com)

15

Micro selection

Once you have identified a potential country from your Macro selection, and a potential industry in your industry selection, it's time to select a company within an industry. So far, we haven't looked at any stocks yet. The Micro selection process should help you quickly identify which stocks to select within an industry.

Most investment books will give you somewhat good advice on how to analyze the fundamentals of a company. This is all very good in itself, but it kind of misses a crucial point. As a retail investor or trader, you are limited on time. You could spend weeks and months analyzing every single company of any exchange. The better way would be to simply analyze a set of tradable stocks (for example the ones shortlisted from your macro and industry selection). From that set of stocks, the quickest way to determine which one is best is simply to compare them against each other.

Even before you look at the balance sheet and income statement of each, you can quickly determine which ones are the potential best simply by looking at industry-standard metrics to compare them against each other.

We are talking about ratios, of course, PE, forward PE, debt/equity, and EV/EBITDA ratios (and many more). Unfortunately, markets are a dynamic place, and what once was, is probably not any longer. Therefore ratios may have worked at a point in time, and not really at other times. The smart way to look at this is to evaluate the metric before using it to evaluate companies. The subsequent two sections, metric auditing, and theory of relativity, are part of the Quantitative selection process.

Metric auditing

Evaluate the metric before using it. I cannot simply give a list of metrics (for example Price per Earnings, Debt to Equity, Return on Investment) and tell you to use them to compare companies for investment selection. Most investment advice given tends to do just that, give a non-flexible, hard set of rules that you should follow forever and will, in return, give you guaranteed results.

I dare not foolishly assume that the reader of this book is a simple person that looks for the simple easy answer, instead of the complex and nuanced reality.

Comparable types of metrics are needed for the quant selection, they have to be numerical, and they have to be comparable units. Nominal amounts like GDP on their own are comparable in one dimension only. Percentages like GDP growth are comparable in more dimensions. Comparing the US nominal GDP against the Mongolia nominal GDP fails to recognize the obvious difference in sizes of these economies, while on the other hand, percentages on growth rates give a level playing field. Comparing apples to apples if you will.

You can go full pro by making advanced macros in excel, on one side of the spectrum, or simply look at online charts and make a visual decision in 5 mins by comparing 2 charts and deciding that they look kinda correlated, and one leads the other. the second one being the other extreme of the spectrum. And not all that stupid after all, considering the number of metrics to be audited and the time constraints put upon you with your own life. Just remember that you fully appreciate the corner cuttings you will take that may lead to mediocre performance.

A good tool to use to audit metrics is the Market scanner available on the Koyfin platform. Metrics can be measured against one another such as total return for example. Before you do though, you will need to appreciate that the correlation between the two is only reflective of past performance and not an indication of future performance. Once you have accepted these shortcomings, you can start pulling samples of stocks within a market.

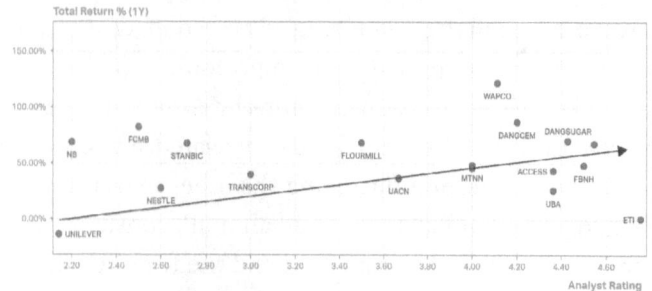

Market scatter of Nigerian stocks, Total return for 1 year against Analyst rating, a slight pattern can be identified. (source: koyfin)

As you can see from the chart above, a sample of Nigerian stocks has been used to measure Total return for 1 year against analyst ratings. A slight pattern occurs, the higher the analyst rating, the higher the performance over 1 year in general. As I mentioned previously, this does not mean that this pattern will occur in the future, but it gives us clues as to what metric may have more weight over others, and which ones don't.

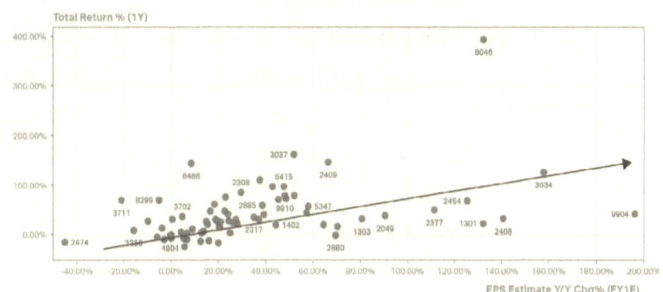

Market scatter of Taiwanese stocks, Total return for 1 year against forward growth of EPS estimates (% growth for next year), a pattern can be identified. (source: koyfin)

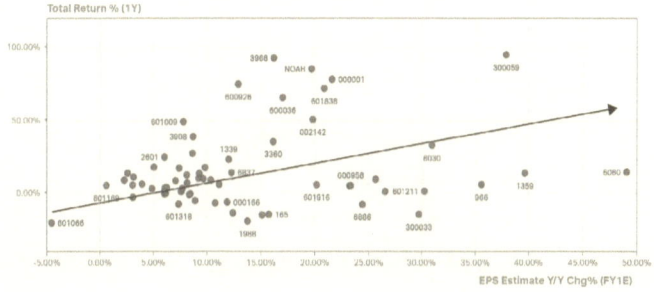

Market scatter of Chinese stocks, financial sector only, Total return for 1 year against forward growth of EPS estimates (% growth for next year), a pattern can be identified. (source: koyfin)

Another point to mention when auditing metrics, is that each metric and ratio will behave differently in different regions and within different industries. Therefore, it would be sensible to audit each market and industry on their metrics instead of auditing metrics once, and using them across all countries and sectors. Think about it, the Financial Services sector in Asia behaves very differently from the financial services sector in Europe. Both sectors will be sensitive to different factors and challenges, and investors will invest in them differently.

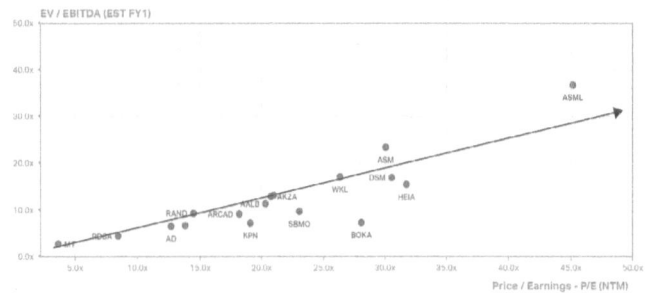

Market scatter of Dutch stocks, Price per earnings against forward EV/EBITDA (source: koyfin)

There is a lot to like about this approach. The greatest part about it is that it is timeless. As we said before, a lot of investing books will give a set of metrics to look at such as PE, on the premise that PE will be important to investors forever in the future. But as we know, markets and markets participants change in an ever-evolving global environment. Auditing your metrics will be as relevant 4 months from now as well as in 40 years from now, where markets will look like nothing today. In 40 years, you can pick up a market scatter tool, audit all metrics again in different markets and regions, and determine what's seems important for investors at this point in time.

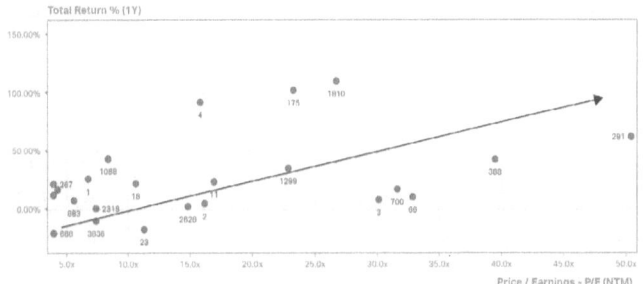

Market scatter of Hong Kong stocks, Price per earnings against total return for 1 year (source: koyfin)

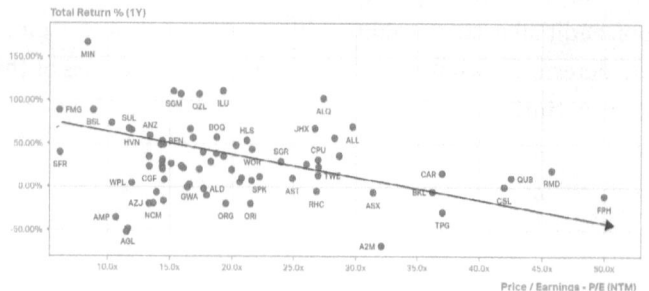

An example of a failed pattern, Australian stocks PE ratio against 1-year return, nothing can be drawn from this chart, another metric should be used for selecting Australian stocks (source: koyfin.com)

The Theory of Relativity

The theory of relativity is made up of two ideas proposed by Albert Einstein in the early 1900s. The first is known as "special" relativity, whereas the second is known as "general" relativity.

Einstein's theory of special relativity is based on two major principles. 1. The principle of relativity: For every inertial reference frame, the rules of physics are the same. 2. The speed of light principle: In a vacuum, the speed of light is the same for all observers, regardless of their relative velocity or the motion of the light source.

What exactly does this imply? Prior to Albert Einstein, physicists believed that all motion happened in relation to a reference point known as the "ether." The ether, according to

Einstein, does not exist. All motion, he argued, was "relative." This meant that measuring motion was dependent on the observer's relative velocity and position.

OK, that's great but what does it have to do with my portfolio? bottom line is, it's all relative.

You cannot expect markets to behave the same every day, and only use a hard set of rules to trade it. The better way is to appreciate that change is constant, that the world is dynamic, and therefore you should simply compare stocks against each other all the time with varying ratios and metrics, and simply picking the best ones. An still, this will not guarantee the best results.

On the next page, you will be able to see a dashboard of stocks in the US, within the Machinery industry. a sample of "important" metrics is displayed for each. None of them are important. But when you look at all of them together, you can start to paint a picture about which stocks look better than others. In the second image, displaying French stocks in the Consumer Discretionary sector, the averages of each industry metric is displayed at the bottom of the table. This is particularly helpful to determine whether a single stock is above or below its industry average for each metric.

EXOTIC MARKETS

Ticker	Name	1Y	Graph 1Y	EV/EBITDA FY1	EV/EBITDA FY2	PE FY1	PE FY2	Debt/Equity	EPS FY1	EPS FY2	Analyst Rating	Vol 1M
Machinery												
CMI	Cummins Inc.	38.45%		9.7x	8.9x	15.0x	12.9x	51.8%	16.09	18.74	3.68	20.35
FLS	Flowserve Corporation	40.52%		13.7x	12.0x	25.0x	20.2x	111.0%	1.61	1.99	3.17	28.73
IR	Ingersoll Rand Inc.	72.68%		19.6x	17.6x	27.9x	23.9x	44.2%	1.75	2.05	4.00	24.46
SPXC	SPX Corporation	46.51%		16.1x	14.1x	25.1x	20.4x	71.7%	2.37	2.92	5.00	25.68
ITW	Illinois Tool Works Inc.	30.87%		18.6x	17.4x	26.5x	24.1x	261.2%	8.49	9.31	3.05	13.68
NDSN	Nordson Corporation	18.79%		19.4x	17.9x	29.0x	26.2x	71.0%	7.53	8.36	4.00	13.79
DCI	Donaldson Company, Inc.	37.50%		16.4x	14.6x	27.1x	23.4x	69.8%	2.32	2.68	3.29	20.50
WAB	Westinghouse Air Brake Tech...	41.83%		13.5x	12.0x	19.5x	17.0x	44.7%	4.20	4.83	4.00	20.82
IEX	IDEX Corporation	42.87%		22.7x	20.9x	35.5x	31.9x	45.5%	6.19	6.87	4.07	15.38
PH	Parker-Hannifin Corporation	68.54%		14.5x	12.9x	20.3x	17.7x	140.4%	14.94	17.12	4.10	22.22
LECO	Lincoln Electric Holdings, Inc.	59.42%		15.7x	14.4x	23.6x	20.9x	96.6%	5.60	6.32	3.55	20.70
TTC	The Toro Company	64.77%		19.6x	18.3x	30.8x	27.7x	78.3%	3.54	3.93	3.33	19.12
CR	Crane Co.	53.65%		10.2x	8.7x	15.8x	13.1x	86.8%	5.76	6.94	4.40	27.61
XYL	Xylem Inc.	85.56%		24.5x	21.8x	43.8x	36.6x	113.0%	2.72	3.26	3.21	16.39
DOV	Dover Corporation	57.80%		15.6x	14.8x	21.3x	19.7x	97.6%	6.99	7.55	3.75	17.40
CAT	Caterpillar Inc.	71.74%		16.9x	13.9x	21.9x	18.0x	245.7%	9.86	12.03	3.44	24.56

Dashboard of US stocks in Machinery, with ratios and comparative metrics (source: koyfin.com)

MICRO SELECTION

Ticker	Name	Graph 3M	3M	Graph 6M	1Y	Graph 1Y	Market Cap	PE FY1	PE FY2	EPS % FY1	EPS % FY2	Revenues % FY1	Revenues % FY2	EPS Rev 1M	EPS Rev 3M	EPS Rev 6M	Sales Rev 1M	Sales Rev 3M	Sales Rev 6M
Consumer Discretionary																			
RMS	Hermès International Société		39.67%		65.17%		$152.41b	68.2	59.4	26.71%	14.69%	24.70%	11.23%	-0.52%	16.59%	21.3%	-2.6%	8.54%	9.05%
SW	Sodexo S.A.		13.70%		30.73%		$15.52b	43.5	18.3	-14.4%	139.34%	-10.54%	17.48%	-0.3%	-27.9%	-47.2%	-3.3%	-3.0%	-8.1%
EL	EssilorLuxottica Société ano		22.02%		36.23%		$91.32b	35.1	30.0	141.43%	17.30%	19.19%	8.17%	0.22%	2.50%	9.87%	-1.8%	5.23%	1.6%
KER	Kering SA		23.99%		52.19%		$109.01b	30.6	26.3	47.79%	16.49%	17.20%	9.78%	0.8%	0.8%	5.0%	-1.3%	7.49%	1.5%
FR	Valeo SE		-21.41%		8.50%		$7.22b	18.7	9.4		98.95%	21.14%	9.29%	-3.21%	-16.64%	-13.6%	-3.0%	0.0%	-8.4%
RNO	Renault SA		-4.89%		50.93%		$10.93b	16.2	4.5		256.69%	9.29%	9.40%	-0.52%	10.8%	-38.11%	-3.0%	-1.1%	-4.9%
ML	Compagnie Générale des Éta		28.16%		45.66%		$28.45b	14.2	11.7	77.42%	21.36%	6.42%	8.04%	1.11%	3.64%	10.62%	-2.2%	3.16%	-3.6%
POM	Compagnie Plastic Omnium		-4.66%		45.23%		$4.55b	12.2	10.2	555.89%	19.55%	11.35%	5.42%	-0.5%	8.56%	36.82%	-3.3%	0.10%	-4.6%
EO	Faurecia S.E.		-17.29%		19.89%		$6.74b	10.5	7.2			10.04%	12.57%	-0.5%	6.7%	1.75%	-3.1%	0.0%	4.7%
AC	Accor SA		6.39%		30.07%		$9.94b		56.7	47.31%	46.69%	37.33%	-0.5%					
UG	Stellantis N.V.		-2.22%		50.90%		$61.47b				11.54%		11.54%			-2.4%	-3.9%	1.99%	113.89%
CDI	Christian Dior SE		49.35%		80.75%		$145.25b					8.27%							
4.46%			12.24%		42.96%		52.56B	27.7X	23.4X	139.13%	70.30%	13.82%	12.49%	-0.50%	0.57%	-0.40%	-2.66%	1.85%	7.04%

French stocks in the Consumer discretionary sector, with averages for each metrics at the bottom of the table (source: koyfin)

Stock qualitative analysis

After having shortlisted a handful of candidates in your stock level research, you can now look at the qualitative side of each company.

This is the part that is much less numerical and requires a bit more digging. But thankfully, a lot of resources are available. In the information age, it is actually quite an overload.

Of course, the first step would be the newsflow about the company. In overseas regions, you may have to look for the local and regional news of the target country and search using the company name. The news flow is useful to start learning more about the company and its operations. Then, I would turn my attention to the annual report of the company, and the quarterly PowerPoint presentations they release for their investors. You see, every public company has a fiduciary duty to keep their investors updated on the company's operations, it's the law in most jurisdictions. And you can expect the same even in emerging countries.

Of course, because these reports are published by management, they will only say goods things about the company in order to reassure investors, and maybe gain new ones. So you will have to read between the lines of all the biased statements telling us how good the company is performing, and will in the future. Nonetheless, these reports give you a wealth of information such as the breakdown of revenue streams (not available on financial websites that only give you the total revenue figure), their potential investments and developments for each department, and their overall business plan will be laid out for you to read about. When you combine this with the knowledge you have gained in your country's research at the macro level, coupled with the knowledge gained on the industry research, you start to gain a very good picture of the potential investment possibilities.

16

The Tide

You now have a small list of the best investments in world. Now it's all about waiting. Waiting for the right moment to present itself, because there will always be a right moment further in the future. In a couple of days, a couple of weeks, a couple of months. You will know when that moment is because all the signals will flash and you will jump on it.

What if you miss that moment? well, you cannot control the tide itself. But you can control what you can do about it. And the tide always comes back anyway.

Technical Analysis

After having identified the ultimate best stock to buy, you shouldn't put the trade on straight away still. You need to wait. You need to wait for the correct entry within the supply and demand of the stock being traded on the exchange. This can be done by looking at a visual representation of the supply and demand, AKA technical analysis, which you may be more familiar with under that name.

That is the problem in a nutshell with technical analysis, people tend to forget or don't even know that technical analysis is only a visual representation of supply and demand and nothing more.

Unfortunately, most online traders getting financial education online end up using technical analysis on their own and speculate blindly on markets based on TA, which can work, but there is no fundamental support for their trades. Therefore rendering the venture highly risky and irresponsible.

Here are few TA tools that you can use after having done all the work previously mentioned, in order to optimize your entry and exit of trades.

Simple Moving Averages

The moving average (MA) is a straightforward technical analysis technique that smooths out price data by calculating an average price that is continually updated. The average is calculated over a set length of time, such as 10 days, 20 minutes, 30 weeks, or any other time period selected by the trader. There are benefits to utilizing a moving average in your trading, as well as several types of moving averages to choose from. Moving average techniques are very popular and can be adapted to any time period, making them suitable for both long and short-term investors and traders.

On a price chart, a moving average can assist reduce the amount of "noise." To obtain a general indication of which way the price is heading, look at the direction of the moving average. If it's slanted up, the price is rising (or recently was); if it's angled down, the price is falling; if it's oriented sideways, the price is most likely in a range.

A moving average can also serve as resistance or support. A 50-day, 100-day, or 200-day moving average can function as a support level in an uptrend, as seen in the chart below. Because the average functions as a floor (support), the price rises when it hits it. A moving average can function as resistance in a downturn; like a ceiling, the price hits the level and then begins to fall again.

In this approach, the price will not always "respect" the moving average. Before reaching it, the price may flow through it briefly or halt and reverse.

If the price is above a moving average, the trend is generally upward. The trend is down if the price is below a moving average. Moving averages, on the other hand, can have variable lengths, thus one MA can suggest an uptrend while another would indicate a decline.

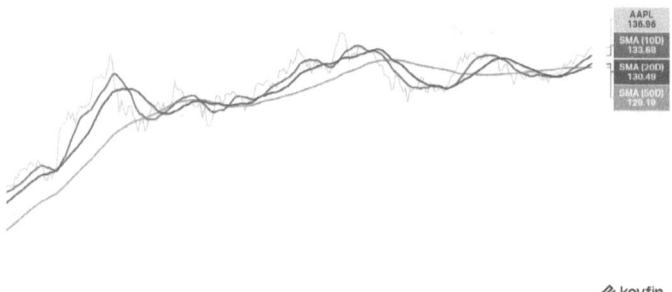

Relative strength divergence

The relative strength index (RSI) is a technical analysis indicator that evaluates the size of recent price fluctuations to determine if a stock or other asset is overbought or oversold. The RSI is represented as an oscillator (a line graph that swings between two extremes) with a range of 0 to 100.

Values of 70 or above on the RSI, according to traditional interpretation and use, a signal that investment is becoming overbought or overpriced, and may be poised for a trend reversal or corrective drop in price. A reading of 30 or less on the RSI suggests that the market is oversold or undervalued.

The stock or asset's principal trend is a useful tool for ensuring that the indicator's findings are correctly comprehended. For example, well-known market expert Constance Brown, CMT, has advocated the concept that an oversold RSI reading in an uptrend is likely considerably higher than 30%, while an overbought RSI reading in a downtrend is likely much lower than 70%.

When the price of an asset moves in the opposite direction of a technical indicator, such as an oscillator, or in the opposite direction of other data, this is known as divergence. Divergence signals that the present price trend is deteriorating, and in certain situations, the price will change direction.

Divergence is used by traders to determine the underlying momentum in an asset's price and the possibility of a market reversal. On a price chart, for example, investors can plot the Relative Strength Index. If the stock is increasing and setting new highs, the RSI should be doing the same. If the stock is making new highs but the RSI is making lower highs, it's a sign that the price upswing is fading. This is referred to as negative divergence. The trader can then decide whether to quit the position or place a stop loss if the price begins to fall.

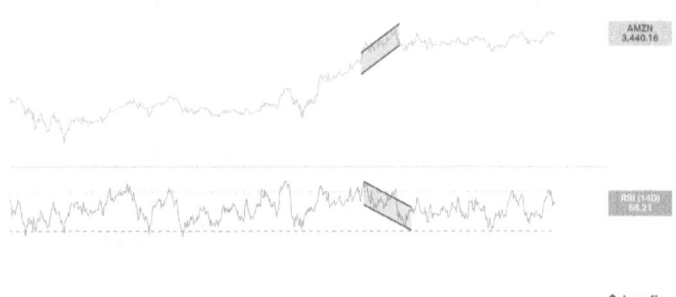

example of a Relative strength divergence, Amazon (source: koyfin)

Volume

Trading volume is a metric for determining how much of a certain financial item has changed hands over a specific period of time. Volume is calculated based on the number of shares traded in stocks and the number of contracts traded in futures and options. Online charts are frequently used to display the numbers and other indicators that rely on volume data.

Looking at volume trends over time might help you determine the strength or conviction behind individual stocks. Trading volume is a sign of an option's current interest, and the same is true for options traders. Volume, in fact, plays a vital part in technical analysis and is one of the most famous technical indicators.

There are typically standards utilized when assessing volume to evaluate the strength or weakness of a move. As traders, we are more likely to participate in powerful moves and avoid weak moves, or we may even look for an entrance in the opposite direction of a weak move. These rules do not apply in every scenario, but they provide a broad direction for trading decisions.

Volume should rise in a rising market. In order to keep driving prices upward, buyers must increase their numbers and excitement. Increasing price and declining volume might indicate a lack of interest, which could signal a reversal. This is a difficult concept to grasp, but the basic reality is that a price decrease on little volume is not a powerful signal. A significant volume price decline indicates that something in the stock has fundamentally altered.

We might witness fatigue motions in a rising or declining market. These are usually significant price movements accompanied by a sharp rise in volume, signaling the end of a trend. Participants who have been waiting and are frightened of missing out on more of the move rush in at market peaks, depleting the supply of purchasers.

Falling prices eventually push away a significant number of traders at a market bottom, resulting in higher volatility and volume. In these instances, we will observe a drop in volume following the surge, but the other volume recommendations may be used to assess how volume continues to play out over the next days, weeks, and months.

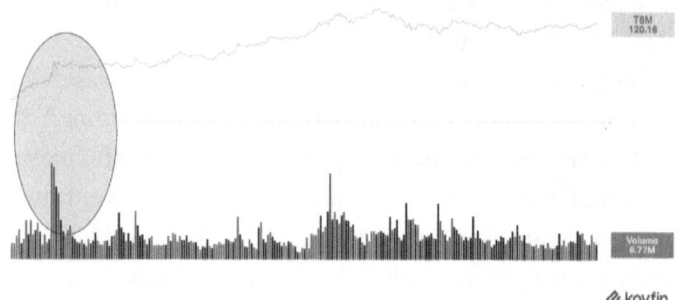

Most people think that sudden big volume is always bearish, Taiwanese company TSMC proves otherwise with a bullish trend for months after the spike in volume.

Fibonacci levels

Fibonacci retracement levels are horizontal lines that show potential areas of support and resistance. Fibonacci numbers are used to create them. A percentage is assigned to each level. The percentage indicates how much of a previous move has been retracted. 23.6 percent, 38.2 percent, 61.8 percent, and 78.6 percent are the Fibonacci retracement levels. 50 percent is also used, however, it is not a Fibonacci ratio.

Because it may be drawn between any two major price points, such as a high and a low, the indicator is valuable. Between those two marks, the indicator will generate levels.

Assume the price of a stock climbs $10 before falling by $2.36. It has retraced 23.6 percent in that scenario, which is a Fibonacci level. Fibonacci numbers may be found all around the world in nature. As a result, many traders feel these figures are also relevant to financial markets.

Entry orders, stop-loss levels, and price objectives may all be calculated using Fibonacci retracements. A trader could see a stock rising higher, for example. It retraces to the 61.8 percent mark after a surge higher. Then it begins to rise again. The trader decides to purchase since the bounce happened at a Fibonacci level during an upswing. A stop-loss may be put around 61.8 percent since a return below that level could signal that the rally has failed.

Unlike moving averages, Fibonacci retracement levels are fixed values that do not fluctuate. The pricing levels' unchanging nature enables rapid and clear identification. When price levels are challenged, this aids traders and investors in anticipating and reacting sensibly. These are inflection points when some kind of price movement, such as a reversal or a break, is predicted.

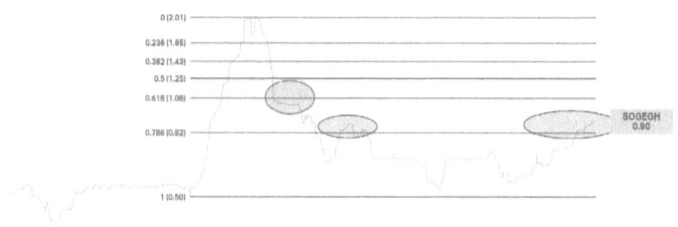

Societe Generale Ghana PLC, Fibonacci levels (source: koyfin.com)

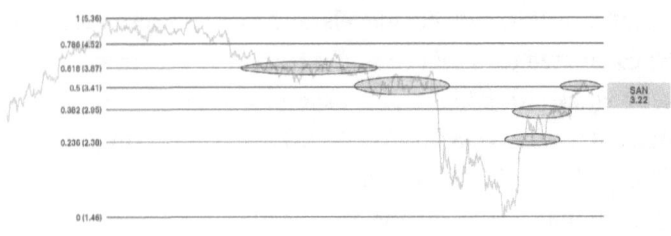

Banco Santander, Spain, Fibonacci levels (source: koyfin.com)

Tea leaves and tarot cards

Ultimately, the whole TA can be summarized into this. People pay too much attention to it when they should be focusing more on what we talked about in previous chapters.

Don't be that trader/investor, because you will not last very long, and it will not be a very interesting profession.

Technical Analysis gone too far, tarot cards and tea leaves

Watchlist

Managing all that research and processes can get very messy very quickly, not to mention that most retail traders and investors also need to manage their day-to-day job or business. You, therefore, need to come up with some organizational skills in order to build your global portfolio quickly and efficiently, in a repeatable manner. So far all the steps in part 2 are pretty self-explanatory and simple to follow on the surface.

The reality is always quite different from the theory, and you will be faced with the challenge of building your portfolio in the most optimal manner while juggling with your own life. A watchlist is nothing more than a simple shopping list at the outset. On the surface, you could have only one watchlist, that keeps tabs on your work-in-progress investment ideas but is not quite ready to put on yet (such as waiting for a good entry in the supply and demand on the exchange).

A more sophisticated approach is to keep a watchlist for every step of the process. For example a watchlist for keeping tabs on your macro research, with your top countries to go long (or short), a watchlist for industries selected within regions, a watchlist for stocks that are work in progress (further digging needed, like qualitative analysis), and finally a watchlist with validated stocks to invest in, but the timing is not quite right yet.

Another trap that I should mention, that I certainly still become a victim of, is that you should also know when *not* to add an item to your watchlist. I, unfortunately, added items to my watchlists so many times when I shouldn't have. The mistake I made was to add items to the watchlist as if my watchlist was simply a reminder to look at it. Then your watchlist becomes not only overloaded but filled with things that don't really matter. Be also concise in the information you log on your watchlist, most of the time you will log too much or irrelevant information.

Quality over quantity prevails, and you should aim for a short watchlist at every step, but that is made up of the best investments ideas you have.

You need to think of when to remove items from your watchlist as well. This is an equally important step. When an idea doesn't work out, it becomes stale and clogs up room in your watchlist for a potentially fresher idea.

17

The buffet

I love a good buffet restaurant. No, I am not talking about Warren Buffet, who's that guy? I am talking about a restaurant where there is a self-service buffet. It's funny because a buffet restaurant has a cheerleader effect, as in when you put all the elements together (the food), they look much better than taken on their own, individually. When I go to a buffet restaurant, I am more excited about the choice I will get, rather than the dishes on their own individual merits. You see, I like buffets because I get to choose what I want, not because the food is necessarily great.

Unfortunately, there is a lot of confusion around which financial instruments to use when trading or investing. I hear a lot of vocal people preaching the merits of owning stocks outright and everything else is bad, and other people just trade options and nothing else. Also, you will hear of people only using CFD contracts and nothing else. The option guy, that only trades options and nothing else has decided at one point, that he understands options best. He appreciates the benefits of options, he is aware of the pros and cons, and has concluded that he will only use options to trade, on all of his positions, exclusively, for the rest of his life.

What these people are doing is not necessarily wrong, but there is a much better way to approach which financial instruments to use: the buffet. What you should do instead is the following, choose the financial instrument as you would choose your meal for lunch. Let me explain, use the financial instrument that is best suited for the particular trade in question. Whenever you have decided to trade a stock, go over the simple task of deciding which instrument to use to trade that stock. Different financial instruments have different characteristics, pros and cons, therefore suited for different situations pertaining to the trade in question. Take the time to learn the basics of each instrument in order to add them to your collection of tools in your handyman's toolbox.

Stocks

Stocks are the simplest instrument and the most available especially in overseas markets. You will have to use this instrument the most simply because of its availability. It is also the safest in terms of investor protection. Its characteristics are simple to understand, therefore it is better to stick with stocks unless you have to. Owning stock outrights makes you a real shareholder of a company but you will have almost zero leverage in your positions.

CFDs

CFDs are Contract for Difference. When you have a CFD contract on a stock, you do not own the stock, you own a contract with the broker that mirrors the price of the underlying asset (the company stock). On that basis, CFDs allow you to take much more leverage than you would with owning simple stocks. But remember, the broker is the counterparty of the contract, so you better make sure that this is a good and fair broker. CFD are not available in the US but they are in Europe.

Some advantages of CFDs include access to the underlying asset at a lower cost than buying the asset outright, ease of execution, and the ability to go long or short.

Options

Options trading may appear intimidating at first, but it's simple to grasp if you learn a few essential concepts. Investor portfolios are typically made up of a variety of asset classes. Stocks, bonds, ETFs, and even mutual funds are examples. Options are a different asset class that, when handled appropriately, may provide numerous benefits that stock and ETF trading alone cannot.

A call or put option gives the buyer the right, but not the duty, to purchase (in the case of a call) or sell (in the case of a put) the underlying asset at a particular price on or before a specific date. Options are used to generate revenue, speculate, and hedge risk.

Because they draw their value from an underlying asset, options are referred to as derivatives. A stock option contract generally represents 100 shares of the underlying stock, although options on any underlying asset, including bonds, currencies, and commodities, can be created.

When options are available in a foreign market that you are interested in, make sure to spend the time to weigh the advantages and disadvantages of using either the stock or the option. Most of the time the determining factor will be price, but you can also weigh the risks and the expected volatility in the future for the asset you are about to trade.

Warrants

Warrants are a type of derivative that gives you the right but not the duty to purchase or sell securities (usually equity) at a specific price before it expires. The exercise price, also known as the strike price, is the price at which the underlying security can be bought or sold. European warrants may only be exercised on the expiration date, but American warrants can be exercised at any time on or before the expiration date. Call warrants grant the right to acquire security, whereas put warrants grant the right to sell a security.

Warrants, unlike options, are dilutive. When a warrant is exercised, the investor receives newly issued shares rather than existing stock. Warrants, as opposed to options, have significantly longer durations between issue and expiration, often years rather than months.

Warrants do not pay dividends or give you the opportunity to vote. Investors are drawn to warrants as a way to leverage their stock positions, hedge against downside risk (by pairing a put option with a long position in the underlying company, for example), or take advantage of arbitrage possibilities.

THE BUFFET

The buffet principle not only applies to instruments, but to everything else mentioned previously, you have a choice of countries, of industries, and of stocks, they are there displayed in the buffet counter, for you to pick and choose what you want.

Also, when you are full, sometimes it's better to stop eating, or you might get sick. Don't overload your portfolio with a thousand positions in different countries. You can do it if you want to, but if you are a one-man show retail investor/trader, you will get overwhelmed and neglect part of the process. Just stick to a few carefully selected choices from the salad bar.

18

Protection

If you are in a foreign country and end up in a situation where you may have intercourse with a stranger, you would probably make sure to have protected sex by buying condoms.

I apologize for the lewd imagery but I have to emphasize that this chapter is important, because it is about protection. After all, even if the thought of bragging at your next socialite gathering about how smart you are investing overseas may sound great, the risks remain.

Position sizing

The first obvious protection you can have is to not put all your eggs in your basket. I apologize in advance for having to mention it, but if you go through the trouble to invest in overseas markets to be geographically diversified, you should also be diversified in terms of the number of opened positions. A simple guideline would be to have between 10 and 50 opened positions at any point in time. Any less and each losing position will be very painful, and any more than 50 will be unmanageable. Also, you can only invest in the stocks that have made through all the steps in your selection process, therefore having too many trades on your watchlist ready to be put on, may indicate a lack of quality research in your process. And if you are happy with the quality of your selection process, you are simply in a great position of being spoiled with choice.

Currency hedging

Economic development, government debt levels, trade levels, and oil and gold prices, among other things, may all impact the value of a currency. Slowing GDP, growing government debt, and a large trade imbalance, for example, might lead a country's currency to depreciate versus other currencies. Rising oil prices might lead to stronger currency levels in nations like Canada, which are net oil exporters and have substantial reserves. If a country imports significantly more than it sells, this is an example of a trade imbalance.

As we are dealing with overseas markets, you will have to deal with foreign currencies. You may have had the best investments in South Africa or Turkey in recent years, but it wouldn't have mattered if you did not hedge the currency risks, because both currencies have been murdered in recent years.

There are a few ways you can eliminate your exposure to the local currency even when buying stocks in that currency. When you eliminate the currency risks, you only have exposure to the price movement of the stock and not the currency of the country.

The first obvious thing to do is to look for ADRs or GDRs (American Depositary Receipts, and Global Depositary Receipts).

Depositary receipts are shares of a foreign firm traded on a different international exchange. Depositary receipts can be arranged in a variety of ways, allowing international investors to invest in foreign firms via their own domestic markets.

The obvious advantage of using such an instrument is that it will be denominated in the currency of your preference, for example, US dollars. The shortcoming of ADRs and GDRs is access, only big companies can afford to be listed in multiple markets.

If no depositary receipts are available for your target stock, you can use either currency swaps, currency ETFs, or hedge currency risk in the forex market directly.

A currency swap is a financial transaction in which two parties exchange an equal amount of money in different currencies. The parties are effectively lending each other money, which they will repay at a certain period and exchange rate. The goal might be to minimize the cost of borrowing in a foreign currency, hedge exposure to exchange-rate risk, or speculate on the direction of a currency.

Currency exchange-traded funds (currency ETFs) are suitable hedging vehicles for ordinary investors who want to protect themselves against currency risk. These currency ETFs provide a more straightforward, highly liquid method to profit from currency fluctuations without the hassle of futures or forex: You buy them on your brokerage account like any other ETF.

If you are dealing with a very exotic currency, probably

none of the above instruments will be available, therefore you will have to go directly in the forex markets to hedge that position manually against the currency of your choice, by matching the nominal amount of the stock investment.

All the above instruments (except ADRs and GDRs) have one main disadvantage. When you hedge currency risk, you need to allocate capital to the hedge, the same capital that could be used for another investment in your portfolio. This means that the return on investment is greatly reduced when you base it on the capital used (capital invested in the stock + capital used to hedge the currency risk).

Pair trading

A very underutilized method of reducing risk in retail traders' and investors' portfolios is pair trading. As the name implies, investments and trades are made in pairs. At first, this approach is a bit remote but familiarity with it can become addictive. The simple premise of a pair trade is that one trade is long, and the other is short. For example, if you buy a stock in the French market, you would eliminate some risks associated with the French market by short-selling another stock in the French market. If a shock happens in that market, both your investments will be impacted, the stock you bought may become a losing position, but your short-selling position will be in profit, therefore absorbing the loss from the long position. The trick obviously is to choose carefully which stocks to go long and which to go short. By looking at the pair trade in a 3 dimensional way, you can structure the pair so that the 2 stocks will behave in your favor, while still protecting you from market risks.

While you were doing research on the French market, you may have identified growing industries and declining industries. If you go long a company in a growing industry and go short in a declining industry, you will protect yourself from market risk, while still taking advantage of the inherent protection of the pair trade on the French market.

Also, what if you remain in the same industry? While you were researching stocks in a particular industry, you may have come across leaders and laggards within a single industry, and structure the pair within the same industry therefore not only protecting you from market risk on the whole French market, but also on the risk of unforeseen shock on that industry as well.

What about going long a country and short another? You can certainly do that too, or even going long a stock in the construction industry in Asia, while going short a stock in the construction industry in South America. You can see that you can get quite creative after getting lots of ideas from your research process.

You may recall in the Macro selection chapter our observation on Sweden's PMI results outperforming Italy's PMI results subsequently to the COVID 19 pandemic.

A simple pair trading position on both country's ETFs (denominated in US dollars, highly liquid) by going long Sweden and short Italy would have resulted in approx +40% over one year, unleveraged.

PROTECTION

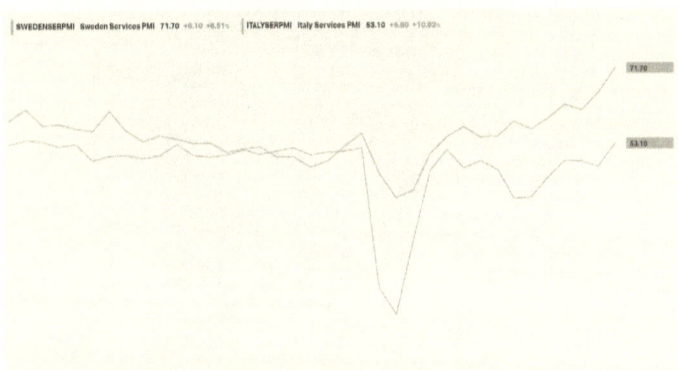

From the earlier chapter, Sweden PMI results much better than Italy PMI results

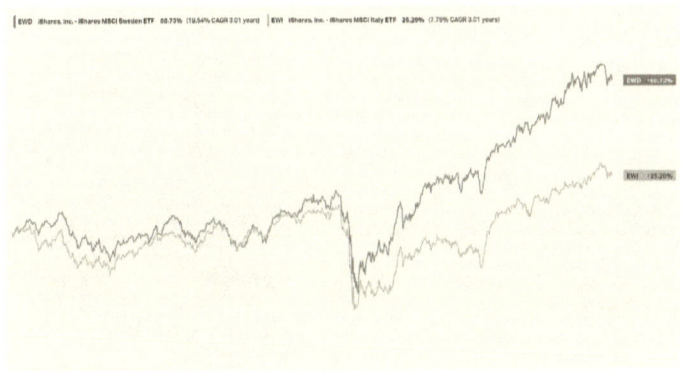

Performance of Sweden and Italy ETFs over 3 years

IV

Part Four

Pudding Proof

19

Think Global

Politics issues

As you may have noticed, I did not mention politics in any parts of the research process, or how you should approach politics in a certain region. I could say that you should follow politics in that region closely and that would be true. Whenever it comes to your investment, you should pay attention, definitely. But in general, and this may shock you, don't bother.

CNN and Fox News are debating on the latest hot political topic vs Floyd Mayweather and Conor McGregor exchanging yo mama slurs before a fight. What's the difference? none. it's payday for both. I don't care anymore unless it's in relation to my portfolio.

I used to care and I got deteriorating health as a result of it. It's quite popular to talk about the "rat race" these days in relation to corporate life denial. I would argue that "choosing your team" race is equally if not more depressing.

And I hate to break it to you but your vote means nothing. I vote with my feet, when things get too much out of hand, I vote for the departure terminal. When doing so, your life dramatically changes in a way that a ballot vote simply cannot compete with. If I don't have a position in the country that I am in, I avoid politics like the plague.

Turns out that not caring does not impact my life in any detrimental way whatsoever, quite the contrary actually. People call me names for doing so, I live better. Ignorance is bliss.

	Beginner	**Experienced**	**Advanced**
Capital	$0-$250k	$250k-$1M	$1M+
Brokerage accounts	1 main US account, 1 secondary account for other region	1 main US account, 2-3 secondary accounts for other regions	Multiple main accounts, 1 account for each sub regions (emerging and frontier)
Regions	Developed Emerging developed	Developed Emerging developed Emerging	Developed Emerging developed Emerging Frontier emerging Frontier
Instruments	Stocks ETFs CFDs Options	Stocks ETFs CFDs Options Warrants Certificates	Stocks ETFs CFDs Options Warrants Certificates
Currency risk	ADRs & GDRs Currency ETFs	ADRs & GDRs Currency ETFs Currency Swaps	ADRs & GDRs Currency ETFs Currency Swaps Foreign Exchange
Taxation & accountancy work	As low as possible	Limited and reasonable	1 main hollistic accountant + multiple locals outsourced in each region

Beginner to advanced levels of investing in exotic markets

A world of hustlers and consumers

Get on a plane and see the world. The best trading ideas are the ones you come across in the real world.

During a recent interview with Bernard Arnaud, the CEO of LVMH, a French conglomerate of luxury goods and spirits, Steve Jobs was mentioned. Mr. Arnaud acknowledges that Steve Jobs is much more widely known among pop culture than he is, but he continued saying that Jobs confessed to him a certain degree of jealousy towards him.

According to Jobs, his company Apple needs to constantly renew itself due to technological obsolescence. He said that Apple customers will change gadgets every year and that Apple is stuck in a chasing cycle to make sure that their customers keep buying Apple products. He said that in 20 years from now, maybe Apple customers will no longer use iPhone products, but will use something else.

He continues by saying that he is jealous of Mr. Arnaud because 20 years from now, more people than ever will open a bottle of champagne for their anniversary (only sparkling wine from a tiny region in France can claim the name of "Champagne").

It was funny to hear about Steve Jobs feeling insecure about such things, while most Americans see Jobs as a guru. This interaction gives us perspective on the world. The world is made of hustlers on one hand, and consumers on the other.

Hustlers will take great effort in improving their lives through enterprise regardless of their location, and the number of consumers will inevitably increase in the years and decades to come.

Some naysayers will say "that's not 100% true, the middle

eastern countries of Islamic faith won't buy champagne! Therefore, your whole paradigm is false." The Middle East is not gonna buy a lot of champagne, that's true. But they have nothing against buying Louis Vuitton bags, which is also owned by Bernard Arnaud by the way.

In my personal experience, I have seen skyscrapers cities being built on barren land within a single year, the same land that was reclaimed from the sea a couple of years prior. Makes me think that at the time my nephew was born about 4 years ago, this ultra-modern Asian city where I am now with kilometers of cemented towers in sight, was still part of the ocean. During the same time, the city where I grew up barely changed.

You have to forgive me, but I come from Europe, where efficiency and competitiveness are not on top of the list. I can only regret witnessing the future downfall of my European middle-class counterparts, that are so unprepared that it's not even funny.

How can I help you?

I can help you in three ways:

Number one, we publish lots of videos on Youtube talking about this stuff so feel free to come and watch our videos.

Number two, Pervasives collects, processes, and publishes a collection of industry data pertaining to international equities. You can browse the data for free, or you can sign up for the pro version to get everything.

Number three, If you need help with international taxes on your portfolio, you have a problem that needs to be solved, we can help you. Contact us at: https://pervasives.com/

How can you help us?

If you have enjoyed this book and would like to support us, you can leave a review of this book on Amazon. This will help us a lot, and allow other people like you to discover this book.

Recommended tools

bne Intellinews: intellinews.com

bne IntelliNews publishes business news and data on emerging markets. They publish news coverage of Eastern Europe, Central Asia, Africa and the Middle East and data and forecasting on more than 72 different countries and 400 industry/commodity categories.

Salaam Gateway: salaamgateway.com

Salaam Gateway is the world's leading news and insights platform on the global Islamic economy. They cover sectors across Islamic finance, halal, and Islamic lifestyle, with an eye on key producer and consumer markets.

Worldbank

The World Bank is an international financial institution that provides loans and grants to the governments of low- and middle-income countries for the purpose of pursuing capital projects. They publish key economic information on their website, as well as a vast amount of economic data for most countries in the world.

OECD

The Organisation for Economic Co-operation and Development is an intergovernmental economic organisation with 38 member countries, founded in 1961 to stimulate economic progress and world trade. They publish a number of economic indicators for each countries on their website.

Koyfin

Koyfin provides free tools to help investors research stocks and other asset classes through dashboards and charting. Their focus on fundamentals is particularly welcomed. Koyfin tries to bring a Bloomberg terminal experience to retail investors and traders.

Seeking alpha

Seeking Alpha is a crowd-sourced content service for financial markets. Articles and research cover a broad range of stocks, asset classes, ETFs, and investment strategies.

Sum Zero

SumZero is an online community for professional investors, which hosts investment research, job opportunities, and capital introduction services. Sign up for their service is limited to industry professionals.

Value Investor Club

Value Investor Club is a forum type of website for quality investment research by its community. Access is also restricted. The website was initially started by Joel Greenblatt.

Bloomberg News

Bloomberg Television is an American-based pay television network centered towards business and capital market programming, owned by Bloomberg L.P. It is distributed globally, reaching over 310 million homes worldwide

IHS Markit

IHS Markit Ltd is an American-British information provider based in London. Their press releases covering country PMIs are of particular attention.

Pervasives

Granular insight on Sectors & Industries Designed for macro trade idea generation. Covering a wide range of geographies.

Finbox

Finbox is an intelligent toolbox, with a wide range of tools for investment research centered around value-investing but not only. Good platform for DCF models.

Google Trends

Google Trends is a website by Google that analyzes the popularity of top search queries in Google Search across various regions and languages. The website uses graphs to compare the search volume of different queries over time

Statista

Statista is a German company specializing in market and consumer data. According to the company, its platform contains more than 1,000,000 statistics on more than 80,000 topics from more than 22,500 sources and 170 different industries.

IBIS World

Expert industry market research to help you make better business decisions. Industry market research reports, statistics, analysis, data, and trends.

Finviz

Stock screener for investors and traders, financial visualizations, all for free.

IMF

The International Monetary Fund (IMF) is an international financial institution, headquartered in Washington, D.C., consisting of 190 countries working to foster global monetary cooperation, secure financial stability, facilitate international trade, promote high employment and sustainable economic growth. They publish a wealth of economic information on their website.

The World Economic Forum

The WEF's mission is stated as "committed to improving the state of the world by engaging business, political, academic, and other leaders of society to shape global, regional, and industry agendas". Their intelligence website section is of particular attention.

Eurostat

Eurostat is the statistical office of the European Union, responsible for publishing high-quality Europe-wide statistics and indicators that enable comparisons between countries and regions.

Trading Economics

View more than 20 million economic indicators for 196 countries. Get free indicators, Historical Data, Charts, News, and Forecasts for 196 countries.

Guru Focus

Value Investing | Market insights and news of the investment gurus. Value investing screens and valuation tools.

Trading view

Live quotes, stock charts, and expert trading ideas. TradingView is a social network for traders and investors on Stock, Futures, and Forex markets

Notion

A tool that blends your everyday work apps into one. It's the all-in-one workspace for you and your team. Great notetaking and organizational for investment research.

Recommended books

SPQR, Mary Beard

The Silk Roads, Peter Frankopan

The Decline and Fall of the Roman Empire, Edward Gibbon *(6 volumes)*

Sapiens, Yuval Noah Harari

Homo Deus, Yuval Noah Harari

The Nomad Capitalist, Andrew Anderson

You can be a stock market genius, Joel Greenblatt

Boomerang, Michael Lewis

CFA Level 1 workbooks

ACCA Advanced Financial Management workbook

Financial advice disclaimer

The information in this book should not be considered tax, financial, investment, or any kind of professional advice. Only a professional diagnosis of your specific situation can determine which strategies are appropriate for your needs. Pervasives can and do not provide advice unless/until engaged by you.

Image credits

1. Book cover. Images were taken from the online financial data platform Koyfin. 2021. Changes were not made on screenshots of the platform, but the screenshots have been reorganized into a mosaic to fit the book cover. https://www.koyfin.com
2. Bank of Namibia. Photograph of specimen $10 Namibian dollar note. "bank of Namibia". bon.com.na
3. Google Search. World Population screenshot. 2021.
4. Germany. Kumar, Ank. Frankfurt Stock Exchange. 17 November 2015. Wikimedia Commons. No changes were made. https://commons.wikimedia.org/wiki/File:Frankfurt_Stock_Exchange_(Ank_Kumar)_01.jpg
5. The UK. The Present Stock Exchange. Image extracted from page 499 of volume 1 of Old and New London, Illustrated, by Walter Thornbury. Original held and digitized by the British Library. Wikimedia Commons. No changes were made. https://commons.wikimedia.org/wiki/File:ONL_(1887)_1.481_-_The_Present_Stock_Exchange.jpg
6. France. Bourse de Paris - Louis et Eugène Roland-Gosselin, agents de change parisiens. 19th century. Unknow painter. Wikimedia Commons. No changes were made. https://commons.wikimedia.org/wiki/File

:Bourse_de_Paris_-_Louis_et_Eug%C3%A8ne_Roland-Gosselin.jpg#filelinks
7. France. Defnsjen. Paris La Défense. 30 September 2019. Wikimedia Commons. No changes were made. https://commons.wikimedia.org/wiki/File:La_D%C3%A9fense_Paris.jpg
8. Italy. Monti, Paolo. Borsa di Milano, 1968. Wikimedia Commons. No changes were made. https://it.wikipedia.org/wiki/File:Paolo_Monti_-_Servizio_fotografico_(Milano,_1968)_-_BEIC_6330455.jpg
9. The Netherlands. Berckheyde, Job. Amsterdam exchange with stockbrokers. Painting. circa 1680. Wikimedia Commons. No changes were made. https://commons.wikimedia.org/wiki/File:Job_Berckheyde_-_Amsterdam_exchange_with_stockbrokers_gri_33125001303870_0037.jpg
10. Belgium. Unknown author. The 1920s. Brussels Stock Exchange. Wikimedia Commons. No changes were made. https://commons.wikimedia.org/wiki/File:Briefkaart_Beurs_Brussel.jpg
11. Austria. Norton, Richard. Wiener Bourse. between 1910 and 1915. Wikimedia Commons. No changes were made. https://commons.wikimedia.org/wiki/File:Wiener_B%C3%B6rse_5642869671_f8971e56c8_o.jpg
12. Spain. FDV. Madrid Stock Exchange. 1 July 2011. Wikimedia Commons. No changes were made. https://commons.wikimedia.org/wiki/File:Bolsa-madrid-010711-1.jpg
13. Ireland. The Little Museum of Dublin. 1924. Wikimedia Commons. No changes were made. https://commo

ns.wikimedia.org/wiki/File:The_Dublin_Stock_Excha nge,_1924.jpg

14. Switzerland. Kuhnmi. Blue Zurich. 29 January 2017. Wikimedia Commons. No changes were made. https://en.wikipedia.org/wiki/File:Blue_Zurich_(3189 5270053).jpg

15. Portugal. Ascenso, Luis. Lisbon Expo. 13 March 2015. Wikipedia. No changes were made. https://commons. wikimedia.org/wiki/File:Lisbon_-_Expo_-3_(169283 56685).jpg

16. Denmark. Kroyer, Peder Severin. Copenhagen Bourse. Painting. 1895. Wikimedia Commons. No changes were made. https://commons.wikimedia.org/wiki/File :Fra_K%C3%B8benhavns_B%C3%B8rs.jpg

17. Sweden. Brorsson. Photograph of Kista science Tower in Kista north of Stockholm City. 2011. Wikipedia. No changes were made. https://en.wikipedia.org/wiki/Fil e:Kistacentralparts_Publish.jpg

18. Norway. Eriksson, Jorn. Oslo at Night. 25 September 2014. Wikipedia. No changes were made. https://en.w ikipedia.org/wiki/File:Oslo_at_night.jpg

19. Finland. Anonymous. Helsinki Stock Exchange. 1965. Wikimedia Commons. No changes were made. https://commons.wikimedia.org/wiki/File:Helsingin-porssi-1965.jpg

20. Latvia. Anonymous author. Riga Stock Exchange. between 1900 and 1918. Wikimedia Commons. No changes were made. https://commons.wikimedia.org/ wiki/File:Riga_stock_exchange.jpg

21. Estonia. Khora. Downtown Tallinn during sunset. 29 May 2012. Wikipedia. No changes were made.

https://en.wikipedia.org/wiki/File:Tln1.jpg
22. Iceland. Bickel, Christian. Von der Hallgrímskirche in Richtung Tjörnin. 3 Dec 2009. Wikimedia Commons. No changes were made. https://commons.wikimedia.org/wiki/File:Reykjav%C3%ADk31.jpg
23. Turkey 1. Anonymous painter. Dersaadet Securities Exchange. circa 1866-1900s. Borsa Istanbul website. No changes were made. https://www.borsaistanbul.com/en/sayfa/24/milestones-in-borsa-istanbul-history
24. Turkey 2. Brutel, Derrick. View of Levent financial district from Istanbul Sapphire. 1 December 2013. Wikipedia. No changes were made. https://en.wikipedia.org/wiki/File:View_of_Levent_financial_district_from_Istanbul_Sapphire.jpg
25. Greece. Cummings, Neil. Agora in action, former Stock Exchange. 2013. Flickr. No changes were made. https://www.flickr.com/photos/chanceprojects/11085839354/in/photolist-BQ2ie-hTBMGJ-hTBRfU-hTBjSR-hTCkfF-hTBPPh-guM5h3
26. Hungary. Katonams. One of the several new-built building of Budapest, next to the Árpád bridge. 8 November 2007. Wikimedia Commons. No changes were made. https://commons.wikimedia.org/wiki/File:Budapest_-_Business_district.JPG
27. Croatia. Suradnik13. Panorama view of Zagreb. 2008. Wikimedia Commons. No changes were made. https://commons.wikimedia.org/wiki/File:Panorama_Zagreb.jpg
28. Serbia. Albatalad. Bird eye view of Belgrade. 24 February 2021. Wikimedia Commons. No changes were made. https://commons.wikimedia.org/wiki/File

:63oGrad.jpg
29. Cyprus. Nicosia Turkish Municipality. Night at Yenişehir, Nicosia. 2010s. Wikimedia Commons. No changes were made. https://commons.wikimedia.org/wiki/File:Night_at_Yeni%C5%9Fehir,_Nicosia.jpg
30. Malta. Vincentz, Frank. The Malta Stock Exchange. 10 March 2013. Wikimedia Commons. No changes were made. https://commons.wikimedia.org/wiki/File:Malta_-_Valletta_-_Pjazza_Kastilja_-_Borza_ta%27_Malta_01_ies.jpg
31. Montenegro. Bitno, Nije. Podgorica, Montenegro. 13 January 2009. Wikimedia Commons. No changes were made. https://commons.wikimedia.org/wiki/File:PodgoricaOverview.jpg
32. Poland. Boczkowski, P. Painting of the Warsaw Stock Exchange. 1877. Wikimedia Commons. No changes were made. https://commons.wikimedia.org/wiki/File:Wn%C4%99trze_sali_zebra%C5%84_nowego_gmachu_gie%C5%82dy_w_Warszawie_przy_ul._Kr%C3%B3lewskiej_(58709).jpg
33. Russia. Chistoprudov, Dmitry. Business center of Moscow. 31 May 2018. Wikimedia Commons. No changes were made. https://commons.wikimedia.org/wiki/File:Business_Centre_of_Moscow_2.jpg
34. Czech Republic. Jakpet7. BB centrum business district Prague. 25 August 2014. Wikimedia Commons. No changes were made. https://commons.wikimedia.org/wiki/File:BB_Centrum,_Prague,_Czech_Republic.jpg
35. Ukraine. Rozhenyuk, Alexander. перший в Україні інноваційний парк. 28 April 2020. Wikimedia Commons. No change were made. https://commons.wikim

edia.org/wiki/File:080_GATE_DJI_0454-Pano.jpg
36. China. Constantin, Adi. Shanghai Skyline. 14 February 2016. Wikipedia. No changes were made. https://en.wikipedia.org/wiki/File:Shanghai_skyline_unsplash.jpg
37. Hong Kong. Trodel, Jim. Hong Kong Skyline. 15 June 2008. Wikipedia. No changes were made. https://en.wikipedia.org/wiki/File:Skyline_-_Hong_Kong,_China.jpg
38. Taiwan. Ynes95. Taipei Skyline. 15 October 2015. Wikipedia. No changes were made. https://en.wikipedia.org/wiki/File:Taipei_Skyline_2015.jpg
39. Japan. Morio. Tokyo Skyline. 25 January 2009. Wikipedia. No changes were made. https://en.wikipedia.org/wiki/File:Skyscrapers_of_Shinjuku_2009_January.jpg
40. Bangladesh. Asaber91. Dhaka. 14 March 2017. Wikimedia Commons. No changes were made. https://commons.wikimedia.org/wiki/File:Dhaka_(33395988311).jpg
41. Pakistan. Nomi887. Clifton Beach Karachi. 24 May 2019. Wikimedia Commons. No changes were made. https://commons.wikimedia.org/wiki/File:Clifton_Beach,_Karachi_-_Pakistan.jpg
42. Mongolia. Billymse. Inside the Mongolian stock exchange. 2012-03-31. Wikimedia Commons. No changes were made. https://en.wikipedia.org/wiki/File:Trading_floor_of_Mongolian_Stock_Exchange.jpg
43. Nepal. Argenberg, Vyacheslav. Kathmandu, Nepal. 5 Dec 2007. Wikimedia Commons. No changes were made. https://commons.wikimedia.org/wiki/File:View_of_Kathmandu_from_Swayambhunath_2,_Nepal.j

IMAGE CREDITS

pg
44. Uzbekistan. Guidecity. Tashkent skyline. 26 April 2020. Wikimedia Commons. No changes were made. https://commons.wikimedia.org/wiki/File:Tashkent_skyline_2019.jpg
45. Azerbaijan. Presidential Press and Information Office. Baku at night. 14 September 2020. Wikimedia Commons. No changes were made. https://commons.wikimedia.org/wiki/File:Baku_city_at_night.jpg
46. Armenia. DavitEG. Elite Plaza Business center. 6 December 2013. Wikimedia Commons. No changes were made. https://en.wikipedia.org/wiki/File:Elite_Plaza_Business_Center_at_Night.jpg
47. Australia. Nazareth College. CBD Melbourne. 13 June 2012. Wikimedia Commons. No changes were made. https://commons.wikimedia.org/wiki/File:CBD_Melbourne.jpg
48. Singapore. Lieu Song, Benh. Singapore Marina Bay. 27 February 2018. Wikimedia Commons. No changes were made. https://commons.wikimedia.org/wiki/File:Singapore_Marina_Bay_Dusk_2018-02-27.jpg
49. Thailand. Lieu Song, Benh. Bangkok night. 20 September 2009. Wikimedia Commons. NO changes were made. https://commons.wikimedia.org/wiki/File:Bangkok_Night_Wikimedia_Commons.jpg
50. Malaysia. Kerwin, James. Petronus towers, Kuala Lumpur. 3 December 2019. Wikimedia Commons. No changes were made. https://en.wikipedia.org/wiki/File:The_Twins_SE_Asia_2019_(49171985716).jpg
51. Indonesia. Magnificient Jakarta. Jakarta skyline. 23 October 2020. Wikimedia Commons. No changes were

made. https://en.wikipedia.org/wiki/File:Jakartaskyline1.jpg

52. Vietnam. Jim . Ho Chi Minh city Skyline. 10 October 2017. Wikimedia Commons. No changes were made. https://en.wikipedia.org/wiki/File:Ho_Chi_Minh_City_Skyline_(night).jpg
53. Sri Lanka. Balou46. Altes Parlament Colombo. 13 January 2018. Wikimedia Commons. No changes were made. https://commons.wikimedia.org/wiki/File:LK-Colombo-altes-parlament.jpg
54. Cambodia. Maharaja45. Phnom Penh skyline. 11 July 2020. Wikimedia Commons. No changes were made. https://en.wikipedia.org/wiki/File:Phnom_Penh_Evening_Aerial_View.png
55. Myanmar. MosheA. The first Lotteria in Junction Square, Yangon, Myanmar. 18 June 2019. Wikimedia Commons. No changes were made. https://commons.wikimedia.org/wiki/File:LotteriaMyanmar.jpg
56. Laos. Christophe95. Vientiane Center. 23 August 2018. Wikimedia Commons. No changes were made. https://commons.wikimedia.org/wiki/File:Vientiane_Center_exterior.jpg
57. Brazil. Galeria de Léo Pinheiro - Picasa. Bovespa Traders. circa 2009. Wikimedia Commons. No changes were made. https://commons.wikimedia.org/wiki/File:Bovespa_Traders.jpg
58. Chile. Falk2. Sanhattan. 22 February 2017. Wikimedia Commons. No changes were made. https://en.wikipedia.org/wiki/File:J28_293_%C2%BBSanhattan%C2%AB.jpg
59. Colombia. Unknow author. Bogota Colombia. Wiki-

media Commons. https://en.wikipedia.org/wiki/File:Bogot%C3%A1Skyline.jpg

60. Argentina. Deensel. High rises of Puerto Madero. 28 February 2018. Wikimedia Commons. No changes were made. https://en.wikipedia.org/wiki/File:High-rises_of_Puerto_Madero_(40022145164).jpg
61. Peru. Sagitario30252. Lima - Peru. 27 October 2016. Wikimedia Commons. No changes were made. https://commons.wikimedia.org/wiki/File:Lima_-_Per%C3%BA.jpg
62. Ecuador. Molina, Alfredo. World Trade Center Guayaquil. 25 February 2008. Wikimedia Commons. https://en.m.wikipedia.org/wiki/File:Wtcgye.jpg
63. Uruguay. Campi, Marcelo. World Trade Center Montevideo. 20 June 2010. Wikipedia. No changes were made. https://en.m.wikipedia.org/wiki/File:World_Trade_Center_Montevideo.jpg
64. Bolivia. EEJCC. La Paz Downtown at dusk. 22 January 2015. Wikimedia Commons. No changes were made. https://commons.wikimedia.org/wiki/File:Centro_de_La_Paz_al_atardecer.jpg
65. Paraguay. Anonymous author. Skyscraper city Paraguay. 10 September 2018. Wikimedia Commons. No changes were made. https://commons.wikimedia.org/wiki/File:Asunci%C3%B3n_Paraguay.jpg
66. Venezuela. Wilfredor. Panoramic view of Caracas night. 9 April 2014. Wikipedia Commons. No changes were made. https://commons.wikimedia.org/wiki/File:Panoramic_view_of_Caracas_night.jpg
67. Mexico, Salvador, Jonathan. A view of Reforma avenue skyline and Chapultepec park. 15 September

2016. Wikimedia Commons. No changes were made. https://commons.wikimedia.org/wiki/File:Mexico_City_Reforma_skyline_(cropped).jpg
68. Panama. JurriaanH. Skyline of the capital of Panama. 19 June 2008. Wikimedia Commons. No changes were made. https://commons.wikimedia.org/wiki/File:Panama_City_skyline.jpg
69. Dominican Republic. Juan C, Jose. Santo Domingo. 11 December 2010. Wikimedia Commons. No changes were made. https://commons.wikimedia.org/wiki/File:SantoDomingoedit.JPG
70. El Savaldor. JMRAFFI. World Trade Center San Salvador. 2 August 2020. Wikimedia Commons. No changes were made. https://commons.wikimedia.org/wiki/File:World_Trade_Center_San_Salvador.jpg
71. Middle East. Starling, Thomas. A map of middle east. 1832. Wikimedia Commons. No changes were made. https://commons.wikimedia.org/wiki/File:Middle_east_map_(1832).jpg
72. UAE. Reckmann, Tim. Skyline of downtown Dubai. 27 May 2015. Wikimedia Commons. No changes were made. https://en.wikipedia.org/wiki/File:Dubai_skyline_2015_(crop).jpg
73. Saudi Arabia. US Department of State. A picture of the view of Riyadh, taken by the U.S. Department of State. Late 2010s. Wikimedia Commons. No changes were made. https://en.wikipedia.org/wiki/File:Al-Riyad.jpg
74. Qatar. Anzola, Francisco. Doha Skyline in the morning. 15 February 2014. Wikimedia Commons. No changes were made. https://en.wikipedia.org/wiki/File:Doha_skyline_in_the_morning_(12544910974).jpg

IMAGE CREDITS

75. Israel. Eytan, Ted. Photos taken from the top of Azrieli Center Circular Tower, currently the tallest building in Israel. 10 July 2016. Wikimedia Commons. No changes were made. https://commons.wikimedia.org/wiki/File:View_of_Diamond_Exchange_Center_from_Azrieli_Center.jpg
76. Lebanon. Marviikad. Beirut, the beloved, from airplane window. 27 July 2015. Wikimedia Commons. No changes were made. https://commons.wikimedia.org/wiki/File:Beirut_close_to_plane_descent.jpg
77. Jordan. Freedom's Falcon. Amman, Jordan as seen from Armenian Quarter. 15 June 2013. Wikimedia Commons. No changes were made. https://commons.wikimedia.org/wiki/File:Amman_from_Armenian_Quarter_2.jpg
78. Kuwait. Calicut, Irvin. Kuwait. 3 February 2013. Wikimedia Commons. No changes were made. https://en.wikipedia.org/wiki/File:All_major_buildings_in_kuwait_in_one_shot_by_irvin_calicut.jpg
79. Oman. Wusel007. Ruwi Muscat. 24 January 2015. Wikimedia Commons. No changes were made. https://commons.wikimedia.org/wiki/File:Ruwi_Muscat.JPG
80. Bahrain. Wadiia. Manama, Bahrain. December 2014. Wikimedia Commons. No changes were made. https://en.wikipedia.org/wiki/File:Manama,_Bahrain_Decembre_2014.jpg
81. Map of Africa. Parry, Rex. Map of African Roads. 17 July 2007. Wikipedia. No changes were made. https://en.wikipedia.org/wiki/File:Map_of_Trans-African_Highways.PNG

82. Egypt. Abdelwahab, Youssef. A view of the CBD (central business district) in Egypt's new capital. 23 October 2020. Wikimedia Commons. No changes were made. https://commons.wikimedia.org/wiki/File:Central_business_district_,_Egypt%27s_new_administrative_capital.jpg
83. Nigeria. OpenEduEd. Victoria Island, Lagos, Nigeria. 9 September 2014. Wikipedia. No changes were made. https://en.wikipedia.org/wiki/File:2014_Victoria_Island_Lagos_Nigeria_15006436297.jpg
84. Morocco. إيان. منظر من أعلى عمارة الحرية في الدار البيضاء 5 May 2019 5. Wikimedia Commons.
85. Kenya. Africanmodern. Nairobi Downtown. 12 February 2016. Wikipedia. No changes were made. https://en.wikipedia.org/wiki/File:Nairobi_economic_capital_of_africa.jpg
86. Zimbabwe. Gamgee, Samwise. Harare Skyline. 2006. Wikimedia Commons. No changes were made. https://commons.wikimedia.org/wiki/File:Harare_Skyline.jpg
87. Tunisia. Bensaad, Youssef. Panorama de Tunis (vue de sidi belhassen). 30 July 2016. Wikimedia Commons. No changes were made. https://commons.wikimedia.org/wiki/File:Panorama_de_Tunis_05.jpg
88. Namibia. McMorrow, Brian. Close-up aerial photo of Central Windhoek. 2005-05-25. Wikipedia. No changes were made. https://en.wikipedia.org/wiki/File:Windhoek_aerial.jpg
89. Botswana. Newman, Henry. iTowers of Masa Square CBD, Gaborone, Botswana. 30 June 2012. Wikimedia Commons. No changes were made. https://en.wikiped

ia.org/wiki/File:CBD1.jpg
90. Sudan. Dohnálek, Petr Adam. New buildings in Khartoum, Sudan. 22 August 2009. Wikipedia. https://en.wikipedia.org/wiki/File:Strato_en_%C4%A4artumo_(Sudano)_003.jpg
91. Ivory Coast. Koffi, Leon Konan. Skyline of the Plateau commune by night in Abidjan, Côte d'Ivoire. 21 July 2016. Wikimedia Commons. No changes were made. https://commons.wikimedia.org/wiki/File:Commune_du_Plateau_de_nuit_Abidjan_C%C3%B4te_d%27Ivoire.jpg
92. Tanzania. Stanley, David. Dar Es Salaam Skyline. 3 January 2017. Wikipedia. No changes were made. https://en.wikipedia.org/wiki/File:Dar_Es_Salaam_Skyline_(34011488084).jpg
93. Uganda. Omoo. Kampala Skyline. 21 December 2016. Wikipedia. No changes were made. https://en.wikipedia.org/wiki/File:KampalaSkyline2.jpg
94. Rwanda. Adrien K. The skyline of central Kigali. 28 May 2018. Wikipedia. No changes were made. https://en.wikipedia.org/wiki/File:Kigali2018Cropped.jpg
95. GDP growth figures & economic data. Trading Economics. 30 June 2021. No changes were made to the screenshot. https://tradingeconomics.com/country-list/gdp-annual-growth-rate?continent=g20
96. PMI charts. Koyfin. 30 June 2021. No changes were made to the screenshots. https://www.koyfin.com/
97. World Map. Asus2004. Map of countries by 2021 Heritage Foundation Index of Economic Freedom. 12 March 2021. Wikipedia. No changes were made.

https://en.wikipedia.org/wiki/File:Index_of_Economic_Freedom_2021.svg
98. Industry charts. Pervasives. 30 June 2021. https://www.pervasives.com/
99. Market scatters. Koyfin. Different markets scatters computed on the Koyfin financial online platform. 30 June 2021. No changes were made on the generated screenshots. https://www.koyfin.com/
100. Tarot Cards. Nosferattus. Photo of a 3 card tarot spread on a table with candles. 25 March 2021. Wikimedia Commons. No changes were made. https://commons.wikimedia.org/wiki/File:Tarot_cards_-_3_card_spread_with_candles.jpg
101.

Notes

EXOTIC MARKETS

Notes

Notes

Notes

www.ingramcontent.com/pod-product-compliance
Lightning Source LLC
Chambersburg PA
CBHW031604210526
45464CB00004B/1418